DISABILITY, THE BODY, AND RADICAL INTELLECTUALS IN THE LITERATURE OF THE CIVIL WAR AND RECONSTRUCTION

During the Civil War, hundreds of thousands of men were injured and underwent amputation of hands, feet, limbs, fingers, and toes. As the war drew to a close, their disabled bodies came to represent the future of a nation that had been torn apart, and how it would be put back together again. In her authoritative and engagingly written new book, Sarah E. Chinn claims that amputation spoke both corporeally and metaphorically to radical white writers, ministers, and politicians about the need to attend to the losses of the Civil War by undertaking a real and actual Reconstruction that would make African Americans not just legal citizens but actual citizens of the United States. She traces this history, reviving little-known figures in the struggle for Black equality, and in so doing connecting the racial politics of 150 years ago with contemporary debates about justice and equity.

SARAH E. CHINN is Professor of English at Hunter College, City University of New York. She is the author of three other books: *Technology and the Logic of American Racism: A Cultural History of the Body as Evidence* (2000), *The Invention of Modern Adolescence: The Children of Immigrants in Turn-of-the-Century America* (2007), and *Spectacular Men: Race, Gender, and Nation on the Early American Stage* (2017), which won the 2017 George Freedley Memorial Award for an exemplary work in the field of live theater or performance from the American Theatre Library Association.

CAMBRIDGE STUDIES IN AMERICAN LITERATURE
AND CULTURE

Editor
Leonard Cassuto, *Fordham University*

Founding Editor
Albert Gelpi, *Stanford University*

Advisory Board
Robert Levine, *University of Maryland*
Ross Posnock, *Columbia University*
Branka Arsić, *Columbia University*
Wai Chee Dimock, *Yale University*
Tim Armstrong, *Royal Holloway, University of London*
Walter Benn Michaels, *University of Illinois, Chicago*
Kenneth Warren, *University of Chicago*

Recent books in this series

193. MARY GRACE ALBANESE
Black Women and Energies of Resistance in Nineteenth-Century Haitian and American Literature
192. JUSTIN PARKS
Poetry and the Limits of Modernity in Depression America
191. OWEN CLAYTON
Vagabonds, Tramps, and Hobos: The Literature and Culture of U.S. Transiency 1890–1940
190. JOLENE HUBBS
Class, Whiteness, and Southern Literature
189. RYAN M. BROOKS
Liberalism and American Literature in the Clinton Era
188. JULIANA CHOW
Nineteenth-Century American Literature and the Discourse of Natural History
187. JESSICA E. TEAGUE
Sound Recording Technology and American Literature
186. BRYAN M. SANTIN
Postwar American Fiction and the Rise of Modern Conservatism: A Literary History, 1945–2008

(Continued after the Index)

DISABILITY, THE BODY, AND RADICAL INTELLECTUALS IN THE LITERATURE OF THE CIVIL WAR AND RECONSTRUCTION

SARAH E. CHINN

Hunter College, City University of New York

Shaftesbury Road, Cambridge CB2 8EA, United Kingdom

One Liberty Plaza, 20th Floor, New York, NY 10006, USA

477 Williamstown Road, Port Melbourne, VIC 3207, Australia

314–321, 3rd Floor, Plot 3, Splendor Forum, Jasola District Centre, New Delhi – 110025, India

103 Penang Road, #05-06/07, Visioncrest Commercial, Singapore 238467

Cambridge University Press is part of Cambridge University Press & Assessment, a department of the University of Cambridge.

We share the University's mission to contribute to society through the pursuit of education, learning and research at the highest international levels of excellence.

www.cambridge.org
Information on this title: www.cambridge.org/9781009442695
DOI: 10.1017/9781009442657

© Sarah E. Chinn 2024

This publication is in copyright. Subject to statutory exception and to the provisions of relevant collective licensing agreements, no reproduction of any part may take place without the written permission of Cambridge University Press & Assessment.

First published 2024

Printed in the United Kingdom by TJ Books Limited, Padstow Cornwall

A catalogue record for this publication is available from the British Library

A Cataloging-in-Publication data record for this book is available from the Library of Congress

ISBN 978-1-009-44269-5 Hardback

Cambridge University Press & Assessment has no responsibility for the persistence or accuracy of URLs for external or third-party internet websites referred to in this publication and does not guarantee that any content on such websites is, or will remain, accurate or appropriate.

For Kris, of course

Contents

List of Figures		*page* viii
Acknowledgments		xi
	Introduction: A New Kind of Nation – Amputation, Reconstruction, and the Promise of Black Citizenship	1
1	Giving Up the Ghost: The Dead Child versus the Amputated Limb	31
2	"Strewn promiscuously about": Limbs and What Happens to Them	71
3	1860 or 1865? Amending the National Body	103
4	"I don't care a rag for '*the Union as it was*'": Amputation, the Past, and the Work of the Freedmen's Bureau	134
5	Shaking Hands: Manual Politics and the End of Reconstruction	159
	Conclusion: Eloquent Emptiness	191
Notes		202
Bibliography		225
Index		239

Figures

I.1 Thomas Nast, "The Union as It Was" *Harper's Weekly*,
October 24, 1874.   *page* 13

I.2 Brig. Gen. Andrew W. Denison, "Good Bye, Old Arm!"
Library of Congress, M1640.H.   18

1.1 Southworth and Hawes, *Postmortem Portrait* (c. 1850).
Courtesy of the George Eastman Museum.   32

1.2 Reed B. Bontecou, *John Parmenter* (1865). Courtesy of
the Burns Archive.   33

1.3 Southworth and Hawes, *Postmortem of Child* (c. 1850).
Courtesy of the George Eastman Museum.   43

1.4 Unknown photographer, *Postmortem Photograph of Girl*
(c. 1855). Courtesy of the George Eastman Museum.   44

1.5 Reed B. Bontecou, *John H. Bowers* (1865). National
Library of Medicine.   52

1.6 Reed B. Bontecou, *Charles H. Wood* (1865). Medical
Historical Library, Harvey Cushing/John Hay Whitney
Medical Library, Yale University.   53

1.7 Reed B. Bontecou, *John Parmenter* (1865). National
Museum of Health and Medicine.   55

1.8 Reed B. Bontecou, *Foot of John Parmenter* (1865). Medical
Historical Library, Harvey Cushing/John Hay Whitney
Medical Library, Yale University.   57

1.9 George Gardner Rockwood, [Sergeant Thomas Plunkett
of Co. E, Twenty-First Massachusetts Infantry Regiment
in uniform with amputated arms] (1862). Library of
Congress, LC-DIG-ppmsca-71017.   59

List of figures

1.10 J. W. Black, [Sergeant Thomas Plunkett of Co. E,
Twenty-First, Massachusetts Infantry Regiment in uniform
with American flag] (1863). Library of Congress,
LC-DIG-ppmsca-49716.   61

1.11 J. Gurney & Son, [Private David H. Wintress of Co. C,
139th New York Infantry Regiment, Captain William A.
MacNulty of Co. A, Tenth New York Infantry Regiment
and Veterans Reserve Corps, and Sergeant Thomas Plunkett
of Co. E, Twenty-First Massachusetts Infantry Regiment in
uniform, displaying their wounds] (1864). Library of
Congress, LC-DIG-ppmsca-70977.   63

1.12 Fredericks & Co, [Sergeant Alfred A. Stratton of Co. G,
147th New York Infantry Regiment, with amputated arms]
(1864). Library of Congress, LC-DIG-ppmsca-53074.   66

1.13 Thomas Nast, "FRANCHISE AND NOT THIS MAN?"
Harper's Weekly, August 5, 1865.   68

1.14 Unattributed, "A Man Knows a Man." *Harper's Weekly*,
April 22, 1865.   70

3.1 Edward V. Valentine, *Recumbent Statue of Robert E. Lee*
(1870).   130

3.2 Edward V. Valentine, *Knowledge Is Power* (1868).
Courtesy of the Valentine, Richmond, VA.   131

5.1 Thomas Nast, "Andrew Johnson's Reconstruction and
How It Works." *Harper's Weekly*, September 1, 1866.   163

5.2 Thomas Nast, "To Thine Own Self Be True." *Harper's
Weekly*, April 24, 1875.   164

5.3 Thomas Ball, *Emancipation Memorial* (1879).   165

5.4 Thomas Nast, "Compromise – Indeed!" *Harper's Weekly*,
January 27, 1877.   166

5.5 Thomas Nast, "The Same Snap – 'Reform Slavery.'"
Harper's Weekly, December 30, 1876.   167

5.6 Thomas Nast, "A Truce – Not a Compromise." *Harpers
Weekly*, February 17, 1877.   168

5.7 Friedrich Graetz, "Insatiable Glutton." *Puck*, December 30,
1882.   171

5.8 Thomas Nast, "Let Us Clasp Hands over the Bloody
Chasm." *Harper's Weekly*, September 21, 1872.   176

x   *List of figures*

5.9 Thomas Nast, "Compromise with the South: Dedicated
     to the Chicago Convention." *Harper's Weekly* on
     September 3, 1864.   181
C.1. Robert E. Lee statue being removed in Memphis, TN.
     Courtesy of CBS News.   199
 C.2 Steve Helber, "Pedestal that once held a statue of Robert E.
     Lee, Richmond, VA." The Associated Press.   200

Acknowledgments

This is the most satisfying part of writing a book: the pleasure of recounting all the help I've had along the way. Over the course of twenty years, I have had the privilege of having my work read by a group of scholars whose astute, insightful, and supportive responses have shaped not just this book but every piece of writing that has made its way into print. Although they might not be visible, the handprints of Jeff Allred, Sophie Bell, Anna Mae Duane, Joseph Entin, Louise Heller, and Meg Toth are all over this book. And when the Covid-19 pandemic pounded our research plans (and attention spans) into mush, our weekly Zoom writing sessions opened up the time and delivered the motivation to keep working on it.

I am beyond grateful to the Civil War Caucus, one of the most collegial groups I have had the good fortune to become part of, for welcoming me into the fold. In particular, many thanks to Kathleen Diffley, the guiding light of the Caucus, and Jane Schultz for their warmth and generosity. Caucus meetings are a model of shared intellectual purpose, and I have learned an enormous amount from Heather Chacon, Benjamin Fagan, Brigitte Fielder, James Godley, Allison Johnson, Gregory Laski, Justine Murison, Timothy Sweet, and Elizabeth Young, to name just a few.

C19, the Society of 19th Century Americanists, has been an intellectual home for me for over a decade. Rodrigo Lazo, Justine Murison, Britt Rusert, Edlie Wong, and Xine Yang made my time on the executive board a pleasure; Anna Mae Duane and Autumn Womack were terrific teammates in the work of imaging the "Reconstructions" conference we all put together in 2022; and Martha Schoolman and John Funchion were exemplary hosts.

Thanks to Shirley Samuels for inviting me up to Cornell to present part of what became Chapter 2, and for arranging for me to look through the revelatory photographs of Reed Bontecou, the core of Chapter 1, as well as for her hospitality, terrific conversation, and delicious tequila. The "Literary Tourgée" conference at the Chautauqua Institute in 2019,

xii   *Acknowledgments*

organized by Robert Levine and Sandra Gustafson, enriched my knowledge and understanding of the work and legacy of Albion Tourgée.

Joseph Straus made me aware of the work Devin Burke had done to
catalogue disability-themed Civil War–era song sheets. Maria Seger gener-
ously shared proofs of *Reading Confederate Monuments* before it was
published, so I could benefit from the research and wisdom of her
contributors. Carolyn Karcher's championing of *Bricks without Straw*,
including her brilliant scholarly editing of the novel, put it on my radar
in the first place.

Thanks are also due to Lenny Cassuto, for encouraging me to bring the
book to Cambridge University Press. His advocacy for this project
reassured me that I was on the right track, and his support and regular
communication were exactly what I needed to bring it to the finish line.
The help of Ray Ryan and Edgar Mendez smoothed the path from
manuscript to physical (and electronic!) volume – thanks especially to
Edgar for answering all my questions with patience and forbearance.

For the past twenty-three years, my professional home has been Hunter
College, part of the City University of New York. Hunter is proof that
students, faculty, and staff can create an exceptional institution even amid
the most challenging of circumstances: ongoing fiscal austerity, crumbling
infrastructure, autocratic administration, disinvestment on the state and
federal levels, and unreliable subways. My students are hard-working,
motivated, and whip-smart, navigating a host of obstacles so they can get
the same access to higher education that their more affluent counterparts
take for granted. Life at Hunter would be nothing without my outstanding
colleagues, who have mastered doing a lot more with a great deal less.
I have cherished my conversations with Tanya Agathocleous, Jeff Allred,
Kelvin Black, Nijah Cunningham, Jennifer Gaboury, Jeremy Glick,
Marlene Hennessy, Rupal Oza, Amy Robbins, Michael Thomas, and
Alan Vardy. During my time as department chair, I would have floundered
without the staunch support of Mark Bobrow, Gavin Hollis, Mark Miller,
Janet Neary, Sonali Perera, Angela Reyes, and Dow Robbins. My fellow
chairs, especially Kelly Anderson, Lisa Marie Anderson, Anthony Browne,
Sam D'Iorio, Paolo Fasoli, Donna Haverty-Stacke, Laura Keating, Elke
Nicolai, Catherine Raissiguier, Mary Roldán, and Howard Singerman,
were excellent co-conspirators. My dearest friends Rebecca Connor,
Lynne Greenberg, and Donna Masini kept me aloft with gossip and good
food and drinks.

My professional and political lives have been enriched by my ongoing
work with *Radical Teacher*. Dick Ohmann, Louis Kampf, and Saul

Acknowledgments xiii

Slapikoff were remarkable examples of lives lived with integrity in every context; they made combining radical hope with a cool awareness of the uphill battle we still face look, if not easy, at least manageable. Allia Abdullah-Matta, Pamela Annas, Sophie Bell, Michael Bennett, Jackie Brady, Erica Caldwell, James Davis, Linda Dittmar, Joseph Entin, Chris Kennedy, Paul Lauter, Frinde Maher, Neil Meyer, Susan O'Malley, Bob Rosen, Jesse Schwartz, and Jocelyn Wills are ideal comrades in keeping this scrappy yet venerable institution alive and healthy.

Closer to home, I have been nourished by a community of friends, both literally and metaphorically. The Club 641 crew – May Watson Grote, Ruth Katcher, Katie Hale, Sheri Holman, and Amy Oztan – have provided great food and even better company. And it has been a joy to travel with Sheri and Amy along the circuitous path of parenting from preschool to college and beyond. Noa Ben Asher, Hannah Faddis, Katrina Foster, Hayley Gorenberg, Pamela Kallimanis, Kathy Kline, Chaia Milstein (leader of the redoubtable Clinton Hill Crokinole League), Margot Pollans, Jessica Rogers, Sonja Shield, and Rosie Uyola are the kinds of friends a girl can usually only dream of. Thank you to Priscilla Wald for talking me off the cliff. Once, early in the pandemic, I invited Anna Mae Duane to a Zoom coffee date; it's three years later, and our Monday morning conversations are still the highlight of my week.

Finally, I have to thank my family, both of origin and of choice. My mother, Carol Chinn, has been a steadfast supporter of my work. As I was finishing up the book, she was diagnosed with a terminal illness and, with typical bravura, faced it with determination, and grace. I am still wrestling with the fact of her loss. My beloved children, Gabriel and Lia, moved during the writing of this book from adolescence to adulthood, even as they grappled with the disappointments and challenges of the COVID-19 pandemic; my pride and delight in them are impossible to contain, let alone measure. I dedicate this book, as always, to Kris Franklin, who has been with me at every turn, and with whom every day offers the possibility of a new adventure.

Introduction
A New Kind of Nation – Amputation, Reconstruction, and the Promise of Black Citizenship

> And now that the war is over, and the four-years' struggle ended, we cannot but inquire whether in that fearful conflict anything has been *gained* for which we should also give thanks; whether any good has come out of the struggle which will go into our future history, and which will make us a greater and a better people; whether the results are *worth* the sacrifices made.
> —Rev. Albert Barnes, "Peace and Honor: A Thanksgiving Sermon"

> Oh, how you have suffered! If retribution could ever teach men to revere justice, it would seem that the late Rebellion could have taught you that.
> —Frederick Douglass, "Govern with Magnanimity and Courage"

> Loss is inseparable from what remains, for what is lost is known only by what remains of it, by how these remains are produced, read, and sustained.
> —David L. Eng and David Kazanjian, *Loss*

Of all the damage wrought by the US Civil War, the most visible was borne by soldiers who had fought and lost arms, legs, hands, feet, fingers, or toes. While the dead evoked the most grief, they were materially invisible, interred away from sight, if not from memory. But amputees carried with them reminders of the conflict's cost.

This is hardly surprising. Tens of thousands of men North and South underwent some kind of amputation as a result of injury and/or infection. The critical literature around this phenomenon has stressed the discourses of loss, destruction, emasculation, immiseration, and impoverishment that resulted from amputation, especially for former Confederate soldiers.[1] And while that isn't wrong, it isn't the whole story either, most notably in the North. Many white Union veterans as well as Northern civilians imagined amputation as part of an economy of reparation and redemption – the lost body part payment for the sins of slavery, and a reminder of what had to be excised from the nation in the wake of the Confederate surrender at

2   Introduction

Appomattox. In this imaginary, amputation served as a catalyst for Reconstruction.

This narrative of amputation as both a reminder of the losses occasioned by slavery and a kind of promissory note for Black emancipation was produced by a specific kind of writer, politician, minister, and/or philosopher: white former radical abolitionists who were on their way to becoming radical Reconstructionists.[2] They held the veteran amputee up as an avatar of a nation from whom the disease of slavery had been cut away, and who faced a new way of living in and understanding his altered body. Along with this physical change came an ethical understanding of the necessity for a rethinking of the racial hierarchies on which the United States had been founded.

Such a reimagining required a firmness of purpose and a refusal to conform to the simultaneous emergent desire for reconciliation, a desire that strengthened over the course of the late 1860s and into the 1870s, until, by the 1880s it was dominant within white American culture. For example, on November 30, 1869, former abolitionist and antiracist activist Wendell Phillips was the featured speaker in the Parker Fraternity series of talks (endowed by and named after Transcendentalist, antislavery agitator, and supporter of John Brown, Theodore Parker). The title of Phillips's speech was "What I Ask of Congress," and his list of requests was short. Primary among them was that the nation's elected officials rethink their policy of reconciliation and forgiveness toward the erstwhile Confederacy. "We have the idea," he opined, "that forgiveness of everybody, in all circumstances … is a virtue." Rather than forgiveness, Phillips argued for the "stern, rigid, indomitable, unmixed idea of justice" that at that moment seemed "intolerable to the American people" (2).

Phillips was joined in his sense of justice by a small, mostly tight-knit group of white radicals who were unusual in several ways. First, they worked closely with Black activists and political leaders before, during, and after the war. Their primary political commitment was to racial equality and, in the years after the war, a variety of stances including reparations, gender equality, and Black citizenship. This book, then, is about those few white radicals who resisted the ongoing rescripting of the meanings of the Civil War and Reconstruction. Like Phillips they argued against the growing desire to forgive and forget not just the war but also the history of slavery itself. Rather than reunite the body politic as though its violent division had never happened, they insisted that the national corpus should not be remade in its prewar image – that the country should

Introduction 3

remember its sins, the price it had paid for them, and the new shape it had to take in the postwar years.

This tripartite mandate for the body politic found its visual representation in corporeal form in amputee veterans of the Union Army. For this politically committed group of white radicals, amputation was the ideal metaphor for the obligations of loss and the reimagination of the national body, its necessary new instantiation. Lost limbs were partial payment for the sins of slavery as well as permanent reminders of what the country owed the newly freed. And stumps left behind told a story of the irrecoverability of the status quo ante, the willed impossibility of going back to the way things were when the Slave Power controlled the country.

In this book I trace a trajectory from the battlefields and hospitals of the Civil War, where arms and legs were separated from bodies to become undifferentiated piles of limbs, to the photographic images of amputee veterans, to novels in which amputees stand in for the radical hopes of what Reconstruction might bring, and to the post-Reconstruction demonization of the veteran amputee and his symbolic disappearance from the national scene. In many ways, this book is about a struggle over definitions of the postwar Union and the meanings of whiteness, as well as what white people owed the millions of newly emancipated Americans, soon to become citizens, after centuries of enslavement. As I hope to show, for these white radicals, this struggle was at the heart of their vision of Reconstruction. They followed the lead of Black activists in adopting what David W. Blight has called "the emancipationist vision" that embraced "the politics of radical Reconstruction ... the conception of the war as the reinvention of the republic and the liberation of blacks to citizenship and Constitutional equality" (2). Forging a discourse that melded a declaration of debt to the formerly enslaved and a vision for a racially just nation, white radicals – whether officially affiliated with the Republican party or operating within a political culture that had its roots in prewar abolitionism – looked around them at the trauma of the war and attempted to construct narratives about what had happened, why it had happened, and what should happen next.[3]

Few of the figures I discuss in these pages are part of the US literary canon as it now stands, although one – especially Albion Tourgée, the subject of Chapter 4 – was a best-selling novelist and major legal figure during his own lifetime (and is now enjoying something of a renaissance). Some, like Anna Dickinson, a well-known fixture on the lyceum circuit in the prewar period who often shared a stage with Frederick Douglass and other famous abolitionists, were already committed political radicals by the time the war ended. Others, like Oliver O. Howard, the director of the Freedmen's Bureau, and Tourgée himself, came to radical politics through the crucible of the Civil War. Better known are Thaddeus Stevens, the radical Republican congressman from Pennsylvania, and the clergyman Horace Bushnell, whose words were often material for national news stories. And a focus of Chapter 5 who also appears in this introduction, Thomas Nast, may have picked up on many of the themes of radical Reconstruction, but he was hardly a reliable ally to Black Americans before or after the war.

Together, I would argue, they constitute what Raymond Williams called a "formation." For Williams, formations were "conscious movements or tendencies (literary, artistic, philosophical or scientific) which can usually be readily discerned after their formative productions" (119). This characterization seems especially apposite for this group of people: while some knew each other, not all did; most of them were part of cross-racial networks of political activists and intellectuals that reached from New England to the Midwest and into the upper South; and they all found their way to the body of the veteran amputee as a trope through which to think the lessons of the Civil War and the necessity for a full and antiracist Reconstruction.

This analytical structure brings with it some important and urgent ethical questions. First of all, as a scholar with deep investments in Disability Studies, I'm alert to the problematics of the deployment of these disabled men as symbols or, as David T. Mitchell and Sharon L. Snyder formulate this operation, "narrative prostheses," a "crutch upon which literary narratives lean for their representational power, disruptive potentiality, and analytical insight" (49). Mitchell and Snyder warn us that too often literature "serves up disability as a repressed deviation from cultural imperatives of normativity," characterized by isolation, degendering, and impotence (8). As Sari Edelstein glosses this concept, as narrative prostheses, people with disabilities are "narratively exploited, used as signposts and markers, rather than represented as multifaceted subjects" (108). I would argue, though, that the amputee occupies a complex and position in the cultural imaginary of the 1860s and 1870s. Neither pitiable victim, figure of emasculation, nor paragon of overcoming, the Civil War amputee represented in the texts I discuss in the book is, rather, a potent representative of the ethos of human interconnectedness that informed the hopeful – if naïvely optimistic – imaginings of white radicals. We might, following contemporary disability theorists, see the amputee as "cripping" the vision of a reunited, reconciled nation, disrupting the white nationalist

Introduction 5

(and implicitly ableist) focus on the perfectly intact white male body as the paradigm of national belonging.[4]

Moreover, like all embodied metaphors, the image of the amputee proved to be disturbingly labile. Mitchell and Snyder observe that "disability provides an important barometer by which to assess shifting values and norms imposed upon the body," which is especially true here (51). The barometer that appraised the figure of the amputee soldier gauged the nation's short-lived commitment to Black emancipation and citizenship. Indeed, as I show in Chapter 5, the trope of the disabled soldier as the sign of Union victory and the defeat of slavery was resignified as Reconstruction was dismantled, and the manly injured veteran became in turn the grasping pensioner, the alibi for white national consolidation, and, ultimately, simply superannuated and rendered redundant.

Still, there is a risk in writing about white actors in the drama of Reconstruction, a period in which Black Americans were briefly empowered to achieve the political power on national, state, and local levels that had so long been denied them. Black formulations of a racially just society represented one of the most progressive plans for education, labor, and social relations that the United States has ever seen. African Americans demanded not only "that they be included in the existing category of citizenship – that they deserved the right to vote, for instance – but also that citizenship ought to be expanded to include social equality, access to education, and economic opportunity" for all Americans (Quigley 2). Moreover, as the accomplished Black abolitionist Charles Lenox Remond argued, for white Reconstructionists, however allied with their Black colleagues as they might have felt, it was "utterly impossible for our white friends … fully to understand the Black man's case in this nation" (qtd. in Levine xvi).

My purpose here is not to push whiteness to the center of the narrative of Reconstruction – not only would that be historically inaccurate, but it would also run counter to the ethos of the narrative that unfolds in this book. The story I'm telling here is comparatively small but important: it's a story of an ongoing partnership between Black and white activists, and how a network of white radicals refused to allow the realities of slavery and white supremacy to be minimized, palliated, or forgotten, even as the majority of white Americans worked to do just that. They used the figure of the amputee as an emblem of their radical hopes for the postwar nation, for the ambitions of Reconstruction, and as a signifier of protest against the active and passive dismantling of Black civil and human rights.

Crucially, most of these figures looked to and learned from their Black counterparts. The model of citizenship they imagined, their view of a nation not divided unequally by race or – for many – by class or gender, and a society that provided unprecedented services for its most marginalized, was powerfully informed by the Black women and men with whom they had worked during the prewar years and strategized during and after the war. They fully acknowledged the terrible toll that slavery had taken, theorized ways by which they could at least in part atone for that profound national wrongdoing, and attempted to both pay back the debt owed the formerly enslaved and keep the promise made to newly inaugurated citizens at the front of the country's mind.

Barely any time had passed after the end of the Civil War before conflict emerged over how – and whether – the country would be restructured. The following decade was consumed by debates over what this restructuring would look like. As Edward Blum observes, "[f]rom 1865 to 1875, a religious, social, and political battle engulfed northern society, as advocates of sectional punishment and racial justice squared off against proponents of sectional harmony and racial oppression" (88). These lines had been drawn well before the war, by abolitionists, on the one hand, and those who valued the wholeness of the Union and/or the institution of slavery, on the other. In the antebellum years, political dominance had lain firmly in the camp of the second group.

The mitigation of the promise of Reconstruction began almost immediately after the surrender of Confederate troops. As David Blight has comprehensively shown, soon after the end of the Civil War, an increasing number of Americans – including their elected officials – edged away from a commitment to Black civil and human rights and toward an "inexorable drive for reunion" (2). Even as notable an antislavery activist as Henry Ward Beecher, who had shipped cases of Sharps rifles to Kansas to ensure that it was established as a free state, started preaching national reconciliation. Indeed, droves of northern clergy "created a counter morality, one that prized national solidarity among whites at the expense of equal inclusion of people of color" (Blum 89).

In Reconstruction, the balance of power shifted several times, each radical change producing reactionary backlash: the initial correlative consolidation of anti-Black violence, as in the rise of the Ku Klux Klan in the late 1860s, sparking efforts at containment by government and activists; and legal action against the Klan, leading to a rededication to white supremacy. In the words of Cody Marrs, Reconstruction was "a historical formation, grounded in violence, through which progress and regress

Introduction

became dialectically intertwined" (409). For African Americans in the South, the gap between the goals of Republican policymakers in Washington and their own experiences of extra-judicial racist violence was painfully wide.[5]

This bitter irony was not lost on the former radical abolitionists who had the highest hopes for Reconstruction. Unlike their more moderate counterparts, they did not see the war as "a triumphal endpoint and moral cleansing of the republic" (Marrs 414). Rather, the Civil War was the necessary preparation for the real work of racial equity, land redistribution, and full enfranchisement. In the early years of Reconstruction, white radicals could not imagine any recursion to the past – the war had put the nation on a forward-looking path toward permanent change. Oliver P. Morton, the radical senator from Indiana, sounded this note in his speech at the dedication of a monument at Gettysburg National Cemetery in 1869, announcing, "Liberty universal soon to be guaranteed and preserved by suffrage universal; the keeping of a nation's freedom to be entrusted to *all the people* and not to a part only" (19). He ended by thundering "HENCEFORTH DISUNION IS IMPOSSIBLE" (40). In milder terms, Horace Bushnell put this perspective simply: "the state-rights doctrine is bled away ... we are not the same people that we were, and never can be again" ("Our Obligations" 328, 331).

Black radicals were, by necessity, more cautious about the irreversibility of the effects of the war and about claims to temporal inevitability more generally.[6] Frances E.W. Harper encapsulates this perspective in her 1871 poem "Words for the Hour," in which she apostrophizes white Northerners as soldiers in an ongoing battle:

> Men of the North! It is no time
> To quit the battle-field;
> When danger fronts your rear and van
> It is no time to yield.

More to the point, she argues, the South is well aware that the war is not yet over, and has regrouped and adapted their tactics for a new dispensation:

> The foe ye foiled upon the field
> Has only changed his base;
> New dangers crowd around you
> And stare you in the face. (185)

Even though, as Greg Laski has argued, the passage of the Thirteenth, Fourteenth, and Fifteenth Amendments, for the majority of white Americans, "encouraged the desire for closure, serving, as it were, as

8   Introduction

signposts denoting the nation's progress toward the moment in which it
could declare itself postslavery"(6), this call to arms was heeded by
Harper's white radical peers, for whom national recidivism was a specter
that haunted them throughout and beyond Congressional Reconstruction.
"The whole fabric of southern society *must* be changed," declared
Thaddeus Stevens, or "[h]ow can republican institutions, free schools, free
churches, free social intercourse exist in a mingled community of nabobs
and serfs?" (qtd. in Foner 236). Given the wholistic vision they had for the
changes the nation had to undergo both North and South, even stasis
represented backsliding. Moreover, as Harper makes clear in "Words for
the Hour," the past of slavery and secession is being renewed and reenacted
by "the foe," so the (white) men of the North must likewise push forward
in order to secure for the future the political gains already achieved.

"The Debt of Justice": Radical Conceptions of Restitution

In the wake of the Civil War, Black and white radicals looked both
backward and forward to assess the task ahead. Up until that moment,
as Alyosha Goldstein has observed (riffing off Cheryl Harris's foundational
analysis that "slavery as a system of property facilitated the merger of white
identity and property [1721]), "[w]hiteness in the United States [had]
been historically constructed not only as a form of property but also as the
capacity to possess" (1077), that is, to possess land, animals, and people.
In his address to Congress in 1865, Henry Highland Garnet articulated
this argument, that "the Scribes and Pharisees of our times who rule the
State" (70–1), by embracing slavery, ventured to "chattleize man; to hold
property in human beings" (73).

Like his fellow abolitionists, Garnet identified slavery as a crime of
property against the enslaved person, who by rights should hold property
in themself. In the rhetoric of abolition, enslavers were "man-stealers" and
"every slave is a stolen man" (Garrison 14); slavery was "theft" and
"robbery" (Garnet 77). When Frederick Douglass first spoke before the
Massachusetts Anti-Slavery Society, he turned this logic inside out, declaring that "I appear before the immense assembly this evening as a thief and
a robber. I stole this head, these limbs, this body from my master and ran
off with them" (qtd. in Quarles 63).[7]

Moreover, responsibility for this theft extended across the nation,
incriminating the North in its complicity with the slave-owning South.
In an 1854 speech, William Lloyd Garrison rejected the claim that slavery
was a sectional issue rather than a national sin:

Radical Conceptions of Restitution   9

> Whatever may be the guilt of the South, the North is still more responsible
> for the existence, growth and extension of Slavery. In her hand has been the
> destiny of the Republic from the beginning. She could have emancipated
> every slave, long ere this, had she been upright in heart and free in spirit.
> She has given respectability, security, and the means of sustenance and
> attack to her deadliest foe.... [T]he sin of this nation is not geographical –
> is not specially Southern – but deep-seated and universal. (25–6)

If the sin was national, then so too was the mandate to repent and provide
restitution. Part of this debt had been repaid by the death of soldiers in the
Union Army: antislavery radicals and even some soldiers themselves (as we
shall see shortly) maintained that blood shed and limbs lost during the Civil
War were in payment for and in order to end slavery. This was not a new
trope. Indeed, the rhetoric of blood compensation had been invoked in the
years before the war, most notably by John Brown, for whom "the act of self-
sacrifice doubled as an act of penance; to suffer in concert with slaves was
also to pay a historical debt for the injuries whites had inflicted on slaves"
(Nudelman 35). And Garrison declared, after serving seven weeks in prison
in 1830 for his antislavery activity, that "[a] few white victims must be
sacrificed to open the eyes of the nation, and to show the tyranny of the
laws" qtd. in (H. Jackson, *American Radicals* 57).

But the years of the Civil War and its aftermath intensified this line of
argument. As the war multiplied that sacrifice by the hundreds of thousands, white radicals saw the fulfilment of their understanding of the
Union as decayed from the inside by slavery and the ransom that had to
be paid to cut out the rot. Pennsylvania Congressman Thaddeus Stevens
characterized the nation under the control of the Slave Power as "the
rotten and defective portions of the old foundations" built at the inception
of the Union that had to be "clear[ed] away" in order for justice to Black
Americans to be done (qtd. in Blight 55). Massachusetts Senator Charles
Sumner invoked the massive losses of the war as a promissory note for the
abolition of slavery, since "[t]he soil of the Rebellion is soaked with patriot
blood, its turf bursting with patriot dead.... There can but one failure, and
that is the failure to end slavery" ("Slavery and the Rebellion" 180–1).
Horace Bushnell, pastor of the North Congregational Church in Hartford,
Connecticut, sounded a similar theme in an 1865 commencement speech
in New Haven commemorating the war dead, whom he characterized as
the "spent ammunition of the war" ("Our Obligations" 322). The death of
so many was necessary "to see that every vestige of slavery is swept clean . . .
We are not to extirpate the form and leave the fact.... We are bound, if
possible, to make the emancipation work well" (352–3).

Frances Ellen Watkins Harper got to the heart of her fellow radicals' vision of both their commitment to racial equality and their belief that such equality was to be earned by not just repentance but also punishment wreaked by the Civil War in her eulogy "Lines to Hon. Thaddeus Stevens," published in her *Poems* in 1871. The first five stanzas of the poem are structured as questions, exploring Stevens's desires for the nation, his "hope to see thy country / Wearing Justice as a crown," as well as his (and Harper's) belief that "the crater of God's judgment / Overflowed the nation's crime" (166).

Toward the end of the poem, Harper takes on the role of prophet, taking Stevens's hopes and extrapolating them with her own vision of what Reconstruction might bring:

> There is light beyond the darkness
> Joy beyond the present pain
> There is hope in God's great justice,
> And the negro's rising brain. (167)

In the final stanza, Harper links her own vision of the future with that of the divine, threading a trajectory from the "crater of God's judgment" to an image of God himself as a combatant in the war who shall protect the struggle in which she, Stevens, and the previously enslaved have toiled:

> Though before the timid counsels
> Truth and Right may seem to fail,
> God hath bathed his sword in judgment,
> And his arm shall yet prevail.[8] (167)

Here Harper mixes an acknowledgment of the wrongs of slavery with hope for a future shaped by divine guidance toward justice. The timidity of moderates must inevitably fall before God's sword "bathed ... in judgment" and the prophesy that "his arm shall yet prevail." Aligning the goals of Reconstruction with God's will, Harper invokes (the famously agnostic) Stevens, the divine plan, and Black liberation.

Nonetheless, according to the poem, slavery had profoundly challenged the divine order of things, to the extent that God was forced to intervene with the instrument of the Civil War. Many white radicals believed that even the losses of the war were not sufficient to pay the debt white Americans owed the newly inaugurated freedpeople, not least because so many Black soldiers had also been injured and died.[9] Instead, they believed that "the [white] nation owed former slaves for their years of involuntary labor" (Faulkner 3). Moreover, mere emancipation could not restore to the formerly enslaved, both present and past, the lifetimes of violence, separation of families, and degradation. In a speech outlining the necessity for the Freedmen's Bureau, Sumner insisted that the nation owed freedpeople anything required to bring them into the polity, since "the debt of justice will not be paid if we do not take [freedpeople] by the hand in their passage from the house of bondage to the house of freedom" ("Creation of the Freedmen's Bureau" 343). Horace Bushnell was even more explicit about what was needed – "negro suffrage appears to be indispensable," he maintained, but that was not enough. "The soil is to be distributed over again, villages are to be created, schools established, churches erected, preachers and teachers provided, and money for these purposes to be poured out" ("Our Obligations" 354).

Crucially, in reckoning this debt, radicals insisted that the nation had to be wholly remade, that, in Thaddeus Stevens's formulation, the decay and rot in the foundations of the Union had to be fully cleared away and a new foundation built. The house had almost been destroyed by the putrefaction of slavery, on the one hand, and the trauma of the Civil War, on the other, but now the process of reconstructing from the bottom up was paramount.[10] Concomitantly, the liberation of enslaved people could be a harbinger of a more comprehensive national emancipation: from white supremacy, from economic inequality, from injustice. As Stevens prophesied, this process "would have so remodeled all our institutions as to have freed them from every vestige of human oppression, of inequality of rights, of the recognized degradation of the poor, and the superior caste of the rich" (qtd. in Foner 254). The key to this liberation was a recognition that the war had caused a near-apocalyptic break from the past, and out of the smoke and chaos would emerge a nation governed by equality before the law.[11]

"The Union as it was – a heinous notion"

Unlike the radicals, moderate Republicans and the vast majority of Democrats were less invested in this characterization of the postwar period as opening up the possibility of a sharp and irreversible break with the past. David Blight points to this as he defines the struggle in the North over Reconstruction as being embodied by "the tangled relationship between two ideas – *healing* and *justice*" (3).[12] At first, many white Northerners focused on questions of justice, not least because "freedpeople seemed to Republicans to be model free Americans, working hard to rebuild the South as they climbed the ladder to economic success, in contrast to Democratic efforts to portray them as 'lazy ne'er do wells'"

(Richardson 32–3). This strategy by Democrats initially backfired, and "a new North emerged ... where a large group of influential political and religious leaders were seriously committed to extending citizenship to people of color" (Blum).[13] In fact, after a rash of anti-Black violence and the refusal of Southern legislatures to ratify the Fourteenth Amendment, "formerly moderate Republicans began to shift over to the previously radical position in favor of government enforcement of black suffrage" (Richardson 43).

Radical Republicans' greatest concern was establishing and then maintaining the massive changes that they believed the nation needed, both North and South, to atone for slavery and push forward toward an equitable society. They achieved this fitfully during Congressional Reconstruction. For them the call for "healing" was a cynical expression of the desire to return to a state of affairs as close as possible to Black enslavement. As Saidiya Hartman has observed, Black attempts to live as free people were regarded by white Southerners as a form of insubordination. Indeed, "[t]he striking similarities between antebellum regulations regarding black conduct and postbellum codes of conduct leave us hard-pressed to discern even those intangible or inchoate expressions of black freedom" (Hartman 148). In his tour of the postwar South, Carl Schurz found a kind of zero-sum equation among white people that "the elevation of the blacks will be the degradation of the whites" (*Report on the Condition* 25).

In reaction to Southern recidivism and Northern calls for reconciliation, white radicals amplified their own refusal to return to any kind of status quo ante. During the early years of the war, moderate Republicans argued for saving the Union without radical change, and "Copperhead" Democrats, who opposed the conflict, adopted the slogan "The Union as it was, the Constitution as it is." Radicals appropriated and inverted that sentiment, deploring the desire to reinstate any vestige of the past. As early as 1863, Albion W. Tourgée (whom I discuss in Chapter 4), condemned the "oft repeated maxim of the Administration – 'We are fighting but for the Union as it was'" as a "sublime hoax" (qtd. in Curtis 189).

Over the next decade, contestation over the form the reconstituted nation should take intensified. In an 1865 speech on Reconstruction delivered in Lancaster, Pennsylvania, Thaddeus Stevens articulated this stance: "'Restoration,' therefore, will leave the 'Union as it was' – a heinous notion" (Stevens, 6). Nearly a decade later, Thomas Nast (whose work I discuss in more detail in Chapter 5) published a cartoon in *Harper's Weekly* entitled "The Union as It Was" that illustrates how Stevens's

"The Union as it was – a heinous notion" 13

Figure I.1 Thomas Nast, "The Union as It Was"
Harper's Weekly, October 24, 1874.

apprehension about "Restoration" was realized by white terrorism and violence (Figure I.1).

Nast's cartoon shows figures representing the Ku Klux Klan and the White League, another white supremacist terrorist organization, joining hands over skull and crossbones, under which is the legend "worse than slavery." A Black man and woman huddle underneath, holding a baby – possibly dead – and a school primer lies in front of them, next to what appears to be a bloodstain. In the background, a Black person hangs from a tree and a schoolhouse burns. And above it all floats an eagle surrounded by the words "the union as it was" and "this is a white man's government."

14 Introduction

It's striking that Nast conjoins the efforts by Black people to gain literacy, represented by the primer and the burning schoolhouse, with the regime of white terror. As I show in Chapter 4, education was a hallmark project of the Freedmen's Bureau and philanthropic and religious organizations. Black literacy posed an existential threat to white supremacy in the South – once freedpeople could read, they had meaningful access to the mechanisms of citizenship: the franchise, informed entry into contracts, the ownership of property. As Nast suggests here, the schoolhouse is the portal to social and political legitimacy – something the Klan and its ilk used violence to counteract.

In this context, "healing" was a hollow promise. How could the country heal while it was infected with anti-Black violence and the violation of freedpeople's recently awarded civil rights? Moreover, public opinion was capricious in regard to those rights, and support soon waned as white Southerners clawed back the measures that Reconstruction had imposed. As Travis M. Foster shrewdly observes, "[w]hite nationalism and sectional reconciliation required Northern whites' inaction even more than their action, their passive consent more than their energetic selection" (78).

In the minds of these white radicals, the body politic was not whole, nor should it be, if wholeness meant reversion to "the Union as it was." If, as Joan Burbick argues in relation to what she calls the language of health and the culture of nationalism in nineteenth-century America, "only the body's health can index how well the republic is functioning," the converse was also true for these radical Republicans – the unhealthy nation is borne out in diseased bodies. Indeed, the nation needed to excise the extremities (in both meanings of the word) through which pulsed the poison of enslavement and white supremacy. What better sign, then, of both the necessary sacrifice of the white body to defeat slavery and the obligation to lop off the diseased remnants of slavery than the amputated veteran?[14]

The amputee was a corporeal reminder that the Civil War had imposed (and should impose) permanent change – there was no recuperating of the lost limb and the amputee had to recreate himself and fashion new ways of being in the world (the Left Armed Corps I discuss later is the epitome of this concept). As Brian Matthew Jordan notes, amputees' "disabled bodies plainly illustrated the unresolved nature of the conflict" and the work that still had to be done ("Living Monuments'" 125). Amputation was the degree zero representation of radical loss and change, and white radical writers and thinkers took it up to articulate their commitment to a transformed, racially and socially just Union. More to the point, the

Military Discourses of Amputation and Emancipation

amputee was a figure that Americans recognized from their towns, their families, and their homes.

"Something more is necessary": Military Discourses of Amputation and Emancipation

Amputation was the most visible signifier of the afterlife of the Civil War embodied in those who had fought. Much like the riven nation, the amputated body represented, in Megan Kate Nelson's words, the "interplay between the whole past and fragmented present" (2). Articulating the sense that the war brought of the uncanny merging of the human, the natural, and the mechanical that Nelson has noted in her analysis of the destruction the Civil War wrought, Oliver Wendell Holmes called "the limbs of our friends and countrymen ... part of the melancholy harvest which war is sweeping down with Dahlgren's mowing machine and the patent reapers of Springfield and Hartford" (567–8). Here, human limbs are reaped by the ship-board Dahlgren gun, designed by Rear Admiral John A. Dahlgren, that spewed shells both onto enemy craft and onto land, as well as by the Sharps rifles that were manufactured in Hartford and the weapons produced by the Springfield Armory.

Of course, amputation was more than a metaphor in the years after the war. Not only were amputated bodies visible, they were omnipresent. The United States had become an amputation nation, one in which amputees were an unavoidable sight. Holmes observed in 1863 that "[i]t is not two years since the sight of a person who had lost one of his lower limbs was an infrequent occurrence. Now, alas! there are few among us who have not a cripple among our friends, if not in our own families" (574). Over 20,000 Union soldiers survived amputation (Clarke 368).[15] Despite the developments in prosthetic technology spurred by the war and heavily subsidized by the federal government, developments that Holmes described at length and with wonderment in his *Atlantic* essay "The Human Wheel: Its Spokes and Felloes," most amputees did not even apply for government-issued prosthetics, and those who did sometimes abandoned them, never able to comfortably wear them (Clarke 364).

It is not surprising, then, that amputation did not just bear the weight of medical discourse (as we'll see in Chapter 2), but was freighted with meaning for the amputees, who saw themselves as both individual combatants and part of a larger plurality. Moreover, the experience of amputation found its way into military and civilian culture from the beginning of the war into the immense changes of the postwar era. As Colleen Glenney

Boggs has written, "the Civil War scaled up disability to a prevailing social condition [and] marks a historical and cultural moment when disability was made central to the construction of national identity and interpersonal subjectivity" (41).

Megan Kate Nelson devotes a significant part of her masterful book *Ruin Nation* arguing this very point. Nelson maintains that "the Empty Sleeve comes not only to symbolize [the] characteristics [of chivalry, courage, and patriotism] but also to represent all the other wounds a soldier could have sustained in battle . . . [T]he transformed, ruined bodies of veteran amputees also became sites for apprehension about many of these same virtues. Soldiers and civilians created a competing narrative – that of the Incomplete Man – as a way to express concern about the masculinity of veterans" (186). Indeed, for Nelson, "amputation emasculated soldiers, bringing them under the healing power and domination of women" (196). There are certainly elements of this fear of emasculation by and about amputated veterans – expressed, for example, in Winslow Homer's 1865 engraving "Our Watering Places: The Empty Sleeve at Newport" and its accompanying story in *Harper's Weekly*. Wounded soldiers themselves worried about being reduced to indigence by their disability – one poem in a hospital newspaper entreated its readers "Let a grateful hand relieve him / Who for us hath lost his leg, / Ever give him home and living / Never seem forced to beg" (*The Cripple* 1.1, 1). And Brian Matthews Jordan observes that once home and in poverty, veterans were not well received: "Most civilians wanted the 'piteous' sight of the one-armed soldier begging in the streets, like the memory of the war, to just go away" (*Marching Home* 59).

Nonetheless, I would argue that amputation signified much more than a loss of masculinity. Several scholars have argued that "[r]ather than negating their identities as men, injury for some amputees constituted the evidence of manhood" (Clarke 366), or at least that there was not an inevitable relationship between amputation and emasculation.[16] As David Serlin observes, "for many of these disabled veterans of the Civil War, the amputation stump, the artificial limb, and other physical markings that proved sustained injury were visual shorthand for military service . . . their permanent uniform" (*Replaceable You* 33).

In large part this was due, as Holmes suggested, to the normalization of amputation as a result of the war. For men in the fight, amputation was part of the lingua franca of the wartime experience. Newspapers produced by injured servicemen in federal hospitals bore titles like *The Crutch* and *The Cripple*, transforming the widespread loss of limb into a commonplace. *The Cripple*, printed "every Saturday at Head-Quarters Third Division General Hospital S. General Hospital, Alexa, VA," as its masthead read, was "published by and for sick and wounded soldiers" at the hospital (2). In the "Salutory" in the first issue on October 8, 1864, the editors even twitted their counterparts in Annapolis about the title of their newspaper: "The General Hospital at Annapolis issues a neat little sheet classed 'THE CRUTCH,' but as there is no use for a Crutch without a Cripple, we have decided to call our paper by the latter title" (2).

Amputation also entered popular culture via cartoons, poetry, and song sheets. As Devin Burke has shown, there were dozens of popular songs that were written in the voice of or represented amputee soldiers and veterans. Songs with titles like "The Wounded Soldier," "I'm Blind!" "Old Arm, Good Bye," "The Empty Sleeve," and "Good-By Old Arm!" found their way into bourgeois parlors, telling stories of military courage and loss (Figure I.2). Several songs covered the same story, in which "a wounded hero" who "awoke from his stupor and missed his arm," asked for it to be brought to him so he could say farewell to it – an indication that this was a popular enough theme to be set to song more than once.[17]

Echoing the debates animating Northern civilian life in the second half of the war, these songs ventriloquized the growing belief among soldiers (as we'll see in Chapter 3) that this was a war to emancipate the enslaved. Although these songs often placed the sacredness of the Union at the core of their message, many explicitly invoked the loss of limb as a sacrifice to end slavery. In Henry Badger's 1864 song, "The Empty Sleeve," the narrator explains the meaning of the eponym: it "points to a time when our flag shall wave / O'er a land where there breathes no cowering slave. / Up to the skies let us all then heave / One proud hurrah for the empty sleeve" (5). In another "Empty Sleeve" song, this time by J. W. Dadmun and P. A. Hanaford, the song prophesies that "In days to come, that sleeve shall be / The good son's joy and pride, / As he shall tell how bravely fought / His sire on Freedom's side" (n.p.). And in "Old Arm Good Bye," published a year after the end of the war, a soldier exclaims, "Oh proud am I to give my mite, / For freedom pure and good!" (Coe and Cooper 4).

As they returned home, amputee veterans themselves made this connection explicit, and "in searching for the meaning of their injuries [they] became especially committed to the cause of emancipation and racial equality" (Jordan, *Marching Home* 3). A significant archive of veteran writings survives in the records of William Oland Bourne, who organized two left-handed penmanship competitions – both with significant cash prizes – for men who had lost their right hands or arms in the war.[18]

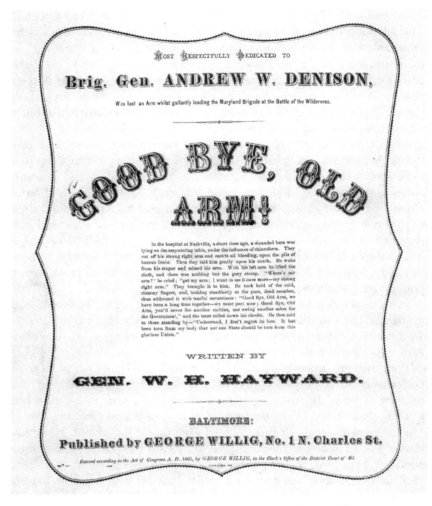

Figure I.2   Brig. Gen. Andrew W. Denison, "Good Bye, Old Arm!" Library of Congress, M1640.H.

Although the contestants, the vast majority of whom were white, were not told what to write about, many of them described their experiences in the war, especially the circumstances under which they lost their arms. Both Black and white veterans often narrated their losses as necessary, even salutary, sacrifices to the cause of emancipation and expanded democracy.

Military Discourses of Amputation and Emancipation

As one wrote, his ordeal "is sacred to those who have been actively engaged in the late war ... because it was between democracy and aristocracy, freedom and slavery, the freedom of the white as well as the black" (qtd. in Jordan, *Marching Home* 117). Similarly, Rufus L. Robinson argued in his competition entry that "[i]t is not sufficient that we have free Institutions, free Speech and freedom of the press, we must have freedom at the Ballot Box ... Not until Universal suffrage becomes a law will our country stand forth in all her greatness and grandeur United, Disenthralled, and Redeemed" (qtd. in Johnson, *Left-Armed Corps* 264–5). In another entry to the left-handed penmanship competition, the writer reproduced the entire Emancipation Proclamation, implicitly forging a connection between his own loss and Black liberation. And several submissions linked their losses to the debt they owed their Black fellow soldiers, "the strong arm and the steady hand of the Negro at a time when his help was sorely needed," and insisted that "the ballot of the loyal black man balance that of the disloyal white" (qtd. in Johnson, *Left-Armed Corps*, 276–7).[19]

Thomas Sanborn, who lost his arm at the battle of Poplar Grove Church in September 1864, sounded a theme that would be repeated by white radicals like Sumner, Stevens, and Bushnell: "In passing from the narrow gauge of slavery to the broad gauge of freedom something more is necessary than to throw away the old rules ... the whole dimensions and proportions are to be remodeled" (qtd. in Johnson, *Left-Armed Corps* 267).

Bourne himself echoed this theme in the banners displayed in the hall where Left Armed Corps handwriting samples were exhibited, one of which read "See the Conquering Heroes Come. The Left Hand. The Empty Sleeve. All Americans Together Not a Fetter in the Clime" (Clarke 389). And the equation of bodily loss and national remaking through emancipation was still in circulation, albeit vestigially, a couple of decades later: the radical novelist and lawyer Albion Tourgée ventriloquized this sentiment in his popular serialized set of sketches written over the course of 1885 from the perspective of a disabled veteran at middle age, later collected as *A Veteran and His Pipe*: "I was ... proud of the folded sleeve, because I had given the limb that filled it for the cause of human freedom" (11).

While the majority of images of amputees (and indeed the number of amputees themselves) were of white men, Black veteran amputees were also enlisted in the discourse of the necessity for Black citizenship, although in subtly different ways. As we'll see in Chapter 1, popular representations of white amputees were primarily photographic, while

20 Introduction

those of Black amputated veterans were allegorical engravings that drew on the discourses of Black self-sacrifice for the good of the race. I discuss this mechanism more fully in Chapter 3, in Anna Dickinson's deployment of Black affliction via sentimental narrative tropes. The logic of Black martyrdom and loss that has its apogee in Harriet Beecher Stowe's *Uncle Tom's Cabin* reemerges in these representations of Black veteran amputees: a liberal discourse that requires Black suffering to legitimate Black empowerment.

However politically dodgy this suturing of Black injury to the expansion of the franchise and citizenship more generally, it contributes to the correlation – and occasional causation – narrated not just by veterans but also by popular culture between the loss of a limb and the struggle to end slavery. And, as we've seen, white radicals maintained an ethos of corporeal sacrifice in the face of the debt owed to the formerly enslaved and were vigilant in the face of backsliding (however ineffective that vigilance might have been in retrospect). But the permanent wound of amputation was more than payment for past sin – it was also a reminder of what was at stake in the project of Reconstruction: full black citizenship. While emancipation was the immediate goal of abolition, passed by Congress before the end of the war, the postwar telos for Black and white radicals alike was citizenship and the vote that went along with it. In Lauren Berlant's words, they were intensely concerned with questions of who would have access to the deep powers of meaningful subjectivity within the postwar state, "whose citizenship – whose subjectivity, whose forms of intimacy and interest, whose bodies and identifications, whose heroic narratives – [would] direct America's future" (6). The body politic from which slavery had been dismembered, embodied in the amputated veteran, was the condition of possibility for a capacious redefinition of citizenship.

"The rights of men and citizens": The Stakes of Black Citizenship

Black claims to and demands for formal citizenship predated the Fourteenth Amendment that formalized it. In 1843, at a Black antislavery meeting in Buffalo, Frederick Douglass's theme was Black people's "Moral and Political Condition as American Citizens" (Levine 33). James McCune Smith argued in 1859 that, contra *Dred Scott*, free Black Americans already enjoyed the benefits of citizenship and hence were citizens: "We must enforce a full acknowledgment of our rights in the free States, and thus obtain a stand point from which we can put in practice the glorious principles, which ... point out in living light our path of duty" (149). Black citizenship was raised by both the readers and editors of the *Weekly Anglo-African*. A September 1861 letter to the editor from "R.H.X." entitled "Formation of Colored Regiments" asked, "Have not two centuries of cruel and unrequited servitude in this country alone entitled the children of this generation to the rights of men and citizens?" (1). Robert Hamilton – cofounder and editor of the paper with his brother Thomas – wrote in support of Black recruitment in 1862, arguing that citizenship was already Black men's sinecure: "we have been pronounced citizens by the highest legal authority, why should not share in the perils of citizenship?" (qtd. in Reidy 221). And one of the products of the Colored Convention in October 1864 was the "Declarations of Wrongs and Rights" that averred that Black Americans should "remain in the full enjoyment of enfranchised manhood, and its dignities" to "claim the rights of . . . citizens" (*Proceedings* 42).

Recently, both Derrick Spires and Koritha Mitchell have argued that a self-conscious, affective Black American citizenship far preceded the Civil War. For Mitchell, Black people constituted a kind of "homemade citizenship" that was organized around individual and communal achievement and "focused more on creating possibility for themselves and each other than on responding to oppression" (3). Mitchell argues that homemade citizenship was and is not a static and constative phenomenon; rather, it is a performative process expressed within "the activities through which besieged communities cultivate success and belonging" (4).

For Spires, citizenship was fostered by connections to both a Black ethos and the larger political world. African Americans "theorized and practiced citizenship in the early United States through a robust print culture" that focused on active engagement with their community. Even as their formal citizenship rights in the North were curtailed over the course of the nineteenth century, Black writers, ministers, publishers, and everyday people imagined themselves as part of a polity defined by mutual responsibilities and rights. For both Mitchell and Spires, Black citizenship was the definitional opposite of the "necro citizenship" that Russ Castronovo has found in effect in the nineteenth century, which was characterized by "the mass of depoliticized persons and de-authorized memories that U.S. democracy creates" (*Necro Citizenship* xiii).

Even as Black citizenship rights were minimal, formal, white citizenship in the United States in the years between the ratification of the Constitution and the passage of the Fourteenth Amendment was fuzzy at best. Erik Mathisen has called the United States in the early nineteenth century a "government without citizens" (13), in large part because Americans did not imagine their subjectivity as primarily – or much at all – forged within the frame of the nation. Citizenship suffered from both "terminological prolixity and under-conceptualization" that provided little objective guidance as to who a citizen was (Hyde 5): Were white women? Children? Free Black men or women? Moreover, definitions of citizenship were hardly reliable. As Carrie Hyde points out, at bottom "[US] citizenship was juridically unregulated, politically inconsistent, and indelibly shaped by the assumptions, fears, and aspirations of the individuals who presumed to merely describe it" (6).

In large part, the modes of power and powerlessness that limned the boundaries of citizenship were determined by local and regional structures and interpersonal relations. The rights and responsibilities that were invested in early Americans were defined by "personal legal status – office, property, household position, race, gender, infirmity, and age" (Novak 105). Certainly, it was hard in the early years of the republic to identify with a national government whose capital moved from New York to Philadelphia before settling in the swamps of what became Washington, DC. But well into the nineteenth century, "Americans lacked a clear, national definition of citizenship and, by extension, had an equally unclear notion of what connected them to the nation state" (Mathisen 4).

The Civil War inaugurated a new conception of national belonging for both North and South. For Northerners, the war was waged to save "the Union," a free-standing entity that enveloped them and afforded them a specific subject position. Likewise, as Sharon D. Kennedy-Nolle argues, the "South ... was never a unified cultural entity" until the Confederacy was formed (15) (indeed, Kennedy-Nolle contends that Southern identity as such congealed only around the Confederacy's defeat). And after the war, the passage of the Fourteenth and Fifteenth Amendments codified the meanings of citizenship for all Americans.[20]

The Fourteenth Amendment – which I talk about in more detail in Chapter 3 – permanently reordered the meanings of citizenship. As legal historian Laura Edwards suggests, along with the right to vote, declaration that all people born or naturalized in the United States were citizens with specifically enumerated rights "theoretically altered the legal status of everyone in the Union and moved questions about the rights of citizens from the states to the federal government" (333). Paul Quigley is even more expansive in his analysis of these changes:

> The development of new concepts of citizenship involved Americans far from Washington, D.C.: Americans northern and southern, male and female, black and white, immigrant and native born. This was not simply the top-down imposition of new legal rules. Instead, it was a collaborative

and wide-ranging reassessment of the many meanings of citizenship in the United States. (2)

At the same time formal citizenship is a prickly issue. It is as often used to exclude, taxonomize, and hierarchize as it is to empower or liberate. While the citizen is awarded rights and privileges, defining what citizenship means is also "a hegemonic strategy [that] works to define ... groups or localities, to fix the power differentials between them, and then naturalize these operations" (Secor 354). Just as the state bestows rights, it also expects the citizen to conform to the restrictions citizenship entails. In Elizabeth Rogosin's analysis, although "citizenship offered the opportunity to demand what one was owed by the state ... at the same time, it compelled one to behave in particular ways according to what the state demanded" (39).

For example, Katherine Franke argues that freedpeople were and were not able to translate their partnerships, formed under slavery and in the face of the inability to formally marry, to the bourgeois norms of marriage and only uncomfortably fit the lived experience of the formerly enslaved. On the one hand, in Franke's words,

> The struggles of abject groups to emerge from the obscurity of the legal margins into the mainstream of civil society often materialized through demands for legal recognition by the state, and inclusion in the dominant legal and political institutions of society. (254)

But since "[r]ights both shape political culture and produce political subjects," the various forms of relationships that people forged in the regime of slavery compromised the status of newly emancipated people as legitimate participants in the polis (308).

So, what kind of citizenship did radicals envision emerging from the passage of the Fourteenth and Fifteenth Amendments? Certainly, as Caitlin Verboon notes, Black citizenship connoted a kind of capaciousness of civic status: "narrowly-defined rights – voting, testifying, sitting on juries, holding elected office – mattered enormously, but so did ... equality and full participation within ... communities" (162). While Russ Castronovo – not incorrectly – avers that "the U.S. democratic state loves its citizens as passive subjects, unresponsive to political issues, unmoved by social stimuli, and unaroused by enduring injustices" (*Necro Citizenship* 4), the citizenship imagined by Reconstruction radicals was process-oriented and inspired by a shared commitment to justice. Rhetorician Robert Asen suggests a way of conceiving citizenship that accords with Verboon's characterization. He argues that if we theorize citizenship as "a mode of public engagement," then this "perspective shifts our focus from *what* constitutes citizenship to *how* citizenship proceeds" (194).

This brings us back to Derrick Spires's work on what he calls the "critical citizenship" woven together by free Black communities in the early republic and the antebellum period. For Black Americans before the Fourteenth Amendment was passed and ratified, citizenship rights were uneven and changing.[21] But, as Spires shows, free Black communities practiced Asen's definition of citizenship as public engagement, what Raymond Williams called a "structure of feeling": a congeries of practices, assumptions, social arrangements, and material culture that construct a way of being in the world, with its own protocols and beliefs. For Williams, structures of feeling "are concerned with meanings and values as they are actively lived and felt" in a specific place at a specific time by a specific group of people (132), defined by "a particular quality of social experience and relationship, historically distinct from other particular qualities" (131).

As Spires shows, for free African Americans in the early United States – and, I would argue, beyond the Civil War and into Reconstruction – citizenship was imagined as a complex phenomenon: social, affective, and political. It drew on preexisting notions of American citizenship promulgated in the Constitution, but broadened and deepened them beyond the juridical and into the communal. In this context,

> "citizen" invokes a civic ethos and protocols of recognition and justice that call on audiences to think about their relation to citizens and others as one of mutual responsibility, responsiveness, and active engagement, a relation in which membership and individual rights come with moral obligations to a collective. (Spires 5)

This is the kind of citizenship that white radicals drew on when they imagined a postslavery America: the inverse of how US citizenship had been constructed so far, as "a long political and economic process of selective inclusion and exclusion requiring constant institutional and cultural maintenance" (Spires 25). In the debate over the passage of the Fourteenth Amendment, radical Nevadan Republican Senator William Stewart derogated this formulation of citizenship in the past, in which the revolutionary generation established "a declaration of rights for all men, but a Government of white men only. The theory was good, the practice in this respect fatally defective" (*Congressional Globe* 2799). Passage of the Amendment, however, would effect a new kind of nation, one that in its juridical structures ensured "the equality of every man in the right to life, liberty, and the pursuit of happiness, and the perfect equality of every man to strive to equal and strive to excel his neighbor in everything great, good, and useful" (*Congressional Globe* 302).

The amputated veteran was the avatar of this aspiration toward "perfect equality," a palimpsestic figure who, as I have shown, embodied multiple radical principles at once: the debt to be paid for enslavement, the excision of the gangrene of slavery, the vow never to return to the world before emancipation, and the promise of a full, equal, and engaged Black citizenship rooted in mutual respect and responsibility.

My goal in this book is not to argue #notallwhitepeople in relation to Reconstruction and its aftermath. Indeed, one thing that Reconstruction can show us is that, just as happens today, white public opinion about racial justice can shift enthusiastically toward and then just as precipitously away from a commitment to equity.[22] By 1874 white support for Reconstruction was already on the wane, and William Wells Brown observed that "there is a feeling all over this country that the Negro has got about as much as he ought to" (qtd. in Blight 131). By the end of the nineteenth century, one would have had to look very hard for a white supporter of Black political and social equality, let alone someone who paid close and respectful attention to Black political, philosophical, or social thought. Most Northern whites looked to their Southern counterparts to represent Black hopes, abilities, and culture to them.[23]

Moreover, despite their full-throated support for Black liberation in all spheres, white supporters of radical Reconstruction often resisted acknowledging the parallels between anti-Black racism and the coterminous violence against other racialized and minoritized peoples, parallels that their Black radical counterparts for the most part recognized. As Edlie Wong shows in *Racial Reconstruction: Black Inclusion, Chinese Exclusion, and the Fictions of Citizenship*, a commitment to Black citizenship did not necessarily translate into support for Chinese immigration, or for Chinese migrants in the United States, Indeed, James Blaine, who had been foundational in shaping and passing the Reconstruction Amendments, argued that Chinese immigrants competed with both Black and white workers, driving down wages (an ironic echo of Free Soil arguments against slavery in the 1850s), thereby "portray[ing] Chinese exclusion as consistent with abolitionism's egalitarian principles" (Wong 71). Similarly, while radical Republican Charles Sumner supported the possibility of citizenship for all inhabitants of the United States, veteran abolitionist Wendell Phillips militated against Chinese migration, citing the need for the United States to remain a Christian nation (Wong 103–4). And while Black leaders shared some of these fears, as Wong shows, "black political sympathy for the Chinese continue[d] to flourish in the face of this perceived difference" (102).[24]

The record of supporters of congressional Reconstruction regarding Indigenous sovereignty is not much better.[25] Oliver O. Howard, the director of the Freedmen's Bureau, moved on to command troops in the West in the so-called Indian Wars, and in 1877 displaced the Nez Perce people from their ancestral lands in what are now Washington State and Oregon to Oklahoma (they were later displaced again to Idaho). General Philip Sheridan, who served as the military commander of the Fifth Military District, which comprised Louisiana and Texas, and feuded with Andrew Johnson over Black voting rights, commanded US troops in the Western plains and oversaw the defeat and displacement of the Kiowa, Cheyenne, and Comanche.[26]

Chapter Outlines

Although thematically focused on Reconstruction, this book ranges from the mid-1850s to the late 1880s. Each chapter forms a section of a chronological arc, beginning in the period just before the Civil War, and its photographic representations of child death, and then lingering in the years of the war itself through contemporaneous and retrospective literary texts. The heart of the book – Chapters 3 and 4 – addresses the historical and novelistic phenomenon of amputation as a trope adopted by white radicals to corporealize their understandings of the war and their hopes for Reconstruction. Chapter 5 and the Conclusion take stock of the initial (if uneven) struggle against and ultimate concession of white America to the revanchist and recidivist energies of white supremacy, which laid the foundation for ongoing denial of civil and human rights to Black Americans.

Chapter 1, "Giving Up the Ghost: The Dead Child versus the Amputated Limb," traces the antebellum faith in the non-finality of death and its antithesis in the irreparable change wrought by amputation. To make this argument I contrast antebellum postmortem photography and images of amputees and amputated limbs. Postmortem photography of children, in particular, reinforces the sense that the family has not *really* been ruptured, that death isn't *really* the end. Photographs of amputee Civil War soldiers do quite the opposite. Certainly, the comparison

Chapter Outlines 27

between these two photographic genres is incomplete: many of these images of amputees played quite a different role, less commemorative and more documentary, especially those pictures taken for medical research. But rather than operating as postmortem photography does, as a mediator between the living child, its dead body, and the family left behind, the portrait of the amputee is insistently in the present, even as the lost limb is consigned to an irrecuperable past. While nineteenth-century pictures of dead children often encouraged the fiction that the photograph's subject was only sleeping and an ongoing member of the family, amputation photography – both medical and vernacular – insists on the permanence of bodily change.

In Chapter 2, "'Strewn promiscuously about': Limbs and What Happens to Them," I explore several accounts by Civil War nurses and surgeons – represented through first-person nonfiction, lightly fictionalized narrative, sensationalized memoir, and fiction. The central texts in this chapter are Walt Whitman's *Memoranda after the War* (based heavily on his wartime journals), Louisa May Alcott's *Hospital Sketches* (drawn primarily from her letters home), John Brinton's *Personal Memoirs* (a narrative of his experiences as a field surgeon and the founding director of the Army Medical Museum), Susie King Taylor's *Reminiscences of My Life in Camp*, and S. Weir Mitchell's short story "The Case of George Dedlow." I'm especially interested in how these narrators represent amputation in different ways, especially the scene of amputation itself, the image of a basket or trough of dismembered limbs, and amputee reflections on the relationship between their remaining bodies and their absent limbs, and the physical and metaphysical permanence of amputation. The chapter ends with a discussion of the Army Medical Museum, in which amputated limbs were catalogued, stored, and often displayed as examples of the anatomical damage done by gunshots and shells. This dovetails with a reading of "George Dedlow", in which the protagonist's legs, stored in alcohol at the Museum, return to him briefly during a séance, absurdly marrying hopes for bodily resurrection with spiritualism's belief in a humanized heaven.

Chapter 3, "1860 or 1865? Amending the National Body," focuses on a now little-read but in her time central abolitionist and antiracist activist, lecturer, and novelist, Anna E. Dickinson. My interest in this chapter is Dickinson's first novel, *What Answer?* (1868), which follows an interracial couple, William Surrey and Francesca Ercildoune, from their first meeting in 1861 to their deaths in 1863 at the hands of a New York Draft Riot mob. It ends with a climactic scene in which Francesca's brother, the biracial Robert Ercildoune, accompanied by his friend William's cousin Tom Russell, attempts to vote in a local 1865 election and is barred by racist poll-goers. The chapter's title comes from Tom's assurance to Robert that it is 1865 not 1860 and, in the wake of the Thirteenth Amendment abolishing slavery and the Civil Rights Act Congress attempted to pass in 1865, he should not be concerned about the legitimacy of his vote in Pennsylvania. In *What Answer?* the body amputated and amended, either by the empty sleeve or by prosthetic leg, holds out hope for an amended Constitution and an amended nation. The novel ends on this very note. Dickinson ventriloquizes all those Civil War veterans disabled by the war: "Here we stand, shattered and maimed, that the body politic might be perfect!" (298). This perfection is not a reconstitution of the prewar nation, but, rather, the spiritual and ethical perfection represented by its amputee characters. Ultimately this novel, published during the process of the ratification of the Fourteenth Amendment, looks toward the possibility of an amended nation.

Chapter 4, "'I don't care a rag for the *Union as it was*': Amputation, the Past, and the Work of the Freedmen's Bureau," deals primarily with the period of Reconstruction and the importance of the Freedmen's Bureau. Using Albion Tourgée's 1883 novel *Bricks without Straw*, Oliver Otis Howard's first-person account of his time as director of the Freedmen's Bureau, and archival records of the Bureau itself, I read the novel as a fictional reenactment of the work of Reconstruction.

In *Bricks without Straw* Tourgée returns again and again to the amputated bodies of Union soldiers and sympathizers as the agents of reparation and justice for Black citizens. But this justice is not just the work of white radicals and sympathetic Northerners. It is struggled for by Black characters, who lay claim to the rights accorded them by the Thirteenth, Fourteenth, and Fifteenth Amendments. In the novel, amputation forces readers to focus on the present and move beyond the past, in recognition that the past of the intact body is irrecoverable. The past of a South organized around the enslavement and exploitation of black Americans is buried, just as white protagonist Hesden Lemoyne's lost arm is discarded, on a Civil War battlefield, or in a pile of other dismembered limbs, in favor of a future that puts Black self-determination at its core. This echoes Tourgée's own goals for Reconstruction: he rejected the goal simply of preserving the Union, avowing, "I don't care a rag for '*the Union as it was.*' I want and fight for the *Union better* than '*it was.*'"

Chapter 5, "Shaking Hands: Manual Politics and the End of Reconstruction," traces representations of hands – disembodied, amputated, and multiplied – as Reconstruction was debilitated and eventually dismantled. Using the political cartoons of Thomas Nast that appeared in *Harper's Weekly* I track Nast's repeated deployment of hands to illustrate the changing fortunes of Reconstruction. Hands also figure in narratives of the twenty-fifth anniversary of the Battle of Gettysburg. One of the most common tropes of the better-known fiftieth reunion, Union and Confederate veterans shaking hands, was already ubiquitous in 1888 at the twenty-fifth, and it's this iterative discourse that I explore. The chapter ends with a reading of William Dean Howells's 1889 novel, *A Hazard of New Fortunes*, focusing especially on the German American veteran Berthold Lindau, who lost his hand during the Civil War. An 1848 refugee with radical racial and class politics, Lindau is portrayed as a holdover from the past who is incapable of adjusting to modernity in the form of massive wealth inequality, urban decay, and the calcification of white supremacy north and south. Lindau's death at the end of the novel is the literary nail in the coffin of radical Reconstruction, which Howells has already consigned to the dustbin of history.

Along with corporeality, I also engage with questions of temporality. The commitment to radical Reconstruction entailed a deep remembering of the past at the same time that it required a clear-eyed understanding of the present and an investment in an equitable future. White supremacy, by contrast, invoked a wholly reworked past, in which slavery was either forgotten or transformed into a benign institution. It looked forward to a future that as closely as possible reiterated the racial power relations of the prewar past and insisted on a present in which time could stand still. The conflict between anti-Reconstruction revanchists and white advocates for Black liberation was not just political per se – it was a struggle to remake the meanings of time itself: the relationships between past, present, and future. While the radicals I focus on here insisted on a total break with the past to fashion a new nation that would endure into the utopian antiracist future, increasingly, white Americans blurred the boundaries between pre- and postwar racialization, so that antebellum enslavement slid effortlessly into Jim Crow white supremacy.

In this book I try to invert the white supremacist claim that Black gain is white loss. My goal is to show that white loss in the Civil War could have been a harbinger of white *and* Black gains, a comprehensive, generous definition of citizenship and the rights of citizens to land, education, and dignity. US constructions of whiteness brought with them genocide, enslavement, and brutal violence: the gangrene that is white supremacy. I would hope that we can imagine a world in which that necrotic limb is cut off for good.

CHAPTER I

Giving Up the Ghost
The Dead Child versus the Amputated Limb

The photograph is arresting in its beauty: a young girl, maybe three or four years old, sleeping gently on a chair draped with a sheet. Less than seven by nine inches, the image is a daguerreotype from the 1850s, a typical carte de visite of the era (although a little larger than usual),[1] a small photograph to be collected in an album of such pictures. The child seems to be sleeping, her chubby arms folded over a crumpled white dress adorned with large bows at the shoulder and embroidery on the bodice, her bare feet tucked under slightly, one leg folded over the other. Her right hand holds a ribbon with a cross attached to it.

Of course, we know that this child is not sleeping, but dead, and that this photograph is not capturing a sweet moment of childhood but memorializing a lost loved one (see Figure 1.1). Postmortem photography was a small but profitable field for practitioners in the mid-nineteenth century, especially pictures of children who had died. While not all the photographs were as aesthetically successful as this one, made by the Boston studio of legendary partners Albert Sands Southworth and Josiah Johnson Hawes, they mostly shared in a similar aesthetic. In the majority of these images, the dead are posed as though just sleeping, and the viewer holds her breath so as not to wake the dozing child.

Southworth and Hawes's artistry (or that of their staff photographer, unnamed) is such that the photograph has a kind of timelessness to it, a stillness that is intensified by the technology of the 1850s, when this photograph was taken. Formed on a glass plate and printed with albumen silver, the image has both sharpness in the foreground and penumbral depth in the background, which is typical of the genre.[2] The picture is both hyperreal and romanticized at the same time, each dimpled knuckle and fold of fabric clearly reproduced, even as the girl's hair melts into the darkness on the edges of the print.

Let us contrast this image with one taken about a decade later. A medical document that is part of Civil War doctor Reed Bontecou's

31

32   The Dead Child versus the Amputated Limb

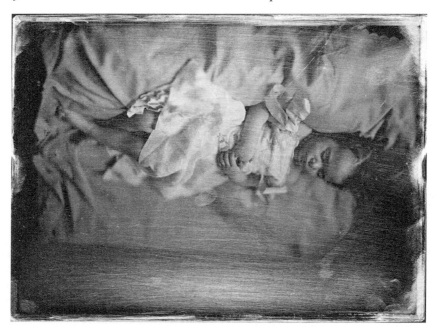

Figure 1.1   Southworth and Hawes, *Postmortem Portrait* (c. 1850).
Courtesy of the George Eastman Museum.

extensive collection of surgical photographs, many of which he took himself of surgeries he had performed, this picture (which I discuss in more detail later on in the chapter) also shows a recumbent figure, that of John Parmenter (Figure 1.2). But it could not be more different from the postmortem photograph above.

Some of the differences are obvious, although (arguably) incidental: the subject of this image is male, not female; he is half naked rather than fully dressed; he is attended by another man, not alone. Others take a moment to sink in. The child in the first image is dead; Parmenter is merely anesthetized. Whereas our unnamed child is beautifully dressed, her hair arrayed around her face, the couch on which she lies covered with undulating draperies, the man in Bontecou's photograph, John Parmenter, is only partly covered by a shirt. His left leg rests on a box, the foot surgically removed and placed beyond the box, so swollen and gangrenous that it is almost unrecognizable.

While the Southworth and Hawes picture has a timelessness to it, emphasized by the shading into darkness of the edges of the image, the

The Dead Child versus the Amputated Limb

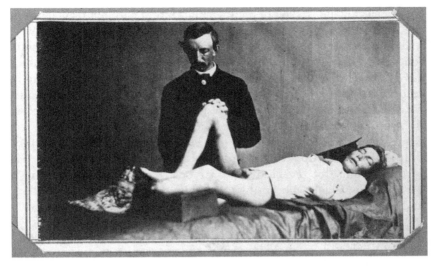

Figure 1.2   Reed B. Bontecou, *John Parmenter* (1865).
Courtesy of the Burns Archive.

Bontecou photograph is fixed at a very specific moment: the brief period after surgery but before Parmenter regains consciousness. His body itself tells a story of a past, in which his infected foot was attached to his body, and a present in which that foot has been permanently removed from the end of his leg. Even if he wanted to (which is highly doubtful, given that gangrene almost inevitably leads to systemic sepsis and death), Parmenter cannot return to the state he was in before this picture was taken, let alone before he was injured at all.

I start with these photographs as an entry point into my argument in this chapter that focuses on photographic representations of amputation, and their rhetorical power. As I argue here, the amputation photograph offers an alternate narrative to, if not a repudiation of, the discourses around loss, death, and the possibility of recuperation that the Civil War made virtually impossible. If, as Drew Gilpin Faust has argued, the mass anonymous death of the war rendered the "good death" an unreachable goal for many of those who died on Civil War battlefields, the losses of amputation argued for an unrecuperability of the past and the need to move into a restructured, reconstructed future. The photograph of the amputee is the discursive opposite of the images of the dead child and all they represent in the sentimental mythos of the mid-nineteenth century.

In what follows, I explore photographic and literary representations of the dead child and its antithesis, the amputee. The intense desire by so many Americans to imagine reconciliation after death provided a blueprint for the discourse of national reconciliation that accompanied the end of the Civil War: change that was not really change, a past that could easily be recuperated into a future, the immutability of social relations even after massive transitions. Of course, the desire for reconciliation at the expense of Black liberation found its roots in other sources, not least of which was a white supremacist social structure that Reconstruction could not successfully unseat. But I would argue that even antislavery white Americans had in the discourse of the dead child a model for how to simultaneously mourn material and emotional losses, refuse the permanence of that loss, and imagine a world in which little if anything actually had to change.

For both sets of images, we have to grapple with ethical issues, since the distinction between viewing and voyeurism can become vanishingly thin.[3] Apart from the studio photographs of amputees that I discuss toward the end of this chapter, these images were not created for wide public consumption. The photographs of dead children, some portrait-sized but most produced as cartes de visite, were intended for family and close friends as a remembrance. The medical photographs had an equally limited, although more formal purpose – illustrating surgical procedures and, later, undergirding pension applications. How, then, are we positioned as viewers and how do we position ourselves? Are we applying an inappropriate aestheticizing lens?

My sense is that for the images of dead children, the ethics of aestheticizing the suffering of others obtain less – these pictures are by definition aesthetically self-conscious as well as memorial objects. As I argue in the next section, they conform to an aesthetic, religious, and affective script shared by mostly white, mostly bourgeois families about the meanings of death and loss. While these photographs were not designed for view by strangers, they were intended to circulate somewhat, and speak openly and with pathos to viewers, narrating a very specific discourse of death.

The ethical questions surrounding the medical amputee photographs are more thorny. While I found no reports of the subjects of these pictures being coerced in any way, at the same time we can imagine that the sitters had little choice in being laid open to the gaze of the photographer and/or surgeon, who were often one and the same (the photograph of John Parmenter is a prime example of this: Did he consent, pre-surgery, to a photograph in which the lower half of his body is so exposed that his penis is visible to the viewer?). And the images were captured for instrumental rather than aesthetic reasons. With this in mind, I try as much as is possible to take into account the subjectivities of the men being photographed – how they address the camera and, by extension, the viewer. While some men look away, most confront this experience and seem to be looking as much as they are looked at. These men, that is to say, are more than their wounds, even as their likenesses are taken precisely to memorialize their injuries and the surgical interventions taken to heal them.

"So shalt thou in a brighter world, behold / That countenance which the cold grave did veil": The Immortality of the Dead Child and the Inevitability of Reunion

In order to work through the disjuncture between these two sets of images – dead white children[4] versus white amputees – it is important to dive into an archeology of the aesthetics and, indeed, the phenomenology of death and mourning in the mid-nineteenth-century United States. Death was ever-present for nineteenth-century Americans of all classes: in Mark S. Schantz's words it was "intimately familiar . . . [They] had seen it in their homes and witnessed it in their streets. They had washed the corpses of loved ones and laid them out in parlors. . . . They had watched at the bedsides of friends as spirits had departed" (9). This was even more the case for the death of children, "which was a commonplace occurrence in the mid-nineteenth century" (Schantz 12). And these deaths were repeatedly narrativized. As Karen Sánchez-Eppler has argued, "Dying is what children do most and do best in the literary and cultural imagination of nineteenth-century America" (101). Certainly, child mortality was a reality for all classes of Americans in the mid-nineteenth century: of every six children born in the 1850s, one died before the age of five (Sánchez-Eppler 107). But even so, child death occupied a disproportionate amount of cultural and imaginative real estate . From best-selling novels like Susan Warner's *The Wide Wide World* and Harriet Beecher Stowe's *Uncle Tom's Cabin* to consolation literature such as Theodore Cuyler's *The Empty Crib* and Nehemiah Adams's *Agnes and the Key to Her Little Coffin* to the poetry of Lydia Huntley Sigourney to the multiple photographs of dead babies, toddlers, children, and teenagers, representations of dying and dead young people were a significant strand of nineteenth-century American culture. And the conventions of how one talked about dead children suffused the letters and poems of everyday Americans.

The dead child invoked two interrelated but separate phenomena: consolation literature and the denial of death. Consolation literature lingered on the material effects of the now-gone child: the crib, the clothing, even the coffin itself. These material objects stood in for the child but were also superannuated by the promise of an eternity in which parents and children would be reunited for good. Nehemiah Adams's *Agnes and the Key to Her Little Coffin, by Her Father*, published in Boston in 1857, is a paragon of the genre, using the key to toddler Alice's coffin as a keepsake and an "emblem and a pledge of readmission to her. She is ours still" (64). The key here plays a double role. On the one hand, it literally locks up the coffin, as though to reinforce how Agnes is in death closed off from her parents and the world of the living. On the other hand, it is a metaphorical key back to her that unlocks the promise of eternity to Agnes's parents. As Adams maintains, it is a key to heaven, in which Agnes and her parents will be reunited as though nothing had happened:

> What scenes there must be in heaven every day, in the meetings of parents and children, and relatives and friends, but among them all I do think that to meet a little child, who died in infancy, and has been for years in heaven, must have as much of surprise and gladness in it as anything. (185)

Adams doesn't elaborate on what would constitute this surprise, but I would imagine it is the reunion of the now elderly parents with their still-baby child. The unchangingness of heaven contrasts with the passage of time on earth, preserving Agnes in her infant state. And the key is a reminder of that stasis; no matter how the parents may change and age, no matter what happens on the earthly realm, heaven is as real and as graspable as the key itself, and as immutable.

Theodore Cuyler, in *The Empty Crib: The Memorial of Little Georgie, with Words of Consolation for Bereaved Parents*, published eleven years later in New York, follows a similar theme. Made up of an initial narrative of the life of little Georgie and then letters and poems from sympathizers (although it's hard to know how many of these are actual letters and how many Cuyler wrote himself, since the narrative voice is quite similar), *The Empty Crib* melds condolence for Georgie's death with consolation by way of assurance of his reunion with his parents in heaven. As "J.B.S." says in a letter to Cuyler, "'Oh, what a child that will be when you meet him again!'" (68–9). To support this point, Cuyler quotes Horace Greeley, offering a prayer that looks forward to reunion and familial reconstitution after death: "God keep me worthy of thy love through the weary years, till I meet thee and greet thee in that world where the loving re-unite, to be parted no more forever" (75–6).

The Dead Child and the Inevitability of Reunion 37

These sentiments often found their way into poetry, written by both amateur and professional poets. In *The Empty Crib*, Cuyler cites a poem on a gravestone in Greenwood Cemetery, where little Georgie is buried:

> Under the daisies two graves are made
> Under the daisies our treasures are laid
> Under the daisies? It cannot be thus
> We are sure that in heaven they wait for us. (152)

This kind of vernacular poetry was commonplace among middle-class nineteenth-century Americans. As Mary Louise Kete has shown, composing and sharing poems was itself a pastime many of the bourgeoisie participated in, especially but not only women. And a large number of these poems were about death and dying. In her excavation of the poetic archive of a rural Vermont family, Kete finds the same theme over and over again, what she calls "the utopian promise of sentimentality – of non-violated community, of restored losses, of healed wounds" (47). This desire for reunion and the non-finality of death can be found in a poem by one of Kete's writers, Abigail Gould Howe, dedicated to her recently dead son, Wayland:

> And if to God we faithful prove
> And act the Christian part
> We'll join them in that world above
> Where we shall never part. (5)

An intrinsic part of the sentimental ethos was an evangelical Christianity centered in large part around the promise of heaven. Here Howe spells out the almost transactional nature of that faith: obedience to God and Christian conduct lead to reunification with loved ones in the afterlife. But as Kete points out, there was more at stake than religious belief. The poem illustrates a larger, psychological need that sentimental Christianity served, the desire "to reattach symbolic connections that have been severed by the contingencies of human existence . . . to imagine the bonds between [Wayland] and herself as different than they really were: as eternal, not temporary; as necessary, not arbitrary" (6). While earthly existence is ephemeral, by maintaining Christian faith and the self-sacrifice and submission to God's will that required, Howe anticipates that her separation from Wayland is brief in comparison to their eternity together.

Abigail Howe and her family members did not lack for models for this kind of poetry. One of the most popular poets of the day, Lydia Howard Huntley Sigourney, was the author of innumerable poems about dead and dying children and their mothers. Long scorned for her sentimental poetry, "The Sweet Singer of Hartford" was in fact a multifaceted writer who penned essays, pedagogical works, and what we would now call ethnography. Moreover, her poetry ranged from topics as broad as the removals of Indigenous peoples in the 1830s to abolition to environmentalism (her poem "Fallen Forests" begins "Man's warfare on the trees is terrible"). At the same time, she often focused on the death of children, especially babies – not surprisingly, since she lost three of her own five children. While Sigourney certainly did not invent the genre of sentimental poetry, she was its most prolific and influential practitioner.

In her 1834 volume of poems, Sigourney revisits this theme again and again. She effortlessly inhabits the narrative of the grieving parent, such as in her poem "To a Dying Infant." Rather than begging the dying baby to live, the unnamed parent bids her child to "Go to thy rest . . . Go to thy dreamless bed" (138). In part, the speaker of the poem wants to spare the child the possibility of sin, a life in which "thy heart might learn / In waywardness to stray" and would rather send the infant to "thy home of rest / In yon celestial sphere" (138). In the final stanza, the speaker muses wistfully on the child's beauty and the love the child evoked, but foreswears that love as a reason for the baby to stay on earth, asking,

> Shall Love with weak embrace
> Thy heavenward flight detain?
> No! Angel, seek thy place
> Amid yon cherub-train. (138)

In this poem, Sigourney presents a set of binary choices to which there is only one right answer. Should the child remain in the world, "thy feet could turn / The dark and downward way" that is a possibility for all mortals. So, "[e]re sin might wound the breast," the parent only partly reluctantly lets the child go to be among the angels. The poem has many of the hallmarks of the sentimental aesthetic: the innocent baby, "gentle and undefiled," half-angel already; the fear of following a worldly path that offers nothing but temporary pleasures (the flowers around the baby's bed "so quickly fade," after all); and the pull toward heaven. And it sets the scene for other poems in the volume that explore more fully what the promise of heaven means, where loved ones are finally reunited.

Paradigmatic of this scenario of heavenly repair of broken bonds is Sigourney's poem "On the Death of a Mother, Soon after Her Infant Son." Sigourney tells the story of a beloved child, "the precious one / The prayed for, the adored," who is the focus of his mother's love and attention (121). She educates him on topics both religious and secular: "For him the

The Dead Child and the Inevitability of Reunion 39

paths of knowledge she explored, / Feeding his eager mind with seraph's bread, /Till intellectual light o'er his fair features spread" (122). But the child quickly dies, followed soon by his mother.

In the narrative of the poem, while the child's death is deeply mourned, the mother's is far less tragic, since it entails her reunion with her dead baby: "Now is her victory won, / Her strife of battle o'er, / She hath found her son – she hath found her son, / Where Death is a king no more" (122). Sigourney uses the conventional language of "the victory" to signify death in salvation, a usage that would have been familiar to her readers. But this victory is twofold: not only is the "battle" of life over, and resolved into eternal life in Christ, but also "she hath found her son, / Where Death is a king no more" (122). God's victory secures her the ultimate reward: the reconstitution of the mother-child bond. Indeed, Sigourney encourages her readers who are bereaved mothers to use this story as a guide to their own ultimate reward. "Look up! Look up to the bountiful sky," she implores them; "Ye have sown in pain – ye shall reap in bliss" (122). The prize of heaven is salvation, yes, but even more importantly it is the reunification of the grieving mother and her dead child (the father seems irrelevant in this poem – his grief over the loss of his wife and child go unmentioned, and he is absent from the scene of the poem altogether).

For Sigourney, the link between mother and child is interrupted by death, but not broken. She acknowledges the intense grief occasioned by the loss of a child, and at the same time sees that as a temporary condition compared with the ultimate prize. With her eye firmly fixed on the hereafter, she encourages women to think beyond the here and now and into eternity, even as she sensitively represents the agonies of bereavement. "'Twas but a Babe," for example, is set at the mouth of the grave of a newly buried child, berating the heartless bystander who dismisses the loss as minimal since the child was so young. Far from it; Sigourney identifies (some might say fetishizes) the pain of losing a child of any age:

> What know ye of her love
> Who patient watcheth till the stars grow dim.
> Over her drooping infant . . .?
> What know ye of her woe who sought no joy
> More exquisite, than on his placid brow
> To trace the glow, of health, and drink at dawn
> The thrilling lustre of his waking smile? (142)

Nonetheless, Sigourney reassures her readers that this tragic separation is only momentary – in an apostrophe to the grieving mother she exclaims, "Can ye not hope, / When a few hasting years their course have run, /

To go to him, though he no more on earth / Returns to you!" (143). It's especially striking that these lines do double rhetorical work. Structurally, they function as a question – one would imagine the phrase "Can ye not hope" would end with a question mark – even if it is a question whose answer is a predetermined "yes." But Sigourney goes one further than that, transforming the question into an affirmation, one intensified by an exclamation mark. Implicitly she's saying, "Yes, you *can* hope," that it is certain that this child will return to their mother intact.

This hope holds for children as well as parents (or, more precisely, mothers). In "Baptism of an Infant, at Its Mother's Funeral," Sigourney offers the same comfort to the motherless child. Indeed, she implies that the reunion between mother and child might even be preferable to the relationship they could expect on the terrestrial plane:

> So shalt though in a brighter world, behold
> That countenance which the cold grave did veil
> Thus early from thy sight, and the first tone
> That bears a mother's greeting to thine ear
> Be wafted from the minstrelsy of heaven. (183)

The relationship of mother and child will play out in a "brighter world," inflected by heavenly music, rather than amid the stresses and strains of everyday life. Sigourney contrasts the joys of heaven with the grief invoked by the mother's death by bookending the "cold grave" with promises of paradise as a "brighter world" on one side and "the minstrelsy of heaven" on the other, as if to say that the grave itself is a short stay compared with the surrounding eternity of the afterlife. And heaven itself engages not just the eyes but also the ears – it allows the child, in death, to "behold" its mother's face, and hear "a mother's greeting" and heavenly music. The poem begins with a celebration of life – a baptism – but quickly dispenses with the living of that life to focus on its end, and the reunion of mother and child. And baptism itself looks toward that reunion, since it is a moment in which the child is given access to the Jesus who saves souls for the hereafter.

Sigourney pushes this logic even further in her poem "A Mother in Heaven to Her Dying Babe," in which the speaker of the poem beseeches those on Earth to release her child into her keeping: "Heaven hath no throb of pain / Heaven hath no tempter's charms, / Friends! Friends! – why will ye thus detain / My darling from my arms?" (216). As in "To a Dying Infant," the speaker judges heaven as a better place for a child to "grow up" (or whatever a dead child in heaven would do) in the care of its mother, free from earthly temptations. By locating the voice of the poem within the persona of the already-dead mother, Sigourney reverses the positionalities of previous poems: rather than identifying the mother with grief and loss through death, this poem views death as a gain, a reorienting of the balance of familial relationship toward its ideal form of a child in its mother's embrace.

In all these poems, the irreversible change of death is actually a way to preserve the status quo. The innocent baby is never corrupted by the "tempter's charms," the mother never ages, and the child never grows up. Heaven is a place in which time stops and growth is arrested, in which mourners are reunited with their loved ones and we are all our best selves. In her poems of grieving mothers and reconstituted families Lydia Huntley Sigourney offers us a blueprint for the architecture of childhood death that played out in literary, musical, and visual artistic objects. But nowhere is the figure of the dead child more poignant than in photography. Photographs had to encapsulate Sigourney's layered message – that the death of a child occasions both intense grief and equally intense hope for reunion – in a single image. It did this in a variety of visual tropes that appeared throughout the mid-nineteenth century, none more powerful than the representation of children as not permanently gone but simply resting, waiting for reunion.

Asleep in Jesus: Postmortem Photography and the Denial of Death

Although it is rare today, postmortem photography was a booming business in the mid-nineteenth century. As Jay Ruby has shown, photographs of the recently deceased were a common element of photographic businesses, often advertised as part of their array of services (55). In his 1855 article for *The Photographic Fine Art Journal*, "Taking Portraits after Death," N. G. Burgess was matter-of-fact about what an intrinsic part of the professional photographer's life postmortem portraiture was. "The occupation of the Daguerrean Artist," he stated, "necessarily brings him into contact with the endearing feelings of the human heart, more especially is this true when called upon to copy the 'human face divine'" (80).

Photography played a complex role in the rituals around death, since it both represented the reality of death – the image of the corpse – and at the same time could participate in the fantasy that death was not final. In Ruby's words, "the motivation for the [posthumous] image contains a fundamentally contradictory desire – to retain the dead, to capture some essence of a being now gone, to deny death" (29). This is especially true of photographs of dead children. Burgess hints at this in his instructions to photographers of the deceased, advising that "if the portrait of an infant is to be taken, it may be placed in the mother's lap, and taken in the usual manner by a side light representing sleep" (80). "In the usual manner" is a striking phrase here – there is so little aesthetic distinction to be made between a child who is dead and one who is sleeping that the technical approach toward both subjects is the same, and hence the result would not be so different.

This methodology of photographing the corpses of children dovetailed with the sentimental insistence that death was not, in some profound way, real or permanent. Photography undergirded "sentimental efforts to keep the dead present" (Sánchez-Eppler 130), not only by providing a permanent token of the lost child, but by constructing an image that obfuscated or even obscured the material reality of death. As Mark Schantz has shown, there was a "lively" debate during the antebellum years over the literalness of the resurrection of the body in heaven, but there was no question that death was not the end of human connection (53). The postmortem photograph did double duty, both "acknowledg[ing] that the child has died" while at the same time "invit[ing] its viewers ... to retain the living child at least as an image" (Sánchez-Eppler 119). As Mary Louise Kete puts it, "[p]hotography promised to bridge the distance of time, of the grave," not just offering the potential of reunion in heaven but also performing the belief that the dead were simply "asleep in Christ," temporarily unavailable to their loved ones but not truly gone. The photographic image of the dead child was an "act of conservation [that] entailed ... a successful act of creation or generation that denied the event of death" (Kete 157).

This visual, emotional, and cultural work done by the photograph of the dead child is evident in another 1850s portrait by Southworth and Hawes (see Figure 1.3). The girl, who seems to be about five, is dressed up in her Sunday best – an off-the-shoulder dress with white lacy petticoat and pantaloons, patent leather shoes, and a beaded bracelet. Despite the formality of her clothes, though, there is a casualness to the portrait – her bottom leg is folded at the knee, under the top leg. While her hair is neatly parted, her hands are laid loosely one on top of the other, as though she had laid down after church and fallen quickly asleep. The portrait feels even more intimate than the one I discussed previously (Figure 1.3), in large part because the child seems to be laid in her own bed, rather than on an abstract, fabric-draped couch that more closely resembles something that might be found in the photographer's studio than the family home.

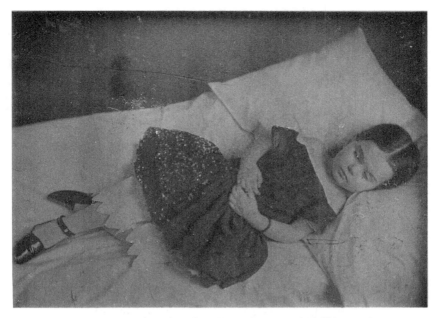

Figure 1.3 Southworth and Hawes, *Postmortem of Child* (c. 1850).
Courtesy of the George Eastman Museum.

This picture (and the many others like it) is in marked contrast to postmortem photographs of older people. In those portraits, the subjects lie straight, arms either by their sides or folded over their chests. There is little sense that they are "just sleeping" – the poses are stiff and formal. In this photograph, however, there is a tenderness implicit in the way the child is positioned. Someone – a parent? the photographer? – moved her arms and legs into gentle asymmetry, as though to embody how this girl might nap quietly on a Sunday afternoon.

A similar portrait by an unknown photographer makes this point even more directly (Figure 1.4). The picture lies in an ornate gutta-percha gilded frame.[5] The child in the image is about three years old, and the girl's skin is painstakingly tinted a rosy flesh color. While tinting was not an unusual technique for nineteenth-century photography, it was mostly partial, shading cheeks pink, for example. In this photograph, however, all of the child's skin that is visible has been colored: face, chest, arms, and hands are all a lifelike hue. Her hair is set in loose ringlets, with a neat central part but slightly disarranged. Her arms lie lightly over her stomach, hands resting close to each other.

Figure 1.4   Unknown photographer, *Postmortem Photograph of Girl* (c. 1855).
Courtesy of the George Eastman Museum.

Once again, the viewer is struck by the tenderness implicit in the pose. Did the photography studio do the tinting to make the child look as though she had just laid down to sleep, or was it one of her grieving parents? Who moved her arms into that position, or arranged her hair? This photograph reinforces the sense that postmortem portraits aren't representations of mourning as much as placeholders for the child itself. They suggest the impermanence – or even the immateriality – of death by constructing an alternate reality that the child need only be awoken for reunification with their grieving parents.

It is this love, this tenderness, that is the foundation of the phenomenon of the postmortem photograph of a child. Love itself becomes a force that can defeat death: not just Christ's love, which by definition is eternal and empyrean, but the more quotidian value of familial love. As Lucy Frank argues, photographs of dead children "offered comfort by reinforcing the sacredness of family love and reaffirming the notion that the strength of

The Gates Ajar *and the Promise of Reunion*   45

affective ties could exceed death" (169). This photograph tells a very specific kind of story about hope and faith, but also about the lack of distinction between the past of the child's life, the present of the child's death, and the future of reunification in heaven. Whatever has been lost will be rediscovered, virtually unaltered.

Postmortem photography of children creates a vernacular visual vocabulary around loss and grief that does double work: making the child's death physically part of lived experience and denying it in the photographic image. The labor of the parent and/or photographer in dressing, grooming, and positioning the child is an embodied reminder that death is real and permanent. Yet the image itself runs counter to that experience, rescuing the child from the finality of the grave. It is both an artifact of grief and a relief from it. The photograph of a dead child preserves an eternal near future in which the child is *just about* to wake up, *just about* to open their eyes, *just about* to be returned to the family – it shifts the focus from an unbearable present in which the child is totally lost.

In other words, poems about child death and these postmortem photographs are designed to mollify the bitter reality of loss. It is certainly true that middle-class nineteenth-century Americans surrounded themselves with the signifiers of grief,[6] but, as these examples show, they also attempted to translate their grief by recuperating the image of the lost object and projecting a reunion in the future. By mixing up these tenses in their experience of death, they were able to construct a narrative that embraced grief – what Dana Luciano has called "the affective residue of the vanished past in the present tense" (2) and "a painful longing to return to a wholeness located in the past" (30) – while denying the actuality of death.

"No fearful looking for separation": *The Gates Ajar* and the Promise of Reunion

The apogee of this belief in the impossibility of permanent loss can be found in Elizabeth Stuart Phelps's *The Gates Ajar*, a novel published in 1868 as a direct response to the carnage of the Civil War. Phelps's childhood biography points us toward her mature attitudes about the ways that death cannot break familial bonds. Phelps was originally named Mary Gray Phelps. When she was eight, her mother died, and the young Mary asked to take on her mother's name, which she went by and published under, even after her marriage. This choice by the young Phelps suggests a nascent belief in the impermanence of death – Elizabeth Stuart Phelps *mère* remains alive through her daughter who bears her name.

46 The Dead Child versus the Amputated Limb

The Gates Ajar amplifies, intensifies, and materializes this wish that death is not really the end, that the past endures into the present, and that the future is in many ways a recapitulation of the past. Moreover, it creates a material and knowable heaven, one onto which, in Mark S. Schantz's words, "Americans could inscribe their most profound hopes and aspirations" (47). The protagonist Mary Cabot is brought back to the world from a deep and bitter sorrow at the death of her soldier brother Roy by the promise, offered by her Aunt Winifred, that Roy isn't really dead but watching over her from heaven. Roy's spirit can imaginatively replace and even improve on his body, give him access to knowledge and acquaintance he would never have had on Earth (at one moment in the text Mary "wonder[s] if Roy has seen the President. Aunt Winifred says she does not doubt it. She thinks that all the soldiers must have crowded up to meet him and 'O,' she says, 'what a sight to see!'").

The Gates Ajar takes the logic of Lydia Sigourney's poems and the postmortem photographs to a new height. Not just the reward for faith and virtue on Earth, heaven is represented the structural opposite of death: whereas the discourse of mourning that suffuses much pre–Civil War sentimental writing invokes fragments of the past in elements of the lost love object (materialized in permanent artifacts such as hair brooches, photographs, or poetry[7]), heaven reconstitutes the grieved-for person in a narratively knowable future. In Phelps's heaven, the present falls away and the future recuperates a complete and unambivalent past. As Cindy Weinstein observes, Phelps's goal "is to make the absent present, to transform what has passed into the here and now" (57). For Weinstein, "Heaven's tense is in the present" (58), but I would complicate that a little to say that heaven is simultaneously past, present, and future – it is a timeless place where loved ones have been and are, and we and they will be, into an endless future.

According to Mark S. Schantz, mid-nineteenth-century Americans had complex materialist beliefs about heaven. For Schantz,

> The modern heaven could be distinguished by four key features: (1) its proximity to earth; (2) its sheer materiality; (3) its insistence on progress and growth; and (4) its emphasis on the reconstituting of human communities, including both families and wider civic institutions. (39)

Elizabeth Stuart Phelps shared in all these beliefs, and they are clearly in evidence in *The Gates Ajar*. For Phelps, absence by death is just another kind of presence, one that guarantees the memory of a lost past that endures into the now. Mary's greatest fear is that in heaven Roy will be

The Gates Ajar *and the Promise of Reunion*   47

so occupied by his spiritual worship that he will no longer think of her or be present for her. But *The Gates Ajar*'s primary concern is to insist on the simultaneous materiality of heaven and the availability of the dead. As Aunt Winifred reassures Mary, "'Our Father, for some tender, hidden reason, took [Roy] out of your sight for a while. Though changed much, he can have forgotten nothing'" (87).

While Aunt Winifred is careful to warn against wishing that the dead be *physically* present with us, believing that that, like praying for the intercession in front of the statue of a saint, would be an invitation toward idolatry, she is certain that they are always spiritually and emotionally present, guiding us through life until we are able to join them in a future that they can already see.[8] A conversation between Mary and Winifred works through this belief:

> "Then you think, you really think, that Roy remembers and loves and takes care of me; that he has been listening, perhaps, and is – why, you don't think he may be here?"
>
> "Yes, I do. Here, close beside you all this time, trying to speak to you through the blessed sunshine and the flowers, trying to help you, and sure to love you, – right here, dear. I do not believe God means to send him away from you, either." (97)

Like the postmortem photographs, *The Gates Ajar* tarries with the fantasy of presence to deny the absence that death brings. It goes beyond promising the reunion in heaven that Sigourney and the other poets offer and elides the reality of separation at all. The word that recurs again and again in reference to the afterlife is "pleasant" – it is pleasant to think of heaven, pleasant to imagine reunion between the beloved dead and ourselves, pleasant to imagine paradise as a place where our earthly wishes will be fulfilled.[9] After a lengthy discussion on whether the souls in heaven will recognize each other and still love each other as individuals (the answer to both is yes), Mary exclaims "How pleasant – how pleasant this is!" (83).

What is it that is so pleasant here? I would argue that the pleasantness of heaven is its uninterrupted continuity with the earthly realm, only without all the human foibles that characterize our everyday lives. As Winifred explains,

> "You will talk with Roy as you talked with him here, – only, not as you talked with him here, because there will be no troubles, nor sins, no anxieties nor cares, to talk about; no ugly shades of cross words or little quarrels to be made up; no fearful looking for separation." (81)

48   The Dead Child versus the Amputated Limb

Visiting Roy's grave, Winifred goes beyond the claim that Roy and Mary will be reunited in heaven to argue that they are not in fact even separated. Not only does Roy watch over Mary, but "'our absent dead are very present with us . . . [God] must understand the need we have of them. I cannot doubt it'" (88). At the end of the chapter, Phelps even resurrects Roy's voice, in which Mary hears him calling to her: "'Mamie! little Mamie!'" (98).

Further conversations fill out the impossibility of the annihilation of the self in death. A long discussion about the place of the physical body in resurrection leads Aunt Winifred to conclude that St. Paul's prophecy that "It is sown a natural body; it is raised a spiritual body. There is a natural body, and there is a spiritual body" (KJV, Corinthians 15:44) means that the spiritual body is as material as the natural body. After all, she argues,

> "What would be the use of having a body that you can't see and touch? A body is a *body*, not a spirit. Why should you not, having seen Roy's old smile and heard his own voice, clasp his hand again and feel his kiss on your happy lips?" (117)

All the rest of Winifred's (and Phelps's) theology of the afterlife stems from this belief. Once she establishes that the dead are as present, as fully embodied, and as eager for communion with their loved ones as the bereaved living are, everything else is simply detail to be filled in.[10] This logic allows Phelps to imagine a heaven that is barely distinguishable from its earthly counterpart, landscaped with mountains and trees, populated with families living in beautiful cottages with gorgeous scenery and spectacular sunsets, playing the piano and eating cookies (although Winifred does hedge her bets by declaring that *Something that will be to us then what these are to us now*," rather than claiming a one-to-one correspondence between earthly life and heavenly existence [144]).

Needless to say, *The Gates Ajar* was profoundly comforting to its readers. It sold over 100,000 copies in its first year of publication, and even generated an array of *Gates Ajar*–themed souvenirs (Schnog 21). In part, as Nancy Schnog argues, this is because *The Gates Ajar* speaks explicitly to female readers, valuing their affective needs for reassurance and familial intimacy over the abstract, male-dominated discourse of orthodox Christianity. Lisa A. Long points out that *The Gates Ajar* is careful to avoid representations of actual bodies – we never see Roy's corpse in his coffin and Winifred's revelation of her breast cancer is covered by ellipses – as a way to "assuage the anguish of readers who might be doubly afflicted by a dead body that is mangled, diseased, or simply missing" (787). Heavenly reembodiment eases this anguish, a crucial intervention "even more necessary in times of war, when precious human bodies are so vulnerable, so cheap" (Long 788).

I don't want to trivialize the important emotional work *The Gates Ajar* did for its readers, especially its female readers. As Long argues, Winifred's "heavenly 'pictures' combat the photographs of Matthew Brady and Alexander Gardner, which were circulating images of blasted landscapes and decomposing bodies throughout the country at this time" (791), giving mourners an opportunity to engage in grieving practices that felt meaningful and authentic. Rather, I am arguing here that *The Gates Ajar* invokes and then intensifies and materializes a cultural practice that emerged in the antebellum period and continued through and after the Civil War: a desire to evacuate death of the horror of its finality, and a narrative of reconstitution of the dead and reunion of the mourner and the mourned. Moreover, as I show throughout this book, that discourse was co-opted in the postbellum years to efface the memory of the nation's division over the fate of its enslaved Black inhabitants, and to diminish to almost nothing newly freed Black people's claim to citizenship. The necessary emotional and firmly established cultural work of grieving the dead became, as we shall see, an alibi for white supremacist nostalgia for a unified nation that never really existed.

"The Illustration of the Wound": Theorizing Photographs of Amputees

Photographs of Civil War amputees work to interrupt this alibi. In both medical photographs and images commissioned by the soldiers themselves, the raw fact of the irreversible loss is the inescapable subtext. The richest archive of these pictures is in the work of Reed B. Bontecou, an army surgeon who kept meticulous photographic and written records of the men who came through his care at Harewood Hospital, a US Army unit in Washington, DC. These records were so complete that they were included in the multivolume *Medical and Surgical History of the War of the Rebellion* and were later used to verify pension claims by disabled veterans.[11]

Equally fascinating are the photographs that the wounded veterans posed for in commercial studios, either makeshift facilities near battlefields and hospitals or established businesses. These photographs provide a semiotically complex field for the viewer to parse: How do the subjects of these images – who were paying for the pictures, after all – pose themselves, use the props and furniture available to them, and interact with other people within the photograph? What is the larger discourse of amputation that emerges out of these images? Is the "body's very embodiedness ... effaced or enhanced when it is taken as the illustration of a wound"? (Samuels 63).

Before I embark on a reading of the photographs themselves, I want to theorize what these images of Civil War amputees might mean in the context of my analysis throughout this project. As Allison M. Johnson points out, the amputation stump itself is "death in the midst of life, invested with discursive power because of its corporeal and metaphorical substance" (*Scars We Carve* 6). What happens to the discursive significance of the stump once it is both rendered incorporeal (that is, two-dimensional) and at the same time held in temporal stasis?

Photography, especially medical photography, as a phenomenon plays a crucial role here, in terms of what photographer-surgeons such as Bontecou and their subjects expected the camera to do.[12] In Bontecou's pictures, the camera picks up where the bone saw, scalpel, and sutures leave off. To that extent it is itself a medical instrument, interacting intimately with the body of the soldier it represents. As Tanya Sheehan points out, the discourse of photography in the mid-nineteenth century overlapped significantly with that of medicine and surgery: photographers often called the process of sitting for a portrait an "operation," for example (50).[13]

Andrea Zittlau argues that medical photography is inevitably patholo-gizing and "enfreaking," creating an implicit analogy between the images of amputations, skin conditions, and the like and the promotional photo-graphs of freak show performers. She is not wrong that in many of these images, "[t]he medical gaze produces both the celebration of medical victory and the display of physical curiosity" (553). But I don't agree that "[t]he medical gaze clandestinely becomes an enfreaking gaze. The medical context, supposedly objective, ultimately turns into the physician's fanta-sies" (554). As we shall see, Bontecou's subjects engage the viewer (and, one supposes, the photographer), often looking directly at us, acknowledg-ing their changed bodies without being pathologized by them.

One reason for this might be that the soldiers' injuries were incurred in a war organized in large part around a discourse of righteous combat, whether in the name of preserving the Union, ending slavery, or both.[14] These amputations are not simply the result of accidents (or at least the majority of them are not – one frequent subject of postwar photography, David Wintress, was injured by an accidental gunshot from a fellow soldier) or bad luck. They represent loss that has ideological and affective meaning.

Moreover, unlike the later medical photographs of the postwar period, these images rarely "create an illusion of privacy mimicking the private studio portrait" (Zittlau 545). The men represented in these pictures are not explicitly posed, and there is very little in the way of props or furniture, beyond a chair or bed and perhaps a small slate with the soldier's details written on it. And these photographs are not synecdochally connected to the condition they illustrate; they are not deployed to represent a part of a larger whole in the way that pictures in medical textbooks stand in for all manifestations of a given disease or condition. Rather, they are metonymically linked, one to the other, by association with the injury that the war has caused, forming a long chain of hundreds of thousands of men, of whom these photographed soldiers are just a segment.

As I will show in the remaining part of this chapter, these images of amputees are not what we might call, after Barthes, "photography degree zero" – that is, aesthetically neutral and outside culture. Rather, they are part of the discourse of amputation that suffuses this book, a narrative that takes amputation as the irreversible corporeal sign of the change that the Civil War wrought. The clear-eyed gaze of each subject of these photographs speaks of the impossibility of going back in time to a whole body and – however ambivalently – an acknowledgment of a new reality.

Imaging the Amputated Body

Commissioned as a major in the Second New York Regiment in 1861, Reed B. Bontecou served both on the battlefield and, starting in 1863, at the Harewood US Army General Hospital. Harewood was by far the largest of the military hospitals, treating up to 3,000 patients at a time, so Bontecou had a wide range of injuries to choose from when selecting subjects for photography (Rogers 116). He took scores of images, pioneering the use of photography in representing injury and surgical outcomes, collecting them into albums. In some of the photographs, for example, those held by the US National Library of Medicine, the trajectory of the bullet wound is traced by a red arrow (and occasionally, for extra drama, drawing in some blood from the wound), and Bontecou has included handwritten notes as well as a printed description of the image (Figure 1.5).

In other versions of these volumes (for example, those held by Cornell and Yale Universities), the photographs are untouched, and the documentary information about the wounded soldier appears on the verso side of the photograph. Less rough and ready than the images with glued-on

Figure 1.5   Reed B. Bontecou, *John H. Bowers* (1865).
National Library of Medicine.

identifying labels and handwritten notes, these pictures conform more closely to the conventions of nineteenth-century US photographic portraiture, down to the oval framing and careful matting, like the image of Charles H. Wood shown in Figure 1.6.[15]

Theorizing Photographs of Amputees 53

Figure 1.6 Reed B. Bontecou, *Charles H. Wood* (1865).
Medical Historical Library, Harvey Cushing/John Hay Whitney Medical Library, Yale University.

At the same time, these photographs are stark – rather than the pictures that the soldiers themselves commission, which are staged in photography studios or other furnished and ornamented spaces, Bontecou's images contain minimal other furniture beyond a utilitarian chair or bed. Their

The Dead Child versus the Amputated Limb

purpose is to focus on the wound (the two-volume collection that Bontecou assembled out of these photographs was called *Gunshot Wounds Illustrated* and contains not just images of amputation but the evidence of every kind of injury, organized by body part). And yet they tell an additional story beyond the fact of the wound. Each picture within the two albums is framed by an oval border, much like a professional carte de visite, with the details of the soldier's name, rank, age, battle in which he was injured, the extent of the injury, and its outcome (in the short term, at least) on the reverse side. And yet in these images, the soldiers emerge not just as medical subjects, but as actors in their own lives.

I begin with an image of Charles Wood, nineteen, of the Fifty-Third Pennsylvania Volunteers, wounded in the Battle of Petersburgh on March 31, 1865 (Figure 1.6). Wood is stripped to the waist, missing his left arm almost to the shoulder, and grasps the chalkboard with his identifying details with his remaining hand, which is tanned a dark brown. According to Bontecou's notes, his arm was amputated in a field hospital, and he came to Harewood to recover. His medical condition is good – as the notes assert, "On admission, the stump was in good condition. Constitutional state of patient was also good." Private Wood looks directly at the camera, eyes slightly squinting. He is handsome and not as thin as many of the soldiers Bontecou photographed – given his age of nineteen, he might be a more recent recruit.

The viewer's eye moves back and forth between Wood's face and his stump. There is a knowingness in his face, an acknowledgment of this enormous and irremediable change that his body has undergone. The abbreviation of the stump is, to my mind, eloquent – less the remainder of an arm than a different kind of appendage, stationary yet muscled. The composition of the image operates along a series of geometric shapes: the near-perfect oval of his head; the triangle delineated by Wood's chin, right arm, and the end of the stump; the rectangle of the blackboard, the complementary rectangle of his torso not covered by the board; the triangle formed by the bottom of the board and Wood's legs; the triangle defined by his suspender on one side and his hip on the other.

The flatness of these intersecting shapes is deepened by the three-dimensionality of the image, however, especially the shadows under Wood's right and left underarms. We can see, too, where the skin has been brought together to cover his wound, helping it heal, even where the needle has gathered and sewn it. This infolding of skin prevents the eye from imagining the arm restored – the stump exists on its own terms, something that Wood himself, with his direct and unflinching gaze, forces us to concede.

A remarkable triptych of before-and-after photographs, one of which we've seen before, of Private John Parmenter, wounded in the foot at Amelia Springs in April 1865, further establishes the uncrossable line that amputation lays down. By the following June, Parmenter's wounded foot became gangrenous and required amputation, a procedure Bontecou himself did. In the initial image, Parmenter lounges on his stomach in an erotic-seeming pose, as Elizabeth Young says, "welcom[ing] his male surgeon-viewer" (493) (see Figure 1.7).

Again, he gazes directly at the camera, his eyes clear and engaging, his head resting on his hands. As our eyes travel down his body, noting the naked thigh and calf, we are stopped by the grotesque gangrenous foot, so transformed that the infection seems to explode the interior of his ankle and the top of the foot. The pillow the supports Parmenter's leg is heavily stained, probably with blood from a previous soldier-patient. Another pillow under his thigh is marked "HH" – Harewood Hospital, where Bontecou practiced. The image, then, represents the past (the bloodied pillow), the present (Parmenter's foot, the "HH" pillow), and the future

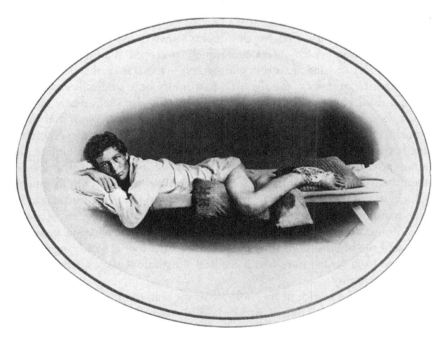

Figure 1.7   Reed B. Bontecou, *John Parmenter* (1865).
National Museum of Health and Medicine.

(the gangrenous foot, soon to be excised), all located in and around the alert and watchful gaze that Parmenter directs at the camera.

The counterpart to this image is the postoperative photograph (Figure 1.2). Here a man – most likely a doctor– gently rests his hand on Parmenter's knee and observes the result of Bontecou's labors. Parmenter is still anesthetized, his naked lower body fully exposed, his legs raised up on a box, revealing the amputation of the foot. Strikingly, the surgeon has kept the foot, and it lies on the bed. This image even more intensely reminds the viewer that amputation is a permanent, immutable alteration of the body. The foot seems to float off the bed, and there is a rectangle of dark negative space created by the side of the box that dramatizes the physical and temporal distance between Parmenter's body and his lost foot.

In some ways, this image resembles the postmortem pictures of children I explored earlier in this chapter. Like those children, Parmenter is supine, laid out on a draped fabric. His eyes are closed, his body limp. But there are significant differences. First of all, the viewer's eye is drawn not to Parmenter's face, but to that of the doctor in the middle of the frame, and the black triangle of negative space created by Parmenter's thin bent leg. Our gaze is also directed by the doctor's own visual attention to the amputated foot, which seems grotesquely oversized. Parmenter himself seems almost incidental to this photograph – the star of the show is the gangrenous extremity – the sign of a past injury now surgically removed.

In a third photograph, Bontecou poses the foot by itself, newly amputated from Parmenter's leg (Figure 1.8). Almost unrecognizable as a human body part, it is a kind of relic that both transmits the power of the body to which it used to belong and bears its own meaning. Unlike the anonymous piles of arms and legs that we will see in Chapter 2, this foot is identified as having belonged to Parmenter and the conditions under which it was removed. At the same time, it is virtually unreadable, a free-standing artifact of the war with no reference point. The circular cut that Bontecou made is clearly indicated in the clean separation between skin and the interior bone, but the necrosis of the foot is so advanced that the foot itself looks more like a medical illustration of gangrene than a human extremity.

This foot is a vestige of the violence of the war and the damage – both direct and indirect – that it wreaked. While the cause of death is rarely visible in the photographs of dead children, here Bontecou's notes and the narrative these three images construct of before and after situate the injury and its surgical relief in a specific moment in time. Moreover, the fact that

Figure 1.8   Reed B. Bontecou, *Foot of John Parmenter* (1865).
Medical Historical Library, Harvey Cushing/John Hay Whitney Medical Library, Yale University.

this wound (and this amputation) was the result of battle locates us in relation to a historical event rather than to an eternal present.

These three images tell several stories. The first is the most obvious: Private Parmenter came to Harewood with a severely gangrenous foot. The foot was removed and the remaining leg formed into a cleanly articulated stump. Parmenter's body and his erstwhile foot are now separate from each other. The second is about Parmenter's subjectivity in relation to the camera. In the first photograph he is actively engaged with the viewer, of a piece with his rotting foot. In the second, he is figuratively transported away from the viewer by the power of ether, and the foot is disarticulated from the rest of him, with the wound sewn up, watched over by a sober-faced doctor whose gaze leads us to the gap between the amputated foot and the remaining leg. By the third image, Parmenter himself is gone, and all that remains is the necrotic foot, remaining evidence of the body that was and the wound whose sequelae still mark it. He has been fully medicalized, removed from the scene altogether, giving way to the real object of interest.

58   The Dead Child versus the Amputated Limb

I propose a third narrative. As the foot moves further and further out of the orbit of Parmenter himself, it becomes decreasingly identifiable as his or as a body part at all. If the intact body is the sign of the prewar body, the episodic representation of the pre- and postamputation foot reminds us that there is no going back: Parmenter and his foot occupy different planes of existence that are irreconcilable. This remarkable set of images literalizes and enacts the discourse of amputation that I am proposing as a larger theme in this book. In the other photographs of amputees I analyze, the "before" image is absent, as is any representation of the excised limb, hand, or foot. There is no one else facing the camera except the amputee himself. In these photographs, the cultural and affective work the amputee can do as a signifier of permanent loss is divided into three distinct moments that stage the increasing, uncrossable distance between Parmenter and his foot – a distance that is always already present for the amputee *tout court*.

Of course, these photographs had a primary purpose, which was to register the various injuries soldiers experienced and the surgical interventions they underwent. While we can't know whether they were coerced into the process, they had little control over the project or their representation, beyond their often-expressive faces. Later on, though, soldiers went to photography studios, to have pictures taken in which they had more autonomy in self-presentation. When – or if – they recovered from their wounds, innumerable men memorialized their bodily losses in photographs that they themselves commissioned, taken in studios, posed, and surrounded by props of their choosing.

Photographing the "Empty Sleeve"

Throughout the war, both before they left with their regiments and after they returned, soldiers had themselves photographed, the images printed as cartes de visite for the families they left behind.[16] These photographs present the viewer with an image of the subject that we can assume he wanted. To the extent that they were kept over decades suggests that they were valued items both to the soldier himself and to his family and descendants. Especially for veterans living with amputations, posed portraits provided men with the opportunity to visually represent themselves as valued participants in the still-raging or erstwhile national struggle.

That is clearly the case for Thomas Plunkett, who had several photographs taken of himself. Plunkett was a sergeant in the Massachusetts Twenty-First who lost both arms at the battle of Fredericksburg while rescuing the regiment's colors, for which he was awarded the Medal of

Honor.[17] A minor celebrity at the time, Plunkett commissioned at least two solo portraits and was part of one group photograph to memorialize his role in the conflict. Both the individual images were taken by well-known photographers in their studios, suggesting that Plunkett's fame made him a worthy subject

One of these photographs is attributed to the Rockwood Photographic Studio, owned by the brothers George Gardner and Elihu R. Rockwood (Figure 1.9). George Rockwood was an innovative photographer who brought the carte de visite format to the United States in the mid-1850s.[18] During the war Elihu served with the Tenth Massachusetts Volunteer Regiment, and George took his studio on the road as a war

Figure 1.9   George Gardner Rockwood, [Sergeant Thomas Plunkett of Co. E, Twenty-First Massachusetts Infantry Regiment in uniform with amputated arms] (1862). Library of Congress, LC-DIG-ppmsca-71017.

photographer. It is possible that the picture of Plunkett was taken at George's field studio – given that it is not dated, it's hard to know whether it originated in the Rockwood Studio itself during Plunkett's visit to the New York Sanitary Fair in 1864 or while Plunkett was still in Virginia.

This picture is hardly as dramatic as the Bontecou images of amputation, but it tells a similar story. Unlike the other two photographs of Plunkett that I will be discussing, this picture is wholly self-contained, with no external signifiers beyond Plunkett's body and clothing. The image is plain and unadorned. The bottom of the picture cuts his body off just at the knee even as the top quarter of the photograph is empty space above his head. This might be a sign of a challenging environment for taking a picture – an argument for the image being recorded in Rockwood's mobile field studio. But the composition seems to condense and intensify the impact of Plunkett's face and body as well.

Although it was taken in some kind of photography studio rather than in a hospital, the photograph has few of the decorations that were typical of the time: pillars, credenzas, drapery, and the like, another clue that this might have been taken in the mobile unit. Instead, Plunkett's body is the sole focus of the viewer's attention. Sergeant Plunkett sits in a chair, turned three-quarters toward the camera. In the absence of his arms, his sergeant's jacket seems oversized, hanging loosely from his shoulders. He looks directly at us, his uniform jacket unbuttoned and pulled over what remains of his arms. While it was the custom to pin or tie up the arms or legs of jackets or trousers over amputated limbs, in this picture Plunkett's sleeves rest on his thighs, emphasizing their emptiness. Indeed, it's not clear where his arms end, especially on the right-hand side.

Most prominent in the photograph are Plunkett's sergeant's stripes, which seem enormous in comparison with his slight frame. The arrow shape of the stripes points down to the empty sleeve, a kind of précis of Plunkett's experience of the war itself. Look, the stripes say, at the losses that this uniform brought with it, losses that cannot be recuperated. Indeed, the point of the photograph is the loss – it is the reason that his image is worth reproducing. Plunkett's story of heroism in a battle is one of loss upon loss: the Battle of Fredericksburg was a disastrous defeat for the Union Army.

The narrative of loss and permanent damage is borne out in another, slightly more elaborately staged, photograph of Plunkett (Figure 1.10). This picture was taken by another prominent photographer, J. W. Black, whose studio in Boston attracted celebrities from John Brown to Walt Whitman, and who was one of the first aerial photographers, capturing

Theorizing Photographs of Amputees 61

Figure 1.10 J. W. Black, [Sergeant Thomas Plunkett of Co. E, Twenty-First Massachusetts Infantry Regiment in uniform with American flag] (1863).
Library of Congress, LC-DIG-ppmsca-49716.

Boston from a hot air balloon.[19] In this picture, Plunkett stands next to the flag he attempted to defend, his empty sleeve resting on the fabric. In three-quarter view again, he stares off beyond the edge of the photograph. His left leg is raised up on a box, and his left foot is level with the tattered bottom of the flag. We can see where his arm ends, as the sleeve makes a downward ninety-degree fold at the point where the arm touches the flag, and the bottom half of the sleeve hangs empty.

The photograph reenacts the traumatic/heroic event that both Plunkett and the flag went through and multiply signifies the embodiment of the irreversible losses brought by the war. The cuff of his hanging left sleeve is level with a hole in the fabric, reminding us of the shell that both damaged the flag and took off Plunkett's arms. But the flag is not just torn and tattered – the edge that hangs down against a pillar is stained, possibly with Plunkett's own blood. If this is the case, Plunkett is using the missing part of his body to support a flag that is marked with remnants of that body. Moreover, just as Plunkett's arms cannot be recovered, this blood cannot be reconstituted – it now belongs to the flag, the sign of the riven nation and, increasingly as the war continued, with the emancipation of the enslaved. In this photograph, then, Plunkett's mutilated body and the mutilated flag tell rhyming stories about the sequelae of the war and of the ravaging of human and national bodies.

The final image of Plunkett is in a group portrait of disabled soldiers who were brought together to help fundraise at the New York Sanitary Commission Metropolitan Fair in April 1864 (Figure 1.11). The Fair itself was immense, taking over both the Fourteenth Street Armory and a smaller space on Union Square, and raising over a million dollars (just under $20 million today). It offered everything from jewelry to agricultural products to kitchen goods. J. Gurney & Son set up a "Photographic Gallery," where fairgoers could sit for a carte de visite or buy views of the Fair (US Sanitary Commission, *A Record of the Metropolitan Fair* 169), and where this portrait was undoubtedly taken.[20]

The photograph features not just Plunkett but also two other soldiers: David Wintress, who was blinded from an accidental gunshot wound to his face, and William MacNulty, who lost his left arm at Fredericksburg.[21] Strikingly, he is the only one in uniform (although both he and MacNulty were wounded at Fredericksburg and would have been released from the army at about the same time).

Plunkett's sleeves are pinned up, and his right arm mirrors with MacNulty's – both posed at the same angle, Plunkett's above MacNulty's. Indeed, we can trace a straight line from Wintress's bare

Figure 1.11 J. Gurney & Son, [Private David H. Wintress of Co. C, 139th New York Infantry Regiment, Captain William A. MacNulty of Co. A, Tenth New York Infantry Regiment and Veterans Reserve Corps, and Sergeant Thomas Plunkett of Co. E, Twenty-First Massachusetts Infantry Regiment in uniform, displaying their wounds] (1864). Library of Congress, LC-DIG-ppmsca-70977.

64   The Dead Child versus the Amputated Limb

hand to the fold in MacNulty's sleeve to the equivalent fold in Plunkett's, constructing a narrative of cumulative loss, from two functioning arms to one to none.

Plunkett once again stares impassively at the camera, his body erect. A straight line runs from where his feet meet, vertically bisecting his body, up through the buttons on his waistcoat, creating an almost symmetrical mirror image of each side of the body. The symmetry is interrupted, though, by the divergent placement of his empty sleeves – one folded to his left side, the other pinned to the front of his coat. This disjuncture makes the loss of his arms seem more material – the disorder between the folded sleeves prevents the viewer from aestheticizing Plunkett's image. Both he and Wintress face the viewer, summoning us as witnesses to their loss. While McNulty's pose is more conventional – it was common for photographic subjects in the nineteenth century to look away from the camera – the other two seem almost confrontational, as though they want their damage to speak directly to the viewer.

Wintress's pose is even more direct than Plunkett's: although his body is turned away, his face is turned frontward. The black lenses of his glasses are a focal point – the only wholly black thing in the photograph – and they compel the viewer to look back at them. And although MacNulty's body overlaps with Wintress's to his right and Plunkett's to his left, each man seems separate from the others, self-contained in his own individual story.

Even more than the solo images of Plunkett, this photograph raises multiple, unanswerable questions. It makes some sense that Plunkett and MacNulty would pose together – they were both soldiers from New York, both lost arms at Fredericksburg, and both might have found themselves at the Metropolitan Fair. But how did Wintress find his way into this picture? Who brought these three men together into a single frame? Was this picture solely for them, or was it produced for sale among the other images J. Gurney and Son offered fairgoers as a reminder of what they were spending their money for?

Finally, what is the story that this photograph tells? It is, after all, a chronicle of significant and permanent loss and suffering. Neither Wintress nor Plunkett was expected to survive his wounds (as well as losing his arms, Plunkett had bled heavily from the chest due to his injuries). There is an implacability to both Wintress's and Plunkett's faces that allows for no sentimentalizing of what has happened to them and that overwrites MacNulty's more typical pose.

Even more frequently photographed than Thomas Plunkett was Alfred A. Stratton, who lost both arms in a charge leading up to the battle of

Theorizing Photographs of Amputees 65

Petersburg in June 1864. A brief internet search brings up at least half a dozen images of Stratton: one a medical photograph showing his post-operative amputations and the rest in uniform or civilian clothes. A soldier with the 147th New York Volunteers, Stratton was nineteen when he was wounded. Among the many images of him is an undated photograph taken at the Fredricks and Co. studio in New York (Figure 1.12).[22] This photograph was widely distributed (it shows up in public collections such as the Library of Congress, in various Civil War museums, and in private hands), and the Library of Congress print seems to be signed by Stratton on the back – quite an achievement by itself, since he lost both arms – which suggests that it was taken and reproduced as a fundraiser to supplement Stratton's disability pension. Posed in a faux parlor, Stratton stands between an ornate side table on which rests a book in a bookstand and a carved wooden chair. Draperies frame him to the left of the photograph.

In the middle of the photograph, Stratton stands, looking at the camera, his sleeves pinned up at what would be his elbows (in fact, Stratton's arms were amputated almost at the shoulder). His hair is neatly parted and pomaded, his jacket buttoned all the way up, invoking an absent assistant who prepared him for this photograph. Stratton's right sleeve points toward the book open on a highly decorated stand, as though to remind the viewer that he can no longer pick a book up to read or turn the pages. Similarly, his left sleeve gestures toward the back of the chair, which is turned toward him as though he might just grab it to sit down. Both of these artifacts index Stratton's loss, the ordinary motions he can no longer make.

Indeed, Stratton seems to occupy a different space from his opulent surroundings. In contrast to the curved and decorated furniture around him, his body is vertical and angular (even the curl of his hair is styled at an almost ninety-degree angle). While the props provided by the studio suggest an idealized home space to which Stratton might return, his stiff pose and uncertain expression suggest that he is out of place within the domestic. It is self-evident to say that his life will be radically different, of course. But, ironically, situating him in an environment that invokes the domestic space intensifies that difference.

This image is uncanny in several ways. First, Stratton's seeming separation or alienation from the "homelike" furnishings of the photography studio recalls two kinds of domestic space: the one on earth, in which he seems supremely ill at ease, and the one in heaven, that has not yet been made available to him. Second, even as he cannot effortlessly slip back into

Figure 1.12   Fredericks & Co, [Sergeant Alfred A. Stratton of Co. G, 147th New York Infantry Regiment, with amputated arms] (1864).
Library of Congress, LC-DIG-ppmsca-53074.

Theorizing Photographs of Amputees 67

domestic life, nor can he reenter the military sphere: his amputations exile him from an uncomplicated relationship with either realm. And third, the image seems unusually still, even for mid-nineteenth-century photography. Stratton gazes out of the picture at an uncertain future, unable to go back but seemingly unsure about how to move forward, frozen on the cusp of a new kind of existence that he can't yet predict.

All these portraits of disabled soldiers have a rawness and immediacy that contrasts with the aestheticized and idealized images of dead children I discussed at the beginning of this chapter. Laid out on beds and sofas, the children's bodies are imbricated with an evangelical faith in heavenly reunion that contracts human time even as it arrests its movement from life to death. Texts like *The Gates Ajar* provided a vocabulary in which the wrenching ramifications of mass death in the Civil War could be ignored in favor of a narrative of return to the status quo ante, where no one is really dead and the war's effects are not actually felt. Amputation, however, allows for no such fantasy.

Strikingly, there are not many popular images of Black amputees, although the few that do exist primarily make a connection between emancipation, Black American belonging, and noble sacrifice. Probably the most circulated of these images is a Thomas Nast engraving published in *Harpers* on August 5, 1865, of Columbia, the embodiment of the United States, and a Black veteran who has lost a leg (Figure 1.13). The caption to the image, "FRANCHISE AND NOT THIS MAN?" makes it clear that Black citizenship and enfranchisement are directly linked to the veteran's bodily sacrifice. However, the Black amputee signifies differently from his white counterpart. Whereas the white amputee's loss is a necessary mechanism to foreclose the possibility of returning to a pre–Civil War nation, the Black amputee's wounds are represented as a guarantee of Black male empowerment.

I discuss in more detail in Chapter 3 how sentimental expectations of Black suffering and death limit the political efficacies of Anna Dickinson's otherwise antiracist novel *What Answer?* but I would like to tarry with this image a little before drawing this chapter to a close. The Black veteran here is presented by Columbia to the putatively white viewership, possibly an audience within the diegetics of the image itself. Placing her hand lightly on his shoulder she challenges the taboo on any kind of physical intimacy between Black men and white women. At the same time, the (we can assume) red, white, and blue runner spangled with stars cascades down a series of steps, a significant impediment to the veteran's progress down the path of American citizenship.

68 The Dead Child versus the Amputated Limb

Figure 1.13 Thomas Nast, "FRANCHISE AND NOT THIS MAN?" *Harper's Weekly*, August 5, 1865.

Theorizing Photographs of Amputees 69

Intrinsic to this image, then, is the offered emancipation and political enfranchisement of Black men, insisted upon by Columbia, no less, who effortlessly reaches out to the man she hopes to invest with the vote. In this engraving, Nast appeals to the patriot's sentiment, larding the image with symbols of national greatness (not least the massive column to the right of Columbia and the veteran). Nonetheless, the route to that empowerment is attainable only via obstacles in the built environment that do not take his disability into account. Columbia, then, gives with one gently touching hand and takes away with the other, revealing more than Nast probably intended of the structural barriers to Black men's exercise of their citizenship rights.

A very different kind of allegory is at work in the unattributed cartoon "A Man Knows a Man," also featured in *Harper's Weekly* in April 1865, published less than two weeks after Lee's surrender at Appomattox (Figure 1.14). A white amputee, already in civilian clothes, shakes the hand of his Black counterpart, still in uniform (in fact, this is historically accurate, since Black men were not officially admitted into the Union Army until 1863 and hence had not served their full three years by the end of the war). While it's not explicit who is speaking – neither of the figures' mouths is open – we can infer that the white man is the one who invites the Black soldier to shake his hand: "Give me your hand, Comrade! We have each lost a LEG for the good cause; but, thank God, we never lost HEART." The composition of the engraving creates a perfect symmetry between the two men, each missing a left leg and holding onto a crutch with his left hand while shaking the right hand of the other. The sacrifice each has made is balanced by the equality of affective power, and the masculine camaraderie of battle underlies each man's equal rights to the Union.

Nonetheless, the cartoon is silent about how the Black soldier found his way into federal troops, as well as the fact that he fought in a segregated army. Is he a formerly enslaved person who self-emancipated to reach Union lines, or a freeman from the free or the border states? The lacunae within the image equate these two losses with the implicit expectation that military service has cost them equally, but unlike the Nast image, it cannot imagine a future that embraces both men on the same terms.

Both these engravings speak to amputation as a nexus between a past that has been permanently excised, a present with promise (however equivocal), and a future that stretches out into the possibility of Black and white comradeship. From the medical photographs by Reed Bontecou

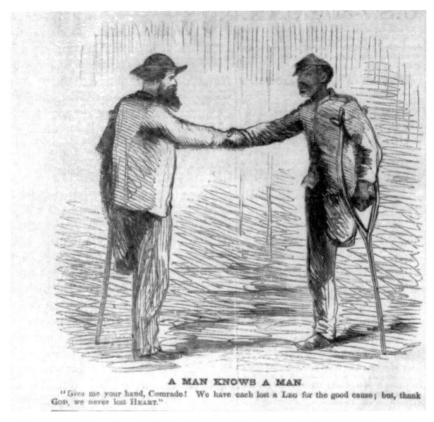

Figure 1.14 Unattributed, "A Man Knows a Man." *Harper's Weekly*, April 22, 1865.

to the portraits of amputee soldiers that they posed for, amputation's irrecoverability is undeniable. The negative space around Charles Wood's stump cannot be filled: we can imagine the arm that would complete it, but nothing will suture it back onto his body. The future will be profoundly different from the past, adjusting to a body that functions in altered ways.

CHAPTER 2

"Strewn promiscuously about"
Limbs and What Happens to Them

In September 1862, Edward O. Hewitt, a veteran of the British War in Crimea and an observer of several battles in the Civil War, visited a field hospital just after the battle of Antietam. Characterizing, in a letter to his mother, Antietam as "really a drawn battle" for both sides – that is, a victory for neither North or South, especially in terms of casualties – Hewitt traveled inside Union lines with a doctor "whose chief interest is of course the hospitals," and ended up in "the main field hospital," a series of large tents receiving the wounded from the battle (Preston 55). Hewitt noted the sheer scale of human injury, with "some 3,000 wretched creatures . . . laying under the trees with a space of say 300 yards square" (55). The hospital was filled with surgeons "without coats . . . covered with blood and dirt, chatting, arguing, and laughing and swearing, and cutting and sawing more like devils and machines than human beings" (55).

Most striking, though, were the result of their labors: "Large heaps of legs and arms were piled here and there, all sizes and stages of decomposition; the odour was fearful and the whole air felt thick and putrid.... I saw about 50 limbs taken off during the 2 hours I remained there" (55). Perhaps even more horrifying was the activity of "Medical Cadets" – surgical trainees – who "the moment a limb was off would pounce on it from behind trees, and fight for it, and in a few minutes it would be cut into little bits for practice.... [W]hen I saw one of these Cadets seize a leg almost before it was off and holding it by the toe run away with it, still quivering and bleeding, and dragging and bumping it along the ground, while the other devils chased him, it made me feel for a little time so sick that I felt myself grow pale and dared not speak for a few minutes" (55–6). Given that Hewitt had fought in the Crimean War, a conflict marked by massive casualties, although more from epidemic diseases than wounds, it's surprising he was so deeply affected.[1] Amputation was certainly widespread and death from infections far higher than those in the US Civil War, but even so, Hewitt was astounded by the speed and rate of

71

amputation. Moreover, the rapacity of the Medical Cadets was clearly a new phenomenon for him: the idea that once separated (or nearly separated) from the body a limb was no more precious than an inanimate object was shocking and sickening.

In this chapter, I want to look more closely at the images of amputated limbs that appear – in piles and heaps, in the imaginations of medical staff and of amputees themselves, as literally and metaphorically disarticulated from the amputee body, as taking on lives and wills of their own – throughout the writing of doctors, nurses, and other habitués of Civil War hospitals. From the development of the Minié ball and the rifled barrel to the shattering of flesh and bone to the chaos and horrors of field hospitals to the imaginative afterlives of amputation, amputated limbs bear the accumulated heft of technology and humanity, of the bodies from which they are removed and to which they can never return.

The chapter returns again and again to the image that Hewitt invokes and that is a constant reminder of the mechanics of wartime injury: the collection of amputated limbs, indistinguishable from each other and in various states of decay. These limbs are more than just the detritus of war; they are the signs of both presence and absence, of irreversible change, and of the corporeal materiality of the change the Civil War ushered in. If, as I have argued, the amputated body is the basis for reimagining the body politic, this chapter asks, What do we make of the limbs that are left behind, under the surgeon's table? I begin with the literal agent of this change, the new military technologies that brought war's damage to new levels, especially rifle and bullet technology. From there I explore how military surgical personnel adjusted to this new reality, primarily through the memoirs of the nurses and surgeons who performed amputations and cared for the soldiers postoperatively.

Most well-known of these medical staff are Louisa May Alcott and Walt Whitman, but I also follow the career of John Brinton, a prominent surgeon. Brinton was also the founding director of the Army Medical Museum, the repository of the largest collection of amputated limbs in the United States. Brinton's focus on the afterlives of the limbs he and others removed from injured soldiers and his vision for the Museum is intimately interconnected but occasionally in conflict with how amputees, nurses, surgeons, and the Union more generally saw the meanings of these leftovers of the formerly intact fighting body.

I end the chapter with a younger contemporary of Brinton's and (in-)famous surgeon and physician in his own right, S. Weir Mitchell.

Military Technology and New Modes of Destruction 73

Although best known as Charlotte Perkins Gilman's doctor and the inventor of the "rest cure," which inspired Gilman's most enduring work, *The Yellow Wall-Paper*, Mitchell had had an illustrious career during the Civil War as a surgeon and a neurologist. Mitchell's work during the war was varied and impressive – he studied amputees closely at the Turner's Lane Hospital, and was the first to closely document "phantom limb," a nomenclature he coined. My focus here, though, is on Mitchell's 1866 story, "The Case of George Dedlow," which I first discussed in the Introduction, in which Dedlow finally encounters his amputated limbs in a spectacular fashion.

Throughout the chapter I consider the narratability of these limbs, which, in their scale and horror, seem to resist narrative. What do these dismembered members say to us about the Civil War, the materiality of the human body, and the integrity of the sense of self? What do they say about loss, those things that cannot be put back together again? Certainly, the Civil War's destructive power changed soldiers' perception of their bodies in relation to the enormity of the destruction and the onslaught of military technology. What Walter Benjamin said of the First World War seems equally resonant for the Civil War: "A generation . . . now stood under the open sky in a countryside in which nothing remained unchanged but the clouds, and beneath these clouds, in a field of force of destructive torrents and explosions, was the tiny, fragile human body" (83).[2]

"Defeat – a somewhat slower – means – / More Arduous than Balls – / 'Tis populous with Bone and stain": Military Technology and New Modes of Destruction

On March 1862 Emily Dickinson wrote to her cousins that her neighbor and her brother Austin's friend Frazar Stearns, the son of the current president of Amherst College, had been "'killed at Newbern' . . . his big heart shot away by a 'minie ball'" (*Letters* 397). Stearns's death hit Emily and Austin especially hard – he was the first of Amherst's young men to fall whom they knew well.

The loss of Stearns had a significant impact on Dickinson's poetry – she wrote several poems that week with death, and wartime death in particular, at their core. Her poem "My Portion is Defeat – today –" speaks specifically to the defeats large and small the Union Army and individual soldiers suffered through in the early years of the war. The poem reflects much of Dickinson's horror over the loss of Frazar Stearns:

> My portion is Defeat – today
> A paler luck than Victory –
> . . .
> Defeat – a somewhat slower means –
> More Arduous than Balls –
>
> 'Tis populous with Bone and stain
> And Men too straight to stoop again
> And Piles of solid Moan –
> And Chips of Blank – in Boyish Eyes – (F704A, J639)

Here Dickinson limns the results of battle – moaning, bodies in rigor mortis ("Men too straight to stoop again"), and blank, dead eyes of young men like Stearns – as well as the slow agony of defeat, more drawn out and slower than death by gunshot ("balls" here refers to bullets, since traditionally ammunition in muskets and other guns was round). But we should be equally alert to Dickinson's specificity in describing the *means* of Stearns's death, which she mentions both in her letter and in this poem: the minié ball. Readers might be surprised to realize how well Dickinson was acquainted with the details of military hardware, that she could name the very ammunition that blew through Stearns's chest.

The minié ball, named after its co-inventor Claude-Étienne Minié, was a new kind of bullet, different from its predecessors in shape, speed, and effect, and often identified by name by observers of the war. As Richard E. Kerr shows, although Minié and his collaborator invented the ball in time for the Crimean War a decade earlier, it was with the Civil War that the minié ball found its way into the US arsenal. Unlike its round, smooth forerunners, the minié ball looked more like current bullets, longer, conical, and with a more pointed tip. While round balls penetrated the body to less depth due to their shape, and tended to be deflected by bone and dense tissue to follow winding routes through the body, the minié ball was more deadly and more damaging (Kerr 15).

The minié ball was not the only change to military hardware, however. The Civil War marked the switch not just in ammunition, but also in rifle technology. Indeed, "rifles" are named after the new development in muskets, the rifled barrel, which was grooved, with raised "lands" separating the grooves. These grooves set bullets into a spinning motion as they were fired, rendering minié balls far more effective and damaging, since they spun into the body, splintering bone as they went (Kerr 17). Unlike round balls, which could jam against the raised lands, the diameter of a minié ball spun easily against the grooves of a rifled barrel, receiving the full charge of the explosion and spin of the shot.

Military Technology and New Modes of Destruction 75

With minié balls, muskets became much more accurate at greater distances – roughly the same at 200 yards, but more than three times as effective at 300 yards and over ten times as accurate at 400 yards, from 4.5 to 52.5 percent (Kerr 19).[3] And the effects were equally devastating at those distances – as Frank R. Freemon points out, unlike a round ball, which maintained its shape after it entered the body,

> the minié ball flattened when it encountered human flesh. It did not pass directly through the tissues as do modern bullets with metal jackets; rather, the deformed bullet tumbled, tearing a terrible swath through muscle and bone. Bones splintered and shattered into hundreds of spinicules, sharp bony sticks that were driven by the force of the bullet through muscle and skin. (48)

The results of the combined power of the minié ball and the rifled barrel were hundreds of thousands of shattered limbs that could not simply be reset and left to heal. Given the extended periods over which battles were fought – sometimes two or three days or even more for the most extensive engagements – wounded and dead soldiers were often left to lie on the ground until the battle was fully over, with the result that wounds could be infected with tetanus or any other bacteria. Added to that the mid-nineteenth-century ignorance of microbe theory and antisepsis, the risks of infection, necrosis, and gangrene were high for every wound.

All of this added up to one thing: surgeons felt compelled to save the lives of soldiers wounded by minié ball fire by amputating limbs. Of course, gunshots weren't the only cause of serious injury: field artillery like Parrott guns and Howitzers also had rifled barrels, and in the hands of experienced troops were remarkably accurate. And some injuries, however caused, were untreatable, especially serious head or chest wounds or internal injuries caused by explosions, and medical staff could do not much more than ease a soldier's suffering, if they reached him at all before death. But gunshot injured and killed more soldiers than any other kind of combat weapon – according to the US Surgeon General's Office the rate of death from gunshot wounds was 14.2 percent – and military surgeons had to adjust in the ways they envisaged injuries to the extremities, which were candidates for amputation.[4]

The experience of the damage wrought by the minié ball shaped the medical discourse around treating survivors of battle, a discourse that developed over time as the war dragged on. Amputation and death rates went down over the course of the war, as field surgeons learned more sophisticated techniques both on the field and from medical manuals that

76   Limbs and What Happens to Them

they brought with them. These manuals reveal a great deal about not just the medical science of the war, but also the expectations about what the war looked like, the assumptions about what constituted appropriate surgery, and the status of field surgeons themselves.

"Derived from their personal experiences": The Medical and Narrative Work of Surgical Manuals

Out of these phenomena a new genre developed: the military surgical manual. In part these manuals were designed to reduce the frequency of amputation on the field. As Brian Craig Miller has shown, amputation rates were particularly high in the early months of the war, as surgeons adjusted to levels of injury they had never witnessed before. At the same time, mortality rates were shockingly high: at the beginning soldiers had not much better than a 50/50 survival rate. As surgeons became more skilled and experienced, both amputation and mortality rates decreased. On the Union Army side, with almost 30,000 amputations the mortality rate for amputees was 27 percent, although that depended on which limb was being amputated and how close to the trunk. Hand and forearm amputations were the least life-threatening; leg amputations at the hip were the most dangerous, with a fatality of 80 percent (Miller 39).[5]

Both the Confederate and Union Armies produced surgical manuals – the North in 1861 and the South in 1863. The Confederate manual identifies its genesis in the surgical tents of battle fields, noting that the "opinions" of the authors "have been derived from their personal experiences" (*Manual of Military Surgery* iii). Not surprisingly, where the opening chapters of the Union manual, written just as the war was beginning, focused on necessary equipment and procedures, the Confederate volume – published with two years' experience in the field – leads off with descriptions of the many infections that follow from injury and surgery.[6] While the Union manual quickly moves into an analysis of the kinds of cases for which amputation is and is not indicated, within the same number of pages, the Confederate manual details the ways that stumps can become infected.

These two manuals implicitly narrate two different moments in the war, and hence two divergent attitudes toward the intact body of the soldier and the possibility and sequelae of amputation. The Union manual takes a leisurely pace toward its main topic, spending several pages on the history of military surgery, its importance both historical and contemporary, and the "qualification and duties of military surgeons" (21). It insists on

The Medical and Narrative Work of Surgical Manuals   77

gentlemanliness of the military surgeon and at the same time his willingness to get his hands dirty – "the white gloved gentry, such as figured in some of the regiments that went to Mexico, have no business in the service" (22). Written within the moment of excitement for signing up, the authors worry that "many medical men, old as well as young, have already been admitted late into the service utterly unfit for office" (22).

The various authors of the Union *Manual of Military Surgery* discourage this kind of wholesale volunteering for medical assistance, recognizing the difficulty and specialization of the work medical surgeons would have to do. They were well aware of the dangers of the new technologies in ammunition, recognizing that conical bullets like the minié ball "commit terrible ravages among the bones, breaking them into numerous fragments, each of which may, in its turn, tear up the soft tissues" (Gross 63). They also prescribe the kinds of equipment a surgeon would need in a surgical kit, including "a full amputating case, with at least three tourniquets, two saws of different sizes, and several large bone nippers; and lastly, a trephining case" for drilling into the skull to relieve brain injuries (36). And the authors had been close enough to war to see the damage done by different kinds of artillery: "Cannon balls often do immense mischief by striking the surface of the body obliquely, pulpifying the soft structures, crushing the bones, lacerating the large vessels and nerves and tearing open the joints, without, perhaps, materially injuring the skin" (64). While not commenting on the cause of the injury, the amputation operation that surgeons performed the most – removal of the leg either just above or just below the knee – was described by the manual authors as "among the most dangerous of accidents, and no attempt should be made to save the limb when the injury is extensive" (67). Ultimately, though, the manual is minimally detailed, drawing up on limited experience by the surgeons and embodying some basic principles of field surgery.

By contrast, the Confederate manual has a kind of you-are-there feel to it. Cannonball fire directed at "a part of the body . . . carries all away before it . . . If it be part of one of the extremities which is thus removed, the end remaining attached to the body presents a stump with nearly a level surface of darkly-contused, almost pulpified tissues" (*Manual of Military Surgery* 38). While both Union and Confederate manuals use the same language of damage – "pulpify," "tear" – the tense they use reveals where they see themselves in relation to the action of war. The Union manual is in the future conditional, that is, these kinds of injury *could* happen in these circumstances. The Confederate manual, written after two years of field experience, is in the present and future indicative: sections of the body are

78 Limbs and What Happens to Them

"carried away," muscles "will be separated from each other and hang loosely"; large chunks of shell "produce immense laceration and separation of the parts against which they strike," and so on (38–9).

Where the Union manual is theoretical and advisory, the Confederate manual is instructive and visual. The Union manual declares "[little] need be said here about the *methods* of amputation," and, indeed, it uses about a page to describe how that should be done. The bulk of its discussion of amputation covers the statistical analysis done in previous wars both domestically and abroad (especially the Crimean War, mainly because it is most recent). Infections like erysipelas and gangrene garner a paragraph each to cover description and treatment.

By contrast, the Confederate manual is both detailed and illustrated: it describes wounds in sometimes disturbing detail, bringing the experience of military surgeons off the field and onto the page, and, unlike its Northern counterpart, includes (admittedly somewhat cartoonish) illustrations of how to execute amputations. Injuries are described floridly as having "a livid-purple tinge" or "dead-like and pale" (39). The authors gather anecdotal evidence of how pain functions in relation to gunshot wounds, for example, that being scraped and bruised by a bullet can be more painful than being shot through, or that hemorrhage can be far more dangerous than a wound itself.[7]

Unlike the Union manual, which moves fairly quickly through different kinds of injury and treatment, the Confederate manual specifies surgical procedures, and accompanies them with clear (if hardly expert) illustrations. The process of creating flaps of skin to cover the leg stump is analyzed in detail over several pages, with each kind of technique compared for effectiveness and long-term care. Essentially, the manual provides step-by-step instructions on how to perform each amputation, with helpful tips for less experienced surgeons (to amputate a foot, for example, the surgeon should "[t]race backwards with the finger the fibular margin of the fifth metatarsal bone [of the toe] ... it is well to bear in mind that the desired point will be found nearly five-eighths of an inch in front of a transverse line" and so on [229]).

The Union manual looks back to the past for examples and forward to the future for implementation. Although it advertises the presence of woodcuts in the book, in fact it has only a few illustrations in the margins of a small number of pages. And these illustrations are of surgical instruments needed to fish bullets out of wounds. While the manual is clear about the kinds of equipment needed for an amputation kit, it barely entertains the importance of such furnishings. In many ways, the manual echoes Northern expectations of the war – that it would be over soon with minimal injuries. The lengthy history of military surgery and emphasis on the importance of experienced and proper surgeons suggests that the editor S. D. Gross and his authors believed that part of their task was to convince the very best surgeons to enter military service.

By 1863, however, the toll of the war on the bodies of troops was clear. Massive death and injury were part and parcel of the conflict, and surgeons needed detailed descriptions and clear images of how to repair arteries, resect cracked bones, and perform amputations. In the Confederate manual, surgical instruments are shown in use, disarticulating fingers, toes, arms, hands, feet, and legs, unlike the amputation kit sitting in its case unused in the Union manual. Strikingly, there are no images of bones being sawed – probably the most iconic image of amputation in popular culture – since that needed little instruction. Rather, the fine work of slicing through flesh, disarticulating joints, and constructing flaps is represented in detail in both words and images.

The Confederate surgical manual is a text produced in the middle of a crisis. We can't know whether it was written before or after the battle of Chancellorville in late April to early May 1863, a decisive victory for the Army of Virginia, or whether it was published after Vicksburg and Gettysburg in midsummer, both significant Union wins. But to a certain extent that's not relevant. The Confederacy was already hemorrhaging soldiers due to desertion and was low on every kind of supply. And most importantly, Antietam and Shiloh the previous year had revealed that modern war itself was the enemy, that the minié ball was the most fearsome opponent.

Despite their differences, though, both of these manuals construct a present tense in which what matters is the damage done to the body and the surgeon's methods for remedying, or at least palliating, that damage. They describe the effects of gun and cannon fire in a present tense that does not consider the future of the body on which they operate. Even the relatively undetailed Union manual narrates the injuries inflicted by minié balls and cannons, leaning on gerunds to do the narrative work: "pulpifying," "crushing," "lacerating," "tearing," "breaking," and so on.

These books are written in a kind of suspended present in which the only reality is the actuality of the surgical process. Of course, neither manual could be expected to anticipate – or, in the case of the Confederate manual, describe – the materialities of amputated limbs that punctuated the surgeons' work. They provide an alternate reality, one quite different from that of the field hospitals described by doctors and nurses who cared for injured men, in which limbs piled up and medical staff were soaked in blood. One might argue that no official manual could prepare for that. And yet they also provide a kind of introduction to the temporality of the field hospital. For these manuals, each patient is himself fungible, defined only by wound and method of dissection or resection, existing in a self-reproducing present. Likewise, as I will show, the amputated limbs themselves become interchangeable, one pile no different from the next, a grim fixture of surgical intervention.

"A naked and ghastly mess of human flesh": Disarticulated Limbs and the Altered Union Body

Neither of these manuals discusses what should happen to the limbs once they have been amputated. This isn't surprising, given that the focus is on saving a soldier's life, and the disarticulated limb is a casualty of the casualty – excised and thrown aside for the greater good of survival. And while the Confederate manual provides detailed illustrations for the most efficient amputation of various extremities, neither text either anticipated or narrated the sheer mountains of human limbs that were discarded over the four years of the war.

At the same time, these piles of amputated limbs are a common feature of memoirs by doctors and nurses working in the field and at more central hospitals, as well as more casual visitors. Usually they are in plain sight, in open-air field hospitals, but occasionally they fill rooms. John H. Brinton, whose work as the first director of the Army Medical Museum is discussed later in this chapter, describes his encounter with the phenomenon in the tone of a gothic novel:

> I found bloodstained footmarks on the crooked stairs [of a small house operating as a hospital after the Battle of Belmont] and in the second-story room stood my friend of Cairo [OH] memory; amputated arms and legs seemed almost to litter the floor.... "Ah, Doctor," said the new-fledged surgeon, "I am just getting on with these," pointing to his trophies on the floor with a right royal gesture. (91)

Amputated limbs take on seemingly opposing meanings in this moment in Brinton's memoir. Initially, we see them as strewn randomly around the room, like leaves on a forest floor. They are literally detritus, fragments of the whole tossed aside. Yet at the same time they are trophies, signs of the young surgeon's skill and prowess, even aristocracy.[8] Are they material proof of conquest like those buffalo pelts and elk horns that white

Americans collected on their hunting trips to the West in the years before the Civil War, items whose value derives from their uniquely American origin and the victory of man over nature?[9] Or perhaps they are prizes awarded for achievement, the speed with which Brinton's friend can detach and discard arms and legs from the trunks of injured soldiers.

In either case, the amputated limbs signify because they are detached from the body to which they originally belonged. More importantly, they are translated into inanimate objects, either derogated (litter) or elevated (trophies), but objects nonetheless. Strikingly, the actual bodies of the troops from which these limbs have been taken are absent from this scene. Brinton's acquaintance identifies his work not with saving the lives of those soldiers, but as "getting on with these" – that is, creating amputated limbs from whole bodies. It is as though the logic of amputation has been turned on its head. Rather than having to remove a limb in order to prevent the death of a wounded soldier, the purpose of amputation is to generate ever larger piles of dismembered arms and legs that can be displayed as trophies to impress a more senior surgeon (incidentally, the surgeon had been an assistant to Brinton in Cairo, and Brinton had been unhappy with his work). The small size and closeness of the room at the top of the crooked stairs only makes this scene more ghoulish.

This gothic tint is either directly or indirectly an element of many accounts of the pile of limbs. Usually the narrator encounters it outdoors in the amputating tent of a field hospital or a larger operating room. Nurse Mary Livermore saw "an ever-increasing quantity of mangled and dis-severed limbs" gather around her after the battle of Fredericksburg (536). The first thing Walt Whitman records in *Memoranda of the War* is "a heap of amputated feet, legs, arms, hands, & c., a full load for a one-horse cart" (8). John Tuttle, a captain in the Union Army, witnesses an intensified version of Whitman's potential "full load" in the aftermath of the fighting at Shiloh in April 1862. For Tuttle, "the most shocking and sickening sight of the day" was "two or three wagon loads of amputated hands, arms, feet, and legs thrown in a heap … a naked and ghastly mess of human flesh" (Miller 1).

Later, while collecting specimens for the Army Medical Museum, Brinton's brush with the gothic intensified, as he enacted a kind of ersatz graverobbing, from a pile that both was and wasn't a place of burial: "Many and many a putrid heap have I dug out of trenches where they had been buried in the supposition of an everlasting rest, and ghoul-like work have I done" (187). Many of the tropes Brinton uses reappear again and again, including the hint of gothic threat. Sophronia Bucklin, for

82 Limbs and What Happens to Them

example, a nurse who served in military hospitals for three years, relates her experience at the amputating tent where "lay large piles of human flesh – legs, arms, feet and hands. They were strewn promiscuously about – often a single one lying under our very feet, white and bloody – the stiffened members seemed to be clutching often times at our clothing" (258).[10]

Once again we see the randomly mixed pile of members of all kinds, in this case not just arms and legs but also hands and feet. This kind of chaos was intrinsic to descriptions of both surgical tents and battlefields more generally. Indeed, several observers of the effects of the war commented on the ways that a wide range of items were thrown about in the wake of a battle. Surveying the battlefield at Gettysburg, Bucklin notes that everything is atomized and blown apart: "Battered canteens, cartridge boxes, torn knapsacks, muskets twisted by cannon shot and shell, rusted tin cups, pieces of rent uniform, caps, belts" as well as body parts (187). This flotsam and jetsam of battle is separated from its original owners – battered and twisted just as hours or days later the limbs of the men will be. Moreover, rather than having fallen to their places on the floor like litter or being dispersed by the power of shot and shell, the limbs have been strewn, scattered by human hand. And unlike Brinton's inanimate arms and legs, these extremities seem to be taking on a ghostly life of their own. Both white and red, exsanguinated and bloody, they seem to be speaking for themselves, grasping at the skirts and trouser bottoms of the doctors and nurses in the tent.[11] At the same time, they are categorically unidentifiable: promiscuous.

For some narrators, the amputated limbs became synecdoches for soldiers themselves, both separated from and signs of the men whose bodies had only recently been whole. Over half a century after the war, German American politician Carl Schurz recalled his "harrowing experiences" witnessing the work of army surgeons after the battle of Gettysburg:

> There stood the surgeons, their sleeves rolled up to the elbows, their bare arms as well as their linen aprons smeared with blood ...; around them pools of blood and amputated arms or legs in heaps, sometimes more than man-high. (*Reminiscences* 39)

In a space full of men lying down on stretchers and operating tables, their blood transferred from their own bodies to the clothing of the men removing their limbs, surgeons bending over them to operate, the pile of arms and legs are the primary signifier of a man standing on two legs. This image is quite different from the undifferentiated piles we have seen before – rather than being totally separated from the human body, these

Disarticulated Limbs and the Altered Union Body 83

limbs constitute another, "harrowing" body that – keeping the etymology of "harrowing" in mind – plows through the intact body to construct a kind of Frankenstein's monster out of discarded spare parts.

Extremities removed from the body lose specificity, region, even gender. Outside Fort Wagner, the site of the heroic if doomed charge by the Massachusetts Fifty-Fourth, the Black regiment commanded by Robert Gould Shaw, Susie King Taylor – herself married to a Black soldier – saw "many skulls lying about . . . the comrades and I would have quite a debate as to which side the men fought on" (30). The irony here is palpable: a formerly enslaved woman and her Black "comrades" implicitly contradicting the white scientific consensus promulgated by Samuel Morton, Josiah Nott, and Louis Agassiz, who looked to skulls to identify what they believed were innate biological and species-based differences between racial groups, known as polygenism.[12]

What are we to make of these piles, heaps, mounds, loads of promiscuously strewn, scattered, littering hands, feet, arms, and legs? Of course, these collections of amputated limbs were a reality of the massive casualties of the Civil War. Tens of thousands of men could be injured in a single battle, of whom thousands would need amputation. In addition, given the lack of any sterile environment (as Michael G. Rhode points out, "[d]octors extracted bullets from wounds by reaching in with their fingers and cleaning out the bullet and any other loose material" [79], moving from man to man without washing their hands or drawing clean water), even if an arm or leg could initially be saved, later infection meant that it might have to be amputated to avoid gangrene or sepsis. That is, these piles are tropes, yes, but they are also actual body parts from actual men.

At the same time, let's return to Susie King Taylor's unburied skulls at Fort Wagner. This scene is actually fairly unlike the others I examine – these are the skulls of men killed in battle, not body parts purposely removed by doctors in the hope of saving a life. They are bare bone, rather than being clothed in flesh (and clothing – Sophronia Bucklin remembers seeing "[b]oots, with a foot and leg putrifying within" [188]). But I would argue that these skulls get to the heart of my argument.

The skulls can only do their symbolic work when they are as far removed from their function on living bodies as possible. For Taylor, the bare skulls have shucked off any signifiers of race or region: they could be the skulls of formerly enslaved Georgians like herself, or upper-class Bostonians like Shaw, or white Southerners. Taylor takes the logic of the disarticulated limb and pushes it even further – in this incident we see the necessity of the separation of the skull from the body to effectuate a

84

nonracial, nonsectional Union. Simultaneously, these skulls are themselves the vestiges of a gesture toward that kind of Union, since at least some of them used to belong to Black soldiers who grabbed their own freedom and entered into a battle for the freedom of their peers. These meanings are not separate from each other, but tightly imbricated one into the other.

At the same time, King forces us to acknowledge that the price that Black bodies pay for this unity is not just loss of limb but loss of life. Indeed, she is clear-eyed throughout her memoir about the suffering of Black troops and the shoddy treatment they received after the war was over, especially in terms of receiving (or, rather, being denied) government pensions. These skulls may gesture toward a non-racial Union, but at far greater cost to Black soldiers than to white.

The pile of limbs reminds us of two simultaneous truths. The first is that the Civil War exacted a terrible price on its combatants, whose bodies were shattered, dismembered, cut up, pulled apart, and even destroyed. And the severity of this price often depended on the racialization of the bodies paying it. But the very anonymity of the pile is also the promise of the war, however grisly the message might appear. Mixed "promiscuously," the pile is no respecter of persons: hands, feet, arms, and legs rub up against each other regardless of race, class, or national origin. The horrific loss carries with it the potential for corporeal coexistence, the kind of proximate equality slavery and white supremacy abhorred.

"These butcher's shambles": Walt Whitman in the Hospital

If, as I have argued, amputation represents not simply loss but also the recognition that the Civil War and its sequelae must acknowledge that the losses of life and corporeal wholeness entailed in war are irreparable and at the same time open up new possibilities to national belonging, these anonymous, promiscuously scattered limbs are the prerequisite for this understanding. Not only must there be something left behind, lost permanently, but it must be structurally impossible to resect limb and body – there can be no going back. The pile of limbs does that imaginative work. There is no way of reuniting body and its parts, since the extremities are now part of a different kind of collectivity, excised and abjected from the body of the soldier and, by extension, of the nation.

This irreversibility is an intrinsic part of Walt Whitman's experiences as an unofficial nurse, a role he took on after finding his brother George in a Washington, DC, hospital, lightly wounded after Fredericksburg. As Peter Coviello argues, Whitman's Civil War memoir *Memoranda during the War* "is ... a story of the simultaneous deformation, and painstaking reassembly, of an idea of America" (Whitman xvii). While Whitman differs from many of the figures in this book in his willingness to sacrifice Black self-determination for national wholeness, something evident in *Drum Taps* and later collections, *Memoranda during the War* reflects on the corporeal losses experienced by Union soldiers as a representation of the larger political questions of the day. The physical dismemberment of troops is an embodiment of the ways that the nation was tearing itself apart through military and political conflict, as Coviello points out: *Memoranda* "is a testament to one man's struggle to sustain his belief in the better possibilities of American life, even as the best of his countrymen set about butchering one another" (li). Or, as Robert Leigh Davis pithily writes, "[b]ody and body politic lose their self-evidence in a Civil War hospital" (38).

Whitman's transcendent faith in democracy was, of course, profoundly shaken by the war. If, in Davis's words, "[d]emocracy is a society without an adequate body" (32), the war literalized the ways in which that body could be rendered incomplete. The whole of the nation comprises many parts: the democratic process, elected officials, the people themselves, the various promiscuous parts that come together in previously unforeseen ways. Each element is insufficient to make up the entirety of the United States; indeed, "the published text, the elected authority, and the afflicted body are importantly incomplete in Whitman, partial realizations of a larger and unrepresented whole" (Davis 24).

For Whitman, the boundaries between amputated limb, ravaged soldier, and shattered nation are paper-thin. He is struck by the common practice of leaving wounded and dead soldiers on the field as battles stretch over days. One man "lay the succeeding two days and nights" after the battle of Fredericksburg, "helpless on the field. It is not uncommon for the men to remain on the field this way, one, two, or even four or five days" (13–14). The men are abandoned, strewn across the field, much like amputated limbs of the Union Army itself, barely distinguishable from each other, reminders of the ruin of the nation and the detritus that ruin leaves behind.

Sometimes Whitman does not make a clear distinction between the damage done by a battle and the act of amputation itself. As hundreds of men arrived from Chancellorsville in May 1862, Whitman recorded his experience of "the camp of the wounded – O heavens, what scene is this? – is this indeed *humanity* – these butchers' shambles?" (24). Whitman's use of the word "shambles" is not simply figurative here, since in the

86   Limbs and What Happens to Them

nineteenth century a shambles still held onto its earlier literal meaning of a stall or table where meat was sold, or more generally a butcher's shop,[13] or, by extension, a metaphorical term for a scene of carnage and slaughter.[14] In fact, it's only in the mid-twentieth century that the word shucks its associations with the slaughterhouse and signifies simply disorder, chaos, and mess. For Whitman, the scene of the wounded is always already a place where men are carved up, limbs are sliced off like so much meat, and the signs of carnage are everywhere. It's not surprising that Whitman's invocation of the shambles is followed immediately by a scene of amputation: "One man is shot by a shell, both in arm and leg – both are amputated – there lie the rejected members" (24–5).

"The rejected members" is a resonant phrase. Of course, Whitman means arms, legs, hands, and feet, parts of the larger body – the original definition of the word. But it's hard not to see the other meaning of "members," people who belongs to an organization or nation. The "rejected" limbs are inseparable from the rejection of the members of the Union by their erstwhile Confederate co-nationalists. Whitman is well aware of the figurative as well as literal stakes of the amputation of the Confederacy from the Union (or vice versa, as this sentence suggests?). Although he is eager to reunite the two sections, he cannot help but recognize the difficulty, if not unfeasibility, of doing so under the current conditions. Within what we might call the regime of amputation, resection is beyond the realm of the possible. The rejected members are everywhere – as hospitals multiply so that "one can hardly look in any direction but these grim clusters [or hospital buildings] are dotting the beautiful landscape and environs," the piles inevitably grow and the dissection of the nation intensifies.

Whitman is well aware of the costs of this new regime – not just the destruction of human bodies but the amputation of the young male population from both the South and the nation as a whole. When a soldier from Connecticut whom Whitman is caring for mentions that he has seen a monument to proslavery senator John Calhoun, Whitman gives a bravura speech lamenting the excision of the South from what it used to be:

> *I* have seen Calhoun's monument. *That* you saw is not the real monument. But I have seen it. It is the desolated, ruined South; nearly the whole generation of young men between seventeen and fifty destroyed or maim'd; all the old families used up – the rich impoverished, the plantations cover'd with weeds, the slaves unloos'd and become the masters, and the name of the Southerner blacken'd with every shame – all *that* is Calhoun's *real* monument. (98)

Whitman's ambivalence about the war and the division and reunification of the nation are in full evidence here. As Ed Folsom observes, "understanding that Whitman abandoned racial for regional reconciliation is central to grasping Whitman's views on race during Reconstruction" (549). Unlike his more radical antislavery contemporaries, Whitman's witness to the horrors of amputation convinced him not of the impossibility of returning to the past but, rather, of the necessity that the nation be reunited at any cost – even if that cost be the liberty of the formerly enslaved. He saw white America as a single unit; indeed, he saw "the actual Soldier of 1862–'5, North or South" as equivalent, "with all his ways, his incredible dauntlessness, habits, practices, tastes, language, his appetite, rankness, his superb strength, animality, lawless gait" (7).

It's not surprising that Whitman returns to the vocabulary and cadence of his prewar writings in this passage, since he sees the men of both armies as former and future members of the United States, no longer rejected but resected.[15] Whitman forces himself to look beyond the piles of amputated limbs toward a fantasized nation in which bodies are somehow stitched back together to form a unified, reconciled nation. Indeed, Folsom reminds us that with its publication date of 1876, "*Memoranda* can and should be read as a Reconstruction document" (551), rather than purely a chronicle of the war. As soon as 1865, the publication date of *Drum Taps*, Whitman was imagining modes of reconciliation between North and South that included both a homoerotic bond between the (white) men on both sides and a collaborative effort at westward expansion. Unlike his radical contemporaries Albion Tourgée, Louisa May Alcott, Anna Dickinson, or Oliver Otis Howard, Whitman can see only one way to deal with the "rejected members" of the Civil War, and that way is the one that privileges a commitment to the white male unity of the past (or, as he puts it in *Calamus*, "the manly love of comrades") rather than forging a nonracial, unpredictable future.

The Afterlives of Limbs

Having witnessed the phenomenology of amputation and the ontology of disseevered limbs, observers wondered about the eschatology of these missing members. In a culture as steeped in evangelical Christianity as the mid-nineteenth-century United States, and one in which millennialist movements thrived, this is not a surprising development – talk about the fate of one's eternal soul was everywhere, and debates about what happened to the body after death and at the Last Judgment were lively.

88 Limbs and What Happens to Them

Amputation complicated those conversations. As Drew Gilpin Faust points out, "[t]he traditional notion that corporeal resurrection would accompany the Day of Judgement seemed increasingly implausible to many Americans who had seen the maiming and disfigurement inflicted by this war" (xvi).

This doubt was intensified by the treatment of amputated limbs that I discussed in the previous section. As arms, legs, and other extremities were separated from their owners and promiscuously combined with and indistinguishable from the discarded parts of other bodies, not only the idea of the integrity of the male body and, by extension, the body politic was threatened. So was the concept of the intact body risen whole from the grave to join Christ in eternal peace. Moreover, if dissevered body parts were to be somehow gathered to their erstwhile bodies, then they always and exclusively belong to the bodies to which they were attached, a very different conclusion from the one of surgeons, who regarded amputated extremities as inanimate objects to be thrown away and disposed of.

Louisa May Alcott's *Hospital Sketches* explores these very questions. As Whitman was caring for his brother and later other men at the hospitals in and around Washington, DC, Alcott – at that point best known as the daughter of Transcendentalist philosopher and education reformer Bronson Alcott – was also making her way to the nation's capital to serve as a nurse. Unlike her protagonist, Tribulation Periwinkle, Alcott was already a published and prize-winning author when she began work at the Union Hotel Hospital in Georgetown, in December 1862. Alcott joined a growing cohort of female nurses: women working as nurses outside the home, especially middle-class white women, were a new phenomenon. Women were not trained or certified as nurses in the years before the Civil War, although Florence Nightingale's service in the Crimean War the previous decade had made the concept more palatable. Of course, women had plenty of experience as home nurses, since most medical care took place in the home and hospitals were reserved for the very poor or those without family to care for them, which often amounted to the same thing.

However, with the Civil War (as with many wars with large numbers of conscripts) the level of need for nurses far outstripped the available number of men who could fill the role. At the outbreak of war, the Union had no army nurses, and initially nursing was taken up by Catholic orders of nuns who were dedicated to nursing, such as the Sisters of Charity, Sisters of Mercy, and Daughters of Mercy (Snoby 158). The first lay female nurses came to the work much as Whitman did, as mothers, sisters, wives, and fiancées, caring for injured and ill family members. By the end of the first year of the war, however, the high numbers of casualties combined with ongoing commitment to the Union moved many women of all ages to volunteer.

While about a third of amputations took place within six hours of injury and another third between seven and twenty-four hours, soldiers sometimes had to wait up to three days to be operated on, and limbs initially not amputated would have to be removed due to infection. So the exclusion of most female nurses from field hospitals did not spare them the reality of amputation (US Sanitary Commission, *Surgical Memoirs* 61). Despite the purported delicacy of bourgeois women, Susie King Taylor noted that nurses soon became inured to the bloody sights they encountered daily: "It seems strange how our aversion to seeing suffering is overcome in war – how we are able to see the most sickening sights, such as men with their limbs blown off and mangled by deadly shells, without a shudder" (31). In *Hospital Sketches* Alcott bears witness to this observation. In her first days at Hurly-Burly House, Trib sees a young soldier "with one leg gone, and the right arm so shattered that it must evidently follow" (37), without so much as a "shudder." Indeed, she ends up attending the weekly amputation sessions as an assistant.

As we have seen, a significant part of this process of habituation involves imagining the injured and amputated parts of the body as separate objects from the body itself. Dr. P., the senior surgeon at the hospital, "through long acquaintance with many of the ills flesh is heir to, had acquired a somewhat trying habit of regarding a man and his wound as separate institutions," not surprisingly, since as often as not that wound was inflicted on a limb that would soon be severed from the man, becoming just another object. Dr. P. implicitly encourages the wounded men to do the same, having them help him examine their own injuries before he removes the arm or leg:

> "Here, my man, just hold it this way while I look at it a bit," [Dr. P.] said one day to [a wounded officer], putting a wounded arm into the keeping of a sound one, and proceeding to poke about among bits of bone and visible muscles, in a red and black chasm made by some infernal machine of the shot or shell description. (98)

Shortly after this, Dr. P. was "whipping off legs like an animated guillotine" (98), himself a machine of destruction turning a metaphorical object into an actual one. Trib sees this trick of imagination extending even to the injured soldiers themselves, although in varying manifestations. One sergeant "was christened 'Baby B.' because he tended his arm on a little pillow, and called it his infant" (94).

At the same time, the soldiers have larger, theological questions about what would happen to their lost limbs. John Brinton was only partly joking when he talked of the limbs he dug out of the "putrid heap" in a trench where they were buried "in supposition of an everlasting rest" (187). The question was, Where would that rest be? And would the rest of them rest in the same place, in the same way? The religious messages they received about the state of their souls and bodies depended on the chaplains who were posted to or volunteered at their hospital. Hurly-Burly House had been assigned a man "who roamed vaguely about, informing the men that they were all worms, corrupt of heart, with perishable bodies, and souls only to be saved by a diligent perusal of certain tracts, and other equally cheering bits of spiritual consolation" (38). This vision of the wholly perishable body might be of comfort for men whose bodies had been shattered and diminished. But Alcott gives us another eschatological narrative, provided by the young man with the missing leg and "arm so shattered that it must evidently follow":

> Lord! what a scramble there'll be for arms and legs, when we old boys come out of our graves, on the Judgement Day; wonder if we shall get our own again? If we do, my leg will have to tramp from Fredericksburg, my arm from here, and meet my body, wherever it may be. (37)

The young man clearly means this as a joke – "[t]he fancy seemed to tickle him mightily, for he laughed blithely, and so did I" – but it does point to an anxiety that the separation of limbs raises (37). It is the inverse of challenge that amputation makes to the convention of the beautiful death and the never-dead child. Rather than focusing on the new body that amputation has made, this soldier zeroes in on the plight of his missing limbs, which would be hard pressed to find the rest of him on Judgment Day.

The scenario he invokes is both ludicrous and horrifying. In the logic of the hypothetical situation he suggests, not only his leg will be traveling North from Virginia and his arm from Georgetown. Hundreds of thousands of arms and legs, with minds of their own and an unerring homing instinct for the bodies of which they were once a part, will be searching for their previous owners, flying across the country in search of them. Like children separated from their parents they will do their best to find

Walt Whitman in the Hospital

their bodies, but the soldier suggests that this effort might be only partially successful. He wonders, not without reason, "if we shall get our own again." This raises an even more bizarre possibility, that these limbs on a mission will fail in their search and have to settle for attaching themselves to other bodies, mixing as promiscuously in the millennium as they did in piles in human time, creating patchwork bodies made up of limbs of various lengths, age, and race.

Dissevered limbs could also serve a more practical, earthly purpose. Since both sides in the war were deploying new technologies, surgeons were learning about the damage those weapons could do on the job. But their knowledge was limited – they knew that minié balls and the new field artillery shattered bone, but they had no opportunity to actually examine the limbs they were amputating so as to have a fuller understanding of how these weapons operated and how injuries might be better treated. That would be the work of researchers who claimed the limbs for themselves, which raised ethical issues about ownership of the body, whether all in one piece or divided into parts.

Enter John Brinton, who had served as a medical surgeon and worked with the Surgeon General, William A. Hammond. In May 1862, Hammond ordered Brinton to "collect and properly arrange [in a Military Medical Museum] all specimens of morbid anatomy, both medical and surgical, which may have accumulated since the commencement of the Rebellion" (Brinton 180). It's striking that Hammond uses the term "accumulated," as though he is invoking the heaps of amputated limbs from which Brinton could choose the most interesting examples. It is also an astoundingly broad order – certainly it wasn't possible to gather together *all* the specimens, since that would require a storage space well beyond the capacities of a museum.

Along with his assistant Frederick Schafhert, Brinton collected, "cleaned, prepared, and mounted" the specimens that struck him as worth preserving. In his *Personal Memoirs* Brinton describes at length the process he and Schafhert went through:

> First of all, the man had to be shot or injured, to be taken to the hospital for examination, and in a case for operation, operated upon.... [T]he bones of a part removed would usually be partially cleaned and then with a wooden tag and carved number attached, would be packed away in a keg containing alcohol, whiskey or sometimes salt and water. Then, when a sufficient number of specimens had accumulated, the keg would be sent to

Washington and turned over to the Army Medical Museum, where the preparations of the specimens would be finished, so that they could take their place upon the shelves. (186)

The commandeering of the amputated limbs for military medical purposes completes the process of alienation of limb from body. The arm or leg becomes a "specimen," not just depersonalized but dehumanized. Occasionally, Brinton or Schafhert was not present at the amputation, and had to extract the limb from the pile or pick it up from the floor. This led to "one of the chief difficulties at this time ...[:] procuring truthful and full histories of the specimens" (186). It's hard to know what Brinton means by "histories" here – is it the story of the injury that caused the limb to be amputated in the first place? The history of the man from whom it was taken? Certainly, Brinton realizes the central problem, that after amputation the excised parts of the body get separated from their pasts. They no longer can tell a story about what happened to them or where they came from – while ontologically expressive (we know what they *are*), they are narratively silent.

Amazingly, soldiers seemed to know the numbers their limbs had been assigned, since visitors would come to the museum where the specimens were displayed and "it often happened that officers and soldiers who had lost a limb by amputation would come to look up its resting place, in some sense its last resting place" (189). There's something jarring about the phrase "its last resting place," given that that place was in a jar of alcohol arrayed on a shelf, for casual visitors to see. In some ways, the bones are lying in state, for all to see. On the other hand, they are scientific specimens to be examined, analyzed, and hypothesized about. This is very different from what one might imagine as a final resting place, and certainly the final resting place for the rest of the body left behind. Here, the bones are both scientific subjects for Brinton and his staff and mementos for the amputees – reminders of a time to which they cannot return.

Not that they didn't occasionally try. Brinton tells a story of a soldier who refused the finality of separation from his lost part:

> On another occasion a soldier, a private, came and examined the Museum, and with the help of the Assistant Curator, found his amputated limb. It seemed to him his own property and he demanded it noisily and pertinaciously. He seemed deaf to reason, and was only silenced by the

> question of the Curator, "For how long did you enlist, for three years or for the war?" The answer was, "For the war." "The United States Government is entitled to all of you until the expiration of the specified time. I dare not give up a part of you before." (190)

The logic in this passage is multilayered and certainly worth unpacking. The private sees his (unspecified) limb – now a bare bone most likely floating in alcohol – as both part of his corporeal self and an inanimate object, his "property." By characterizing it as property, he sees the limb as other than himself: we tend not to think of our body parts as separately identifiable pieces of property that we own, but rather as part of our whole intact selves. To call his limb his "property" conceptually disarticulates from his body what has been literally dissevered.

The curator follows the inverse logic. Since the private has signed up for the duration, every part of him belongs to the Union. While his limb is not part of his body, it is a body part of his to the extent that he claims it as his own. Ironically, by claiming that the limb still conceptually connects to the body from which it was taken, the curator argues for its continued separation from that body (and what the private would want to do with a stripped, partially shattered bone is for us to imagine).

This ambiguity about whom an amputated limb belongs to once it leaves a body comes up again in Brinton's narrative. Brinton hears about "a remarkable injury of a lower extremity" to include in the Museum, an injury to a man who soon died and so remained in ownership of his leg. This raises more complex questions: it isn't just digging limbs out of heaps or shallow trenches. It requires exhuming a whole body and then amputating the limb in question.

Brinton goes first to "his mess mates, explained my object, dwelt upon the glory to a patriot having *part* of his body under the special guard of his country" (191). Here the exposed, analyzed, and exhibited limb casts glory upon its former host. The body of the dead man barely signifies anything – like the heap of amputated limbs, his body is just one among many buried in the wake of some battle,. but the removal of the arm from the body is a sign of patriotism rather than a kind of mutilation. The man's friends are convinced: "the comrades of the dead soldier decided that I should have that bone for the good of the country, and in a body they marched out and dug up that body . . ., the spokesman of the party remarking gravely that John would have given it to me himself, had he been able to express his opinion" (191).

As so often happens when hypothesizing about the fate of amputated limbs, the resolution of this episode is a mixture of ghoulish and surprising. "John's" dead body, which is to say the remainder of the life he gave for the Union, does not adequately signal his patriotism, at least not in the way that his detached leg could. The march out to exhume his body is an ironic reversal of the military funeral – a solemn procession to dig up what had been buried by his comrades at arms. Most bizarrely, the "spokesman" ventriloquizes John, who would have offered up his own arm for the good of the country. John's arm is removed from what was supposed to be its final resting place, attached to his body, to be transformed into an object of scientific inquiry and laid in its actual final home. As Lindsay Tuggle observes, "the specimen assumes a life of its own, independent of the vanishing agency of its 'original possessor'" (78).

In this passage, the arm is a synecdoche, a metonym, and a metaphor for John. The part of John that is his arm stands in for his whole body, radiating the light of patriotism upon him. It also represents him by association – it is no longer actually part of John, but invokes him in the belief that he too would have been willing to surrender it. And it replaces him entirely by erasing his significance in the wake of the value of the arm itself. In all these tropes, however, the arm is separate from John. It is the thing that Brinton wants, that the men have to be convinced to give up, and that carries with it the weight of patriotism.

The sense that the men make of Brinton's request underlies the mission of the Army Medical Museum. The dissevered bones on display in the Museum only tangentially and incidentally belong to the bodies that gave them up, if at all. Most of the men who go to find their own amputated limbs point them out as though they were trophies for performance, not elements of their own being (indeed, in Brinton's descriptions, parts of the Museum seem to resemble nothing so much as a high school trophy case that alumni visit to relive their past glory days and brag to their children). The one man out of the thousands who flocked to the Museum who identifies *and* claims his limb is rebuffed by the government's claim to all the parts of his body, attached or otherwise.

At the Army Medical Museum, amputated limbs live on longer than the men who lost them – indeed, the Museum's holdings still exist in federal facilities. The Museum intensifies the joking puzzle that Louisa May Alcott's patient raises, as to what will happen to all the detached parts of soldiers during the resurrection of the dead. Will they rise as a body out of their alcohol baths to be reunited with their original owners? As we'll see in the next section, one writer imagined what that would look like.

Reconstitutio *ad absurdum*: George Dedlow's Spirit Limbs

This brings us to S. Weir Mitchell, who was fascinated by the neurological effects of amputation, and the body's simultaneous recognition of and ambivalence toward the permanent loss. He wrote "The Case of George Dedlow" in 1866, the same time that he was caring for amputee Union soldiers at the United States Army Hospital for Injuries and Diseases of the Nervous System, just outside Philadelphia (commonly known as "Stump Hospital" by the many amputees who were cared for there), and researching the medical ramifications of nerve damage caused by amputation. The story, "The Case of George Dedlow," is hard to categorize. While it begins as a fairly realistic account of the experiences of a field surgeon in the Union Army, it soon develops into something more strange, surreal, and ultimately absurd.

Wounded while on a mission, Dedlow experiences the amputation of an arm, which is followed by another serious injury and the subsequent amputation of the remaining arm and both his legs. The story is a meditation on the meanings of amputation, especially on the phenomenon of phantom limb, and the contradictory impulses of the self in relation to lost limbs. Throughout much of the story, the feeling that dominates Dedlow's consciousness is pain, whether located in his body, in the amputated member, or in the body's chimerical memory of that part.

After his initial injury, Dedlow's wounded hand is "dead except to pain," as though pain itself is the only sign of life possible under those circumstances. In some ways Mitchell represents the hand as pre-amputated, separated from the rest of his body with its own logic and feeling. Dedlow's pain inheres in the body part itself, rather than in his remaining body. After his first amputation he identifies his recently removed arm as the absent presence of pain: "I dimly remember saying, as I pointed to the arm which lay on the floor: 'There is the pain, and here am I.'" All this suggests what we have seen so far, that the detached part is, even before amputation, an independently operating object, the place where pain is vested. Once the hand is removed, the pain goes with it.

Many readers of "Dedlow" have seen it as either a psychological account of the losses experienced by Civil War veterans (which it surely also is), the first piece of fiction to deal with phantom limb syndrome, or a realistic representation of the horrors of field surgery.[16] While Robert I. Goler begins his excellent discussion of "Dedlow" acknowledging the absurdity of some elements of the story, ultimately he is interested in the more accurate aspects of the text, connecting them to Mitchell's groundbreaking

96 Limbs and What Happens to Them

work on the phantom limb. I would argue, though, that the absurdity of the story speaks exactly to the representations of amputation and amputated body parts that I've been discussing here.

First of all, the central element of "George Dedlow" – quadruple amputation – does not seem to have occurred to anyone in either the Confederate or Union Army, at least not in my own research or the comprehensive photographic collection held by the Library of Congress.[17] Dedlow's limblessness is a pretext for philosophizing about the relationship between a man, his sense of self, and his extremities. But my focus here is the end of the story, a part that few commentators analyze.

The culminating episode of the story begins when Dedlow is invited by a fellow inmate in the hospital where he is recovering to a séance. During the last third of the nineteenth century, as Molly McGarry has shown, Spiritualism, a belief system based on communication with the dead, enjoyed a significant boom, after its fall from popularity a few years earlier when the credibility of its main proponents, the Fox sisters of Upstate New York, came under serious suspicion (suspicions that were later confirmed by the three sisters themselves in the late 1880s, when they confessed that the "spirit rappings" they brought on by communing with the dead were in fact loud percussive sounds made by them cracking the joints in their toes). Deeply entwined with the already-existing cult of mourning in the midcentury United States, Spiritualism was both a religion and a domestic practice: as McGarry shows, "the séance circle . . . was always a more private than public event," held in parlors rather than lecture halls (14). In the wake of the massive death of the Civil War, Spiritualism gained new adherents and new urgency. Indeed, as we saw in Chapter 1, the desire for a Spiritualist solution to the great problem of the hundreds of thousands of dead is a central theme in Elizabeth Stuart Phelps's 1869 novel *The Gates Ajar*, in which the protagonist, Mary Cabot, is comforted by her Aunt Winifred by Spiritualist beliefs. Not coincidentally, Mary's brother Roy was killed during the war, and Aunt Winifred's assurance that death is but a thin veil between the living and the dead, and that Roy is actively accompanying Mary and will lead her to a heaven that looks more or less like the New England town she already lives in, is as immensely comforting to her as it was to Phelps's readers.

Spiritualism as comfort is what, I would argue, Mitchell wants to puncture in "The Case of George Dedlow." The soldier who invites Dedlow to the séance explains Spiritualism's attraction for him:

George Dedlow's Spirit Limbs 97

"It's a great comfort for a plain man like me, when he's weary and sick, to be able to turn away from earthly things and hold converse daily with the great and good who have left this here world. We have a circle in Coates street. If it wa'n't for the consoling I get there, I'd of wished myself dead many a time. I ain't got kith or kin on earth; but this matters little, when one can just talk to them daily and know that they are in the spheres above us."

"It must be a great comfort," I replied, "if only one could believe it."

"Believe!" he repeated. "How can you help it? Do you suppose anything dies?"

"No," I said. "The soul does not, I am sure; and as to matter, it merely changes form."

"But why, then," said he, "should not the dead soul talk to the living?" (103)

Why not indeed? There is a thin, if strictly patrolled, line between evangelical faith in the rewards of heaven and the Spiritualist belief that one can directly communicate with the dead (a line that Phelps's *Gates Ajar* shaves down to a razor-thin distinction). Even such a rationalist as Dedlow believes in the immortal soul and the possibility that physical matter (such as discarded limbs) might live on in different forms. Dedlow agrees to attend a séance the next day, and what follows descends (ascends?) from satire to absurdity.

The other participants at the séance are described in satiric, even cartoonish terms. The whole affair is organized by an "eclectic doctor," a "flabby man, with ill-marked, baggy features and [infected] eyes." The "doctor" is clearly not to be trusted. He had "tried his hand at medicine and several of its quackish variations, finally settling on eclecticism, which I believe professes to be to scientific medicine what vegetarianism is to common-sense, every-day dietetics" (Mitchell, "Dedlow" 104–5). Several women are also present: an "authoress" who was "a good deal excited at the prospect of spiritual revelations" and a young woman "with very red lips and large brown eyes of great beauty" (105). She is, Dedlow later finds out, a "magnetic patient" of the doctor who had left her husband to follow him. Besides the sergeant who brought him, Dedlow meets two other participants – a woman dressed in deep mourning and the medium, a man named Brink, who "wore a great deal of jewelry, and had large black side-whiskers – a shrewd-visaged, large-nosed, full-lipped man" whom Dedlow implicitly suspects to be a charlatan.

With all the characters in place. Mitchell sets the séance in motion. Its focus is initially the woman in black:

> [The eclectic doctor] turned to the lady in black, and asked if she wished to see any one in the spirit-world.
>
> She said, "Yes," rather feebly.
>
> "Is the spirit present?" he asked. Upon which two knocks were heard in affirmation. "Ah!" said the medium, "the name is – it is the name of a child. It is a male child. It is –"
>
> "Alfred!" she cried. "Great Heaven! My child! My boy!"
>
> On this the medium arose, and became strangely convulsed. "I see," he said – "I see – a fair-haired boy. I see blue eyes – I see above you, beyond you –" at the same time pointing fixedly over her head.
>
> She turned with a wild start. "Where – whereabouts?"
>
> "A blue-eyed boy," he continued, "over your head. He cries – he says, 'Mama, mama!'"
>
> The effect of this on the woman was unpleasant. She stared about her for a moment, and exclaiming, "I come – I am coming, Alfy!" fell in hysterics on the floor.

Given that Mitchell was widely read and the intellectual skepticism surrounding both the Fox sisters in particular and Spiritualism generally, readers should take this scene with more than a pinch of salt. Much like television psychics, the medium uses obvious clues to give the woman what she wants. Her full mourning indicates a recent and major loss, either a parent, husband, or child. The effect of the séance on her is "unpleasant," although whether that is because Dedlow feels like she is being swindled or that her "hysterics" are unpleasant in and of themselves isn't clear. However, the presence of a skeptic who, after he is deemed "a disturbing agency," is asked to leave, suggests that Mitchell has injected an element of disbelief into the scene (106).

Soon it is Dedlow's turn. He is asked to think of a spirit to be summoned, and very soon there is a sign.

> For a few moments there was silence. Then a series of irregular knocks began.
>
> "Are you present?" said the medium.
>
> The affirmative raps were given twice.
>
> "I should think," said the doctor, ``that there were two spirits present."
>
> His words sent a thrill through my heart.
>
> "Are there two?" he questioned.
>
> A double rap.
>
> "Yes, two," said the medium. "Will it please the spirits to make us conscious of their names in this world?"
>
> A single knock. "No."
>
> "Will it please them to say how they are called in the world of spirits?"
>
> Again came the irregular raps – 3, 4, 8, 6; then a pause, and 3, 4, 8, 7.

George Dedlow's Spirit Limbs

"I think," said the authoress, "they must be numbers. Will the spirits," she said, "be good enough to aid us? Shall we use the alphabet?"

"Yes," was rapped very quickly.

"Are these numbers?"

"Yes," again.

"I will write them," she added, and, doing so, took up the card and tapped the letters. The spelling was pretty rapid, and ran thus as she tapped, in turn, first the letters, and last the numbers she had already set down:

"UNITED STATES ARMY MEDICAL MUSEUM, Nos. 3486, 3487."

The medium looked up with a puzzled expression.

"Good gracious!" said I, "they are my legs – my legs!"

What followed, I ask no one to believe except those who, like myself, have communed with the things of another sphere. Suddenly I felt a strange return of my self-consciousness. I was reindividualized, so to speak. A strange wonder filled me, and, to the amazement of every one, I arose, and, staggering a little, walked across the room on limbs invisible to them or me. It was no wonder I staggered, for, as I briefly reflected, my legs had been nine months in the strongest alcohol. At this instant all my new friends crowded around me in astonishment. Presently, however, I felt myself sinking slowly. My legs were going, and in a moment I was resting feebly on my two stumps upon the floor. It was too much. All that was left of me fainted and rolled over senseless. (107–8)

Taking into account how juicy this scene is, it is surprising that no critics have fully engaged with it. Mitchell moves from a fairly standard scene of a séance, which is ripe for skepticism, to a much more remarkable episode that shifts the tone of the story from Dedlow's inquisitive, declarative voice to quite another thing. We enter the realm of the fantastic, not to say the ludicrous, and this conclusion to the story raises a variety of questions and conundrums. First of all, the idea that Dedlow's amputated legs have a consciousness of their own is startling, let alone that they can communicate with the medium through the English language. Even more amazing, they can count, read, and write, spelling out their classification numbers and the name of the Army Medical Museum. Second is that they can move between the realm of the spirits and the material world, zeroing in on Dedlow like a dog with a stick, reattaching themselves to his stumps, and animating themselves to help him walk (not to mention that they would have been stripped down to bone, so their ability to support a human being without muscle and skin is questionable). Third, they are fully anthropomorphized and rendered sentient by their drunkenness – the alcohol in which they are immersed is transformed from preservative to intoxicant.[18] Fourth, the story leaves the reader wondering what the end of the scene looked like – were the amputated limbs/bones visible to onlookers? Finally, why does Mitchell end the story with Dedlow tumbling off his reconstituted legs onto the floor, "faint[ing] and roll[ing] on the floor senseless" (invoking the bereaved mother, fainting away at the revelation of her son's spirit)?

Given the implicit skepticism with which Mitchell imbues the entire séance episode, we'd be hard pressed to believe that he wanted readers to take this moment seriously. In many ways, this scene is a complement to Alcott's soldier's supposition that on the Day of Judgement amputated limbs would come looking for their previous bodies. As we've seen, more often than not, once removed, limbs were seen as so much lumber piled up on the dirt floors of surgical tents, tossed into wagons, and thrown into pits. Mitchell's tenure at the Stump Hospital both complicates and underlines this. As a neurologist well acquainted with both the anatomy and the function of different parts of the brain, Mitchell knew that any part of the body removed from the part controlled by the brain was rendered inanimate – feeding into the central nervous system, the brain and associated nerves "convey outwards motor impressions, resulting in voluntary or involuntary motion, as the case may be. They carry centripetally the myriads of impressions which constitute sensations" (Mitchell, *Injuries of the Nerves* 30).

At the same time, he was fascinated by the phenomenon of the "phantom limb," which he called "sensory hallucinations" (348). Mitchell found that he could induce, intensify, or palliate the incidence of phantom limb by applying electrical impulses to the nerves formerly attached to the removed limb. In *Injuries of the Nerves and Their Consequences* (1872), he describes an incident in which he brought on an experience of phantom limb in a patient:

> I recently faradized [treated with electrical current] a case of disarticulated shoulder without warning my patient of the possible result. For two years he had altogether ceased to feel the limb. As the current affected the brachial plexus of nerves, he suddenly cried aloud "Oh, the hand, the hand," and attempted to seize the missing member. (349)

This episode echoes "George Dedlow" in several ways. The cry of "the hand, the hand" invokes Dedlow's exclamation "they are my legs – my legs!" Moreover, the lost hand is brought back into the patient's consciousness by an unseen power, that of electrical current, much like the invisible influence of the medium to bring spirits back to earth. Mitchell continues in terms that are equally evocative of "George Dedlow," relating that "the phantom I had conjured up swiftly disappeared, but no spirit could have more amazed the man, so real did it seem" (349). Even the term "phantom limb" invokes the phantoms called into the room by the medium, as well as the strong implication that the whole séance is an extended exercise in imagination rather than a visitation by actual spirits.[19] As Mitchell defines it, "Nearly every man who loses a limb carries about with him a constant or inconstant phantom of the missing member" (349), as though amputation burdens the rest of the body with a ghost that attaches not to the site of the missing limb but to the survivor himself.

Juxtaposing these two episodes suggests Mitchell's goal in the séance scene in "George Dedlow" is, on the one hand, to question Spiritualism and, more importantly, to underline the physical permanence of the lost limb, on the other. The narrative detail that Dedlow's legs are in the Army Medical Museum, where their connection to a human body is most attenuated, stripped as they are of skin and flesh, preserved in alcohol, and catalogued by number, only reinforces the "thingness" of the lost limbs. The story literalizes the neurological phenomenon of the phantom limb, so that Dedlow does not just feel his amputated legs, but they are, magically, materialized. The fact that his brain believes that they're still there is, ironically, confirmation that they're lost forever, just bones preserved in jars in a medical museum: bones that don't talk, don't spell, don't rap on tables, and don't tuck themselves onto Dedlow's stumps like two artificial limbs.

Dedlow's unconsciousness is like that of the grieving mother: they both fall to the floor after having been abandoned by the spirits they invoked. I'd argue that Mitchell's absurdist logic here – the spirit of Dedlow's legs, preserved in spirits, can be rematerialized in the same way that the spirit of a dead child, preserved in heaven, can visit his distraught mother – puts the brakes on fantasies of reunion, between mother and child (as I discussed in Chapter 1), of the amputated body and its lost limb(s), and of the divided nation.

Ultimately, Mitchell uses satire to make the same implicit argument I have been making throughout this chapter. Amputation is permanent, and the lost limbs are no longer the property of their previous owner, but rather remnants of some irrecoverable past. George Dedlow's limbs soaking in alcohol cannot be resected onto his body, no matter their "spiritual" appearance (I'd argue too that their "drunkenness" is a sign of how separate they are from the body itself – they have an existence independent from Dedlow's). As all these narratives show us, loss via amputation renders the dismembered limb inanimate, mostly indistinguishable within the piles, heaps, mounds, and wagonfuls of its fellows, and even if identifiable, only by number not by name.

What, then, of the body left behind by amputation? How do its meanings change, especially in the context of a conflict whose main theme is the rift of the body politic? As we'll see in the next chapter, the amputated body brings with it its own burdens and, even more importantly, its own promises.

CHAPTER 3

1860 or 1865? Amending the National Body

All this pain, all this loss, all this blood, what was it for? If the goal, to paraphrase Albion Tourgée, was not to reinstate the Union as it was but to (re)create the Union as it could be, what was the payoff for the dissevered limbs and reshaped bodies? In this chapter, I argue that the holy grail of white radicals, the ultimate goal of the architects of Reconstruction, and the implicit or explicit limit case for the costs of amputation was full Black citizenship. That massive rethinking of Black personhood – especially manhood – in the 1860s found its expression, however incomplete and compromised, in the Fourteenth Amendment, which guaranteed American citizenship to all people born in the United States, irrespective of race.

While it also deals with war debt, the rights of former Confederates to the franchise, and the ramifications in terms of congressional representation for states not granting freedpeople the rights of citizenship, the fulcrum of the Fourteenth Amendment lies in its first section:

> All persons born or naturalized in the United States, and subject to the jurisdiction thereof, are citizens of the United States and of the state wherein they reside. No state shall make or enforce any law which shall abridge the privileges or immunities of citizens of the United States; nor shall any state deprive any person of life, liberty, or property, without due process of law; nor deny to any person within its jurisdiction the equal protection of the laws.

Several of the terms in this section, especially "privileges or immunities of citizenship," "due process of law," and "equal protection of the laws" (not to mention "jurisdiction," which led to the first significant weakening of the Amendment in the *Slaughterhouse* cases[1]) have been subject to extensive debate, narrowed and broadened depending on the opinions of federal appeals courts and the Supreme Court.[2] And the language of the Amendment took up weeks of discussion in the Senate and the House of Representatives before it was passed. But at its core, the Fourteenth Amendment was, in the minds of those white radical politicians, activists,

104   1860 or 1865? Amending the National Body

writers, and thinkers, the payoff for the losses of the war: the instantiation of Black equality under the law.

This endorsement of Black citizenship by both Congress and eventually the states was at the center of the work of orator, essayist, and novelist Anna Elizabeth Dickinson. One of the great radical white activists of the 1860s and 1870s, but largely forgotten today, Dickinson packed halls wherever she went, speaking alongside abolitionist superstars like William Lloyd Garrison, Gerrit Smith, and Frederick Douglass. The combination of her youth – she was barely out of her teens when she launched her speaking career – intensity, rhetorical power, and passionate delivery, especially in contrast to her small frame, made Dickinson a sensation, whether she was delivering abolition lectures, stumping for Republican candidates, or headlining the lyceum stage.[3]

While I spend some time on Dickinson's speeches, I am especially interested in her novel *What Answer?* and to a lesser extent her travelogue *A Tour of Reconstruction*. Published in 1868, *What Answer?* engages issues of cross-racial romance, the role of Black soldiers in the Civil War, white racism, and Black citizenship. Although most of the narrative takes place before 1864, with a final scene in 1865, it is, I would argue, a novel that takes up the challenges the Fourteenth Amendment presented to the reshaped nation, and the bodily, political, and moral changes white people across the ideological spectrum needed to undergo in order to make black citizenship a reality.

Equally importantly, *What Answer?* was written as the Amendment was being debated in Congress and then wending its way through the ratification process. The novel is not just a narrative of what white loss and Black liberation could look like, but a kind of primer in antiracism for white readers. While not the most elegantly written novel, *What Answer?*, like its author, has a kind of raw power and radical agenda that force its readers to see the connections between the sacrifices of the war for both Black and white Americans, and the ethical mandate of Black personhood, Black citizenship, Black liberty. At the same time, at key moments it fails these principles, falling back on the discourses of Black sacrifice that informed the sentimentalization of slavery and that characterized much white antislavery effort in the antebellum years.

"A noble and beautiful presence": Anna Elizabeth Dickinson and the Fourteenth-Amendment Roots of *What Answer?*

The stakes of the loss to be endured, the physical wages white Americans must pay for emancipation, are the same in *What Answer?* as they are – as

Anna Elizabeth Dickinson and the Roots of What Answer?   105

we shall see in Chapter 4 – in *Bricks without Straw*. However, for Dickinson, who was born into a Quaker family in Philadelphia, lived her life in the North, and in the antebellum and wartime years traveled extensively up and down the East Coast and into the Midwest,[4] the results of the Fourteenth Amendment extended beyond the destruction of slavery. She was well aware of the restrictive laws in Pennsylvania against Black male suffrage, as well as the routine discrimination against African Americans that was part and parcel of Black Northern life.[5] Indeed, while enslaved people appear in *What Answer?*, the bulk of the novel takes place either in the North or among Union troops. It's no coincidence that the New York Draft Riots feature significantly toward the end of the novel, wreaking racialized proslavery violence on white and Black characters alike. Indeed, while all the characters in the novel who go to war experience amputation, *What Answer?* seems to suggest that Northerners might have to make the ultimate sacrifice to win freedom for all Black people – and even then, the outcome is unclear.

Like the radical republicans in Congress who drafted and debated in favor of the passage of the Fourteenth Amendment, *What Answer?*'s brief is to argue for Black civic and political equality and to link the massive losses of the war, both on the battlefield and closer to home, as the predicate for that equality. Black civil rights were long a theme in Dickinson's speeches – as early as 1864 she gave a lecture that was "a logical vindication of, and impassioned appeal for, the rights of our black fellow-inhabitants, if not fellow citizens . . .; in passages of rare poetic beauty [she] called forth frequent and enthusiastic applause" ("Miss Dickinson's Lecture" n.p.). In this chapter I move back and forth between the novel and the Congressional debates, to show the interconnected threads of argument, both for and against the passage of the Amendment and the thematics of the novel.

Anna Dickinson's oratorical skill was legendary in the years leading up to and the decade after the Civil War. As Elizabeth Cady Stanton noted, "Her power over the audience was marvelous. . . . They followed her with that deep attention which is unwilling to lose a word, but greeted her, every few moments, with the most wild applause, which continued often for several minutes, breaking forth afresh with irrepressible enthusiasm" (499). The *Concord* (NH) *Democrat* described a similar scene when Dickinson came to speak in 1863: "The hall was packed full, there was not a seat on the main floor or in the gallery which was not occupied, and hundreds were standing in the rear of the hall and in the side aisles." Like Stanton, the anonymous reviewer believed that "she possesses oratorical skills of the rarest quality" ("Miss Dickinson's Address").

1860 or 1865? Amending the National Body

A February 1864 article in the *National Antislavery Standard* is even more breathless in its description of the crowds:

> The pressure in the aisles was such, even three-quarters of an hour before the time appointed for the lecture, that the ushers in charge of the reserved seats found it impracticable to discharge the duty assigned them.... It is believed that from three to five thousand people left without gaining admission to the building. ("Miss Dickinson at the Cooper Institute" 3).

And these crowds were, to all reports, adoring. As the same reporter noted, "Miss Dickinson spoke with even more than her usual power, and the most radical sentiments she uttered were applauded to the echo" (28). Moreover, her oratorical palette was not limited to tones of anger and dissent. As the editors of the *History of Woman Suffrage* put it, her style was "bold but tender, and often so pathetic that it brought tears to every eye. Every word came from her heart and went right into the hearts of all" (Stanton et al. 49).

Thanks to the network of lyceums – assembly halls that hosted performances and educational speeches – mid-nineteenth-century audiences had the opportunity to see speakers from Emerson to Frederick Douglass to Anna Dickinson (and, later in the century, Mark Twain). As Angela G. Ray argues, lyceums created a kind of national culture in which "many people, from Maine to Michigan and Minnesota to Maryland, would have seen the same lecturer give roughly the same speech," which would then be reported in local newspapers and reprinted around the country (7). Dickinson was unusual among women who appeared in public in that her message was inextricable from her style of presentation and her personality. Audiences went not only to hear her words about the urgency of social change, but also (perhaps primarily?) to see the phenomenon that was Anna Dickinson. She bridged the gap between abolitionist women like the Grimké sisters, whose power was in their words, and the typical female lyceum performers who were "readers, musicians, or dramatic interpreters, usually performing work authored by others" (Ray 144). Dickinson, the "very acme of fiery eloquence" (Ray 149), combined passionate delivery with heartfelt content, and while she drafted her speeches in detail she spoke without a script, even without notes, giving the impression that her address emerged fully formed from her mind.

This sense that Dickinson's lectures were spontaneous led her observers to see her powers as organic.[6] As one reporter noted, "Miss Dickinson is born an orator. She has the magnetic, dramatic, intense temperament. She has a voice of wonderful strength and responsiveness. She has a noble and beautiful presence" ("Whited Sepulchres" n.p.). However, her critics linked these strengths to what they saw as her weaknesses. While "her intellect is clear, quick, subtle [and h]er intuitions are fine," some saw her as "full of possibilities of greatness," but on the whole falling below her potential. To them, her powers came too easily and generated a "seeming flippancy which often pained, the smartness and repartee that made the unthinking laugh, the begging of questions, the assertion for argument, the climaxes for conclusions" ("Whited Sepulchres" n.p.). Whatever her faults, however, audiences adored her.[7]

In the early years of her career, Dickinson divided her political energies between the fight for women's suffrage and other civil rights on the one hand, and abolition on the other. However, as the war came to an end, and questions of Black emancipation and citizenship came to the fore, she, like many of her women's rights and abolitionist colleagues, felt forced to make a choice between the two causes. Unlike her close friend Susan B. Anthony, Dickinson threw her lot in with Black men's enfranchisement. Anthony tried, to no avail, to include Dickinson in the November 1866 inaugural meeting of the American Equal Rights Association, an organization agitating for women's rights. Anthony's letters implicitly show how far she and Dickinson had grown apart politically, imploring her on August 6, "Annie, if we women fail to speak the *one word* of the hour, who shall do it – no man is able – for no man sees and feels as we do." By November 7, less than a week before the convention, Anthony was reduced to writing to Susan Dickinson asking for a letter from Anna "containing her word of blessing upon our effort to secure to woman as to the negro man, a recognition in the national and state government."

By that time, debates over the Fourteenth Amendment were taking up hours in the Senate and the House, and Dickinson was beginning to work on *What Answer?* Although it preceded the impeachment of Andrew Johnson and the truly radical days of congressional Reconstruction, during which Black men voted, served on juries, and were elected to local, state, and national office, the Fourteenth Amendment was the sine qua non of Black civic and political life. While the Thirteenth Amendment officially ended slavery, it left African Americans in a kind of limbo – American persons but not necessarily American citizens. And it changed nothing for Black people north of the Mason-Dixon Line. The Fourteenth Amendment, however briefly and incompletely, changed Black lives nationwide.[8]

At the same time, as the Amendment's framer, John Bingham, maintained, the first section of the Amendment did little more than extend other elements of the Constitution and Bill of Rights: due process of law is

108   1860 or 1865? Amending the National Body

part of the Fifth Amendment, and the privileges and immunities clause originates in what is known as the Comity Clause (Article IV, Section 2) of the Constitution. However, as Garrett Epps points out, many of the Republican members of the Joint Committee on Reconstruction (also known as the Committee of Fifteen, after the number of senators and congressmen who were appointed to it)

> were operating on an assumption that the cause of the Civil War was neither the institution of slavery itself, nor Northern moral disapproval of it, but a complex political institution called the "Slave Power" – a political term that referred not only to Southern whites who owned slaves but to constitutional provisions and political practices that gave them dispropor-tionate power in the federal government. (12)

For these men, the only way to fully destroy the holdovers of this power was to grant African Americans full citizenship. This mandate took on extra urgency in the wake of the massacre of black inhabitants of Memphis from May 1 to May 3, just as the Fourteenth Amendment was being debated in Congress. As Bernice Bouie Donald shows, the rule of law established by the Constitution was worse than inadequate protection for Black Memphians, forty-six of whom were killed and seventy-five wounded over three days of domestic terrorism. Indeed, the instruments of law, in this case the Memphis police, stood by as the violence occurred, or even arrested Black victims (Donald 1630).

The Fourteenth Amendment was designed, then, to disrupt the pattern of white violence against Black Americans and was authorized by the massive violence of the Civil War itself. Not only was "the antebellum world of racist complacency ... shattered by the Civil War, which rendered imperative the re-examination of the terms of national unity in a new way" (Richards 113), but this new way of seeing depended on that very shattering for its conditions of possibility. As Thaddeus Stevens, the radical Republican co-chair of the Committee of Fifteen argued, taking Abraham Lincoln's image of the house divided and pushing it to its logical extreme, "it is necessary to clear away the rotten and defective portions of the old foundations, and to sink deep and found the repaired edifice upon the firm foundation of eternal justice" (Avins 212).

Part of this clearing away required the excision either of former Confederate States that refused to grant freedpeople their civil rights or of the racism that constituted the "rotten and defective portions." That is, the reconstitution of the national body needed a kind of amputation of white supremacy and a shifting of power from the articulated limbs of the

Black Soldiering, Black Citizenship, and the Cost of Justice 109

states to the central body of the nation. As James E. Bond argues, "the Fourteenth Amendment was revolutionary, not because it redefined privileges and immunities to include the guarantees of the Bill of Rights, but because it gave Congress the power to define and therefore expand the privileges and immunities of citizenship, which states were bound to respect" (255). White supremacy must be cut away from the body politic, and the Constitution live up to its primary purpose as an instrument of the rule of law. In the words of Pennsylvania Representative Leonard Meyers, "Slavery gone, its laws, its prejudices, and consequences should be buried forever" (Avins 193).

At the same time, the Amendment is notable because of what it connotes as much as it denotes. In Deak Nabers's words, it is "carefully poised on the line between the written and the unwritten, the line between natural right and positivist formality" (197). It partakes of both "divine law and positive law" (Nabers 186), to echo Richard Yates, a Union Republican of Illinois, who declared during the debates

> I did not believe the framers of the Declaration meant to exclude any particular class or race of men, when they declared all men equal.... I am for the black man not as a black man; I am for the white man not as a white man, but I am for man irrespective of race or color; I am for God's humanity here, elsewhere, and everywhere. (Avins 148).

What Answer? inhabits these same arguments about Black citizenship, the need to fully dissever the Slave Power from the body politic, and to change both laws and hearts. Like the radical Republicans with whom she shared many opinions, Dickinson saw slavery's reach extending into the homes and souls of white Northerners, whether they be Draft Rioters or liberal New York aristocrats like Will Surrey's parents. Moreover, she believed that she had a role to play in the destruction of white racism and the reshaping of the nation, noting in her private writings, "He who plays with fire becomes an incendiary" (Dickinson, "Speeches and Writings File" n.p.).

"Let this war go on until ... the land be utterly destroyed": Black Soldiering, Black Citizenship, and the Cost of Justice

In many ways, _What Answer?_ is, as Holly Jackson has pointed out, a fairly standard novel of doomed cross-racial romance. It sold well enough – 10,000 copies in the first year – to go through a second printing, although it was praised more for its political power than for its literary achievements

(Gallman 92). In the novel, Will Surrey, the handsome and wealthy heir to his father's successful foundry, falls in love with Francesca Ercildoune, a passionate advocate of abolition and, it turns out, part Black. Francesca is convinced by Will's family to keep away from him before he knows of her racial heritage. But eventually he finds out and despite the threats of his parents to disown him – threats they make good on – he and Francesca marry on his return from the war. His parents are "opposed, and opposed most bitterly; but he was sure that time would soften, and knowledge destroy this prejudice utterly" (184).

Isn't this the fantasy of white liberalism: that time and proximity to Blackness undo white racism and, by extension, white supremacy? Will soon realizes, however, that his hope that his parents would come around is in vain, and it opens up a line of thought that was previously inaccessible to him. Their disavowal of him because of his marriage to Francesca makes him "realize the torture to which, in a thousand ways, the darling of his heart had for a lifetime been subjected" (186).

This is a central insight of *What Answer?* – the need for white empathy with and the recognition of the losses suffered by Black Americans both north and south. And this empathy can only be achieved through meaningful loss in turn: the loss of one's family of origin and/or a part of one's body (both, after all, are cut off; the novel uses trauma and amputation in battle as a sort of repayment in kind of Black suffering by white corporeal shattering). The text also addresses the losses of slavery and the possibility of white reparation.

A significant chunk of the novel is spent on the battlefield either with Will, Francesca's brother Robert, or Jim Givens, the factory foreman who ends up fighting for the Union Army. Each of these characters loses a limb in battle, as part of a larger process of racial enlightenment (on the part of Will and even more so Jim) or the upswelling of national pride (on the part of Robert). I'll discuss each of these incidents later on, but for the moment I would point out that much of the text addresses the losses of slavery and of amputation and the process of shedding white racism through the experience both of war and of Black virtue. Bodily loss and disability either precipitate or are the result of the coming together of Black and white on an even field of engagement. In this way, I argue, *What Answer?* is a novel that thematizes the Fourteenth Amendment at its core.

Strikingly, the first disabled bodies we see in *What Answer?* are Black. The first belongs to Abe Franklin, a clerk at the factory of Will's father. The factory foreman asks Mr. Surrey to fire Abe, or at the very least demote him. As Jim, the foreman says,

Black Soldiering, Black Citizenship, and the Cost of Justice 111

> Nobody here'd object to his working in this place, providing he was a runner, or an errand-boy, or anything that's right and proper for a nigger to be; but to have him sitting in that office ... is what the boys won't stand. (9)

This insult is added to a preexisting injury: Abe has "one lame foot ... shrunken and small and ... the leg was shorter than the other" (17). At the same time, his Blackness is more notional than visible. As Jim says, "his skin is quite as white as mine ... [but] he's a nigger and there's no getting around it" (10). Abe's body is a fascinating palimpsest of visibility and invisibility, a loss of full mobility (which would in fact get in the way of his being an errand boy or a runner) and a surfeit of ostensible whiteness. Abe's Blackness is also a symbol of political allegiance to the cause of abolition – his house is adorned with pictures of radical abolitionists Wendell Phillips and (more incendiary) John Brown. In early 1860s New York, where the Surreys and Franklins live, then, Blackness is linked not just to physical disability but also to a kind of enforced absence from predominantly white arenas.

This same potential banishment from white environments plays out later in the novel in an even more pointed way. A Black soldier, "a large, powerfully made man, black as ebony, dressed in army blouse and trousers, one leg gone," enters a Philadelphia streetcar with the help of Mr. Greenleaf, a Quaker abolitionist. Greenleaf gives him his seat, strikes up a conversation with him, and learns that he lost his leg at the battle of Newbern. "I guess thee is sorry now that thee didn't keep out of it," Greenleaf observes. The soldier responds "'No, sir; no indeed, sir. If I had five hundred legs and fifty lives, I'd be glad to give them all in such a war as this'" (124).

The soldier's heroism and sacrifice for his nation and his own freedom are sharply contrasted with the racism and abuse of a drunken, most likely Irish, "coal heaver" also riding the streetcar, who demands, "what's this nasty nagur doing here? Put him out, can't ye?" (124). But Dickinson does not put racism only at the feet of the Irish, since other passengers pile on: "'Conductor!' spoke up a well-dressed man with the air and manner of a gentleman, 'what does the card say?'" To which the answer is "Colored people not allowed in this car" (124).[9]

The reader would expect the same outcome as with Abe Franklin: concession being made to white racism. But the scene turns in quite a different direction. First of all, both Francesca and Will are on the same streetcar, and Francesca stands up for the disabled soldier and against racism:

> "Of what stuff are you made to sit here and see a man, mangled and maimed in *your* cause and for *your* defence, insulted and outraged at the bidding of a drunken boor and a cowardly traitor?" (125)

Here Francesca flips the script of Black involvement in the war. For Greenleaf and implicitly for the soldier himself, the Civil War is for the *soldier's* cause and *his* defense, especially since so many Black volunteers in the Union Army were themselves formerly enslaved.[10] But as Francesca makes clear, the sacrifices this soldier has made are for his white countrymen, to free them from the sins of the Slave Power and, by extension, of white supremacy. The injustice of the attempt to eject the Black soldier from the streetcar is compounded by the multiple losses he has had to suffer: his freedom, his dignity, his arm, his citizenship. And at the same time, the novel raises a vexing question: Why must this soldier, most likely himself formerly enslaved, suffer even more to earn his freedom and his right to citizenship? How does Black loss signify in relation to white loss?

This question is amplified by the fact that Robert Ercildoune, Francesca's brother, also loses a limb. After all, by the logic we have seen from various white radicals, it would seem that only white loss can atone for Black suffering and provide the nation with the possibility of a new beginning, that the white body must be irreparably altered to teach the lessons of Reconstruction. However, I would argue that Dickinson is making an argument about the trade-offs of national belonging, as she does in the streetcar scene, that partly undergirds her radical antislavery stance and partly compromises it. Throughout the novel, the Ercildoune family engages in a debate both among themselves and with white Americans about the possibility of Black patriotism in the absence of full Black equality. In fact, this debate is the only point of conflict between Will and Francesca:

> All his life, Surrey had been a devotee of his country and its flag . . . the flag, stainless, spotless, without blemish or flaw; the flag which was "far as the sun, clear as the moon," and to the oppressors of the world "terrible as an army with banners." (55)

Francesca feels very differently about her relationship to the nation. Echoing Frederick Douglass in "What to the Slave Is the Fourth of July," Francesca concedes "'I, too, am an American but I do not thank God for it . . . O just and magnanimous country, to feed and clothe the stranger from without, while she outrages and destroys her children within!'"(55). Even as she can pass for white, Francesca chooses not to hide her racial identification from Will. She calls into question America's self-image as a place of refuge and liberty, rhetorically replacing the (presumably European) refugee who flees political violence in, say, Hungary or Poland with the Black child destroyed by slavery.

Black Soldiering, Black Citizenship, and the Cost of Justice   113

The child who is destroyed from within need not even be enslaved. As we see in *What Answer?*, Blackness itself is enough to compromise a character's belonging to civil society and having access to public goods, starting with Francesca herself, and extending to the soldier on the Philadelphia streetcar. Why, then, does Robert Ercildoune, whose losses at the hands of white supremacy are equal to those of his sister or perhaps greater given his darker skin tone, lose a limb in the war along with his white counterparts Will Surrey and Jim Givens?[11]

The answer is suggested in the debate Robert has with his father, having decided to join the Union Army as an enlisted man. Dickinson has already pointed out that both Robert and his father are darker-skinned than Francesca, and "there was still perceptible the shade which marked him as effectually an outcast from the freedom of American society and the rights of American citizenship" (164). Robert insists on signing up as a common soldier, although his father objects, pointing to his "refinement and culture . . . You are made of too good stuff to serve simply as powder" (164). Robert argues that "'Better men than I, father, have gone there, and are there today; men in every way superior to me'" (164).

Mr. Ercildoune is puzzled by Robert's response, since the war is fought by and for "white men, fighting for their own country and flag, for their own rights of manhood and citizenship, for a present for themselves and future for their children, for honor and fame. What is there for you?" (164). Mr. Ercildoune is dry-eyed about the reasons the Union forces would want his son to enlist, arguing that

> "this American nation will resort to any means – will pledge anything, by word or implication – to secure the end for which it fights; and it will break its pledges just so soon as it can, and with whomsoever it can with impunity. You and your children and your children's children after you will go to the wall unless it has need of you in the arena." (165)

Robert's answer looks to a different kind of future, the future of "manhood and citizenship" that the war will usher in:

> "The whole nation is learning, through pain and loss, the lesson of justice; of expediency, doubtless, but still of justice; and I do not think it will be forgotten when the war is ended. This is our time to wipe off a thousand stigmas of contempt and reproach." (165)

Robert points to the logic I've been tracing throughout this book, that Black redemption and emancipation must come through white "pain and loss." Only through the sacrifices made in war can the nation approach justice and erase the "thousand stigmas of contempt and reproach" that

Black people north and south must suffer. Mr. Ercildoune, on the other hand, cannot see the future that seems so obvious to Robert and interrogates the necessity of the sacrifice of another Black body in a white government's fight. He finds it impossible to believe that white people would ever suffer loss for the sake of their Black counterparts, let alone to secure justice for them. After all, he points out, even in Philadelphia, the entire system of government and civil society is engineered to degrade and delegitimize Black citizenship:

> "I pay taxes to support the public schools, and am compelled to have my children educated at home. I pay taxes to support the government, and am denied any representation or any voice in regard to the manner in which these taxes are expended. I hail a car on the street, and am laughed to scorn by the conductor, – or, admitted, at the order of the passengers am ignominiously expelled. I offer my money at the door of any place of public amusement, and it is flung back at me with an oath. I enter a train to New York, and am banished to the rear seat of the 'negro car.' I go to a hotel, open for accommodation of the public, and am denied access; or am requested to keep to my room, and not show myself in parlor, office, or at a table. I come within a church, to worship the good God who is no respecter of persons, and am shown out of the door by one of his insolent creatures.... All this in the North; all this without excuse of slavery and of the feeling it engenders; all this from devilish hatred and malignity." (165–6)

Moreover, Mr. Ercildoune enumerates the unequal ways in which Black soldiers are treated compared with their white counterparts: paid less, given no signing bonus or pension, sent to the most dangerous parts of the battle, and risking murder or (re)enslavement by the Confederate Army if captured. His conclusion is withering:

> "These are the terms the American people offer you, the terms which you stoop to accept, these the proofs that they are learning a lesson of justice!... Let them learn it to the full! let this war go on 'until the cities be wasted without inhabitant, and the houses without man, and the land be utterly destroyed . . . Leave them to the teachings and the judgments of God." (168)

Mr. Ercildoune is not wrong, of course. And he is not alone in his assessment of the price that has to be paid by the nation for not just the sin of slavery but the hypocrisies of Northern racism; he is echoing, after all, the famous words of Lincoln's second inaugural address, which declares,

> Yet, if God wills that it continue, until all the wealth piled by the bondman's two hundred and fifty years of unrequited toil shall be sunk, and until every drop of blood drawn with the lash, shall be paid by another

Black Soldiering, Black Citizenship, and the Cost of Justice 115

drawn with the sword, as was said three thousand years ago, so still it must be said "the judgments of the Lord, are true and righteous altogether."[12]

Even as he makes an enraged and righteous argument, Mr. Ercildoune (avant la lettre for the chronology of the novel, but certainly not for Dickinson and her readers) reinforces Lincoln's logic for the importance of the war to substitute white loss for Black enslavement, and white injury for Black citizenship.

Although the narrative of the novel sides with Robert, this scene seems to support Mr. Ercildoune. Dickinson follows Mr. Ercildoune's peroration not with a response from Robert but with the arrival on the scene of Will Surrey, newly back from the war, as though it implicitly argues that loss should be suffered by white men in the war, not Black. The novel's stance is ambiguous here – does Will's loss of an arm represent the fitting order of things, in which white sacrifice is necessary for Black emancipation? Or does it indicate a route for Robert to follow, a mechanism by which he can be part of the rebuilding of the nation as well through his inclusion in national institutions – in this case the Union Army? Robert notices Will first, as though Will's appearance *is* Robert's response to his father: "'A fine looking fellow! fighting has been no child's play for him,' said Robert, looking, as he spoke, at the empty sleeve" (168). In fact, the reader knows how far from child's play Will's experience of war has been. Fighting at Chancellorsville, "where men fought like gods to counteract the blunders and retrieve the disaster," Will is "stricken down at the head of his command" (118).

Will's experience at Chancellorsville takes him to the brink of death. He is

> covered with dust and smoke; twice wounded, yet refusing to leave the field, – his head bound with a handkerchief, his eyes blazing like stars beneath its stained folds, his voice cheering on his men; three horses shot under him; on foot then contending for every inch of the ground he was compelled to yield; giving way only as he was forced at the point of the bayonet; his men eager to emulate him, to follow him into the jaws of death, to fall by his side, – thus was he prostrated; not dead, as they thought, and feared when they seized him and bore him at last from the field, but insensible, bleeding with frightful abundance, his right arm shattered to fragments; not dead, yet at death's door – and looking in. (118)

We can read the loss of Will's arm as an offering for the suffering of Francesca and by extension Black Americans both enslaved and free, a sacrifice that he takes up almost hyperbolically – the two woundings, the three horses – in order to pay the debt that white Americans owe. The novel has led us to this point by an earlier conversation between Will and other men in his company in which Will argues for the importance of white self-sacrifice for Black freedom. After relating a story about an enslaved husband and wife who had refused payment for rescuing the body of a Union soldier and laying him out for burial, an enlisted man admits to Will that "I began to comprehend what your indignation meant against the order forbidding slaves coming into our lines, and commanding their return when they succeed in entering. Just then we all seemed to me meaner than dirt" (108). Will extends the metaphor even further: "As we are; and, as dirt, deserve to be trampled underfoot, beaten, defeated, till we're ready to stand up and fight like men in this struggle" (109).

Will's insistence that white Americans deserve to be trampled and beaten in payment for the federal regulation forcing self-emancipated slaves to be returned to their enslavers is of a piece with Dickinson's larger argument for white self-sacrifice to atone for slavery. Dickinson traces his trajectory from ignorance of Black suffering to a willingness to enter into the "jaws of death," first due to his love for Francesca and then due to a developing consciousness of the effects of white racism more generally.

If Will's lost arm is in payment for the enslavement of Black people in the South and white racism in the North, why then does Dickinson subject Robert Ercildoune, Francesca's brother, to the same fate? After all, both he and Francesca have survived racial violence and suffered from white supremacy in ways both large and small. Why is it that both must suffer – either loss of limb or, by the end of the novel, loss of life – to ensure Black citizenship, along with the white men who fight against the Confederacy?

"Somebody's to die to get us out of dis": Radical Sentimentalism and Black Death

The reason, I would argue, is that Dickinson sites virtuous citizenship and self-sacrifice on behalf of the nation more firmly with Black characters than white. If white loss must repay the debts of slavery, enslaved people must sacrifice themselves to convince white Americans of their deservingness of equality and justice. This is the sentimental underbelly of abolitionist radicalism, which values suffering as much as (or as a prerequisite for) rights to citizenship. Despite the tough talk of characters like Mr. Ercildoune, the real heroes of the novel are those Black men who give their lives and limbs for the larger cause.

Radical Sentimentalism and Black Death 117

The most striking example of this takes place as Jim Given and his company are trying to escape the notice of Confederate soldiers – the Union soldiers are on a boat and Confederate forces are arrayed on both banks of the river, high up and beyond the reach of Union guns. Suddenly, they get stuck on a sand bar, and someone needs to put the boat off in order for it to continue on its way. But whoever does this puts themselves in danger of becoming a clear target for Confederate fire. Dickinson makes the problem clear: "To stand up was but to make figure-heads at which the concealed enemy could fire with ghastly certainty; to fire in return was to waste their ammunition in the air" (211).

Jim, the escaped slave who has helped Tom Russell – a friend of Surrey's – escape Confederate imprisonment before they join up with Given and his company, takes it upon himself to save the group. As the "hideous shower of death was dropping about them [and] the water was ebbing, ebbing ... leaving them higher and drier on the sands," Jim sacrifices himself:

> "Sirs!" said a voice, – it was Jim's voice, and in it sounded something so earnest and strange, that the men involuntarily turned their heads to look at him. Then, this man stood up, – a black man, – a little while before a slave, – the great muscles swollen and gnarled with unpaid toil, the marks of the lash and the branding iron yet pain upon his person, the shadows of a life-time of wrongs and sufferings looking out of his eyes. "Sirs!" he said simply, "somebody's got to die to get us out of dis, and it may as well be me," – plunged overboard, put his toil-hardened shoulders to the boat; a struggle, a gasp, a mighty wrench, – pushed it off clear; then fell, face foremost, pierced by a dozen bullets. Free at last!

Jim's offering himself up for the salvation of his white companions carries with it echoes of the death of Uncle Tom in *Uncle Tom's Cabin*. Indeed, one critic in the *Christian Recorder* made just such a comparison between the two novels. *What Answer?*, the author claims, "is a book as noble, as enthusiastic, and as brave against America's greatest weakness and crime, Caste – as was 'Uncle Tom's Cabin' against slavery" (1). Dickinson's version of political radicalism means that the Black character who sacrifices himself is a man escaped from slavery, aligning himself with Union soldiers, not a loyal slave beaten to death by the white man who claims ownership over him. But her sentimentalism leads her to a similar place: the change that Black suffering and death make in white lives.[13] After Jim's death, his namesake Jim Given declares that "'the first man that says a nigger ain't as good as a white man, and a damn'd sight better 'n those graybacks over yonder, well –'" (213).

Dickinson's radicalism and sentimentalism meld together in this scene. Like Stowe, she sees Jim's death as his claim to real freedom, of which (self-) emancipation on earth is a pale imitation. At the same time, his self-sacrifice is in the cause not of spiritual but of political salvation of white characters. Jim Given is convinced not of Jim's eternal soul but of his civic and human equality with white people, and superiority to the Confederate soldiers who kill him. His death is a Confederate loss, not just of his body as an enslaved person, but also in the shift in the power of white supremacy. This is in many ways the same logic as the third section of the Fourteenth Amendment:

> Representatives shall be apportioned among the several States according to their respective numbers, counting the whole number of persons in each State, excluding Indians not taxed. But when the right to vote at any election for the choice of electors for President and Vice President of the United States, Representatives in Congress, the Executive and Judicial officers of a State, or the members of the Legislature thereof, is denied to any of the male inhabitants of such State, being twenty-one years of age, and citizens of the United States, or in any way abridged, except for participation in rebellion, or other crime, the basis of representation therein shall be reduced in the proportion which the number of such male citizens shall bear to the whole number of male citizens twenty-one years of age in such State.

Section 3 makes clear the equivalency between political losses suffered by Black men as voters and the white South as an electoral power. Not only is there a one-to-one relationship – just as one dead Black person leads to the change of heart in one white person, the loss of one Black vote leads to the equivalent loss of representation by Southern states – there's also the same slippage of actual loss to metaphorical loss. That is, the actual loss of life by Jim is evened out by the ideological loss of one white man to white supremacy, just as the material loss of the franchise to an actual Black man is equated with the symbolic loss of one unit of representation.

This is not necessarily a failing of the section of the Amendment. After all, Southern states were well aware of the importance of their disproportionate representation in Congress under the three-fifths clause of the Constitution, which many antislavery activists saw as the prime weapon of the Slave Power in the federal government. And it takes Black political power seriously, either in the franchise or as being adequately represented in Congress. But it is symptomatic of the signal weakness of some white radicals like Dickinson, who see Black loss as ennobling to Black lives and instrumental to white political salvation.

Radical Sentimentalism and Black Death

This formula helps explain Robert Ercildoune and his own losses. We witness Ercildoune's heroism first through the eyes of a "little fellow from Massachusetts" (215) in Given's regiment and later through the narrative of the novel itself. "Johnny" tells of Ercildoune's resistance to the lower pay provided for Black soldiers, which Ercildoune characterizes as "the badge of disgrace, the stigma attached, the dishonor to the government" (217). His strongest objection, though, is that "'it's *our* flag, and *our* government now, and we've got to defend the honor of both against any assailants, North or South ... The United States government enlisted us as soldiers. Being such, we don't intend to disgrace the service by accepting the pay of servants'" (217). Ercildoune's argument rests on the same rhetoric as Section 3 – Black loss of dignity results in white governmental loss of honor.

Conversely, Union gains in the war lead to Black gains in equality. As an officer in Given's regiment argues, "He sees plain enough that this war is going to break the slave's chain, and ultimately the stronger chain of prejudice that binds his people to the grindstone, and he's full of enthusiasm for it, accordingly" (218). We see proof of this in Ercildoune's participation in the Massachusetts Fifty-Fourth's doomed attack on Fort Wagner, the most dramatic example of the principle that Black self-sacrifice must be met in equal measure by white commitment to racial equality. Seeing the Fifty-Fourth's colors where they have fallen from the hand of a struck standard-bearer, "Ercildoune, who was just behind, sprang forward, seized the staff from his dying hand, and mounted it upward" (225).

This act of heroism is immediately followed by injury:

> A ball struck his right arm, yet ere it could all shattered by his side, his left hand caught the flag and carried it onward. Even in the mad sweep of assault and death the men around him found breath and time to hurrah.... He kept in his place, the colors flying, – though faint with loss of blood and wrung with agony, – up the slippery steep; up to the walls of the fort; on the wall itself.... Here a bayonet thrust met him and brought him down, a great wound in his brave breast, but he did not yield; dropping to his knees, pressing his unbroken arm upon the gaping wound, – bracing himself against a dead comrade – the colors still flew; an inspiration to the men about him; a defiance to the foe. (225)

If Ercildoune's motives were unclear, Dickinson makes sure we understand what happened. As he drags himself down the hill from the fort, he "gasped out, 'I did – but do – my duty, boys – and the dear – old flag – never once – touched the ground'" (227). His heroism is matched by the fate of the body of Robert Gould Shaw, the white commander of the regiment, which is tossed in a mass grave along with his men. As Dickinson comments, "It was well done, Slavery buried these men, black and white, together, – black and white in a common grave. Let Liberty see to it, then, that black and white be raised together in a life better than the old" (228).

What Answer? melds white and Black sacrifice in the same way that it combines white radicalism and white sentimentalism. The former requires white loss in order to atone for the violence and pain of Black enslavement, while the latter depends on Black suffering to redeem the nation. But this equivalence is inequitable from the start: After all, what benefit do the enslaved gain from white loss? Why must it be met by Black self-sacrifice? Dickinson may invoke a future of multiracial equity, but it is her Black characters who bear the greatest burden for the construction of that future.

This dual mechanism of loss and of the push and pull of Dickinson's allegiances to both radical Republicanism, on the one hand, and bourgeois sentimentalism, on the other, is played out in the deaths of Will and Francesca toward the end of the novel, both victims of the New York Draft Riots of 1863. Will has just signed up to lead a Black regiment, which he considers "'God's service'" (234) that will "'end slavery and the war more effectually than aught else'" (235), and to which Francesca gives her initially reluctant but ultimately fervent blessing.

Into this narrative come the Draft Riots, in Dickinson's telling a perversion of the kind of sacrifice required to redeem the nation. Rather than offering themselves up for the sake of ending slavery and securing Black citizenship, the rioters "steep themselves" in "rapine and blood," especially the blood of Black New Yorkers (250). Rather than being injured, they cause ruin and celebrate in it, which "made the whole aspect of affairs seem more like a gathering of fiends rejoicing in Pandemonium than aught with which creatures of flesh and blood had to do" (252). In harsh contrast with the work of God that Will Surrey surrenders himself to in leading a Black regiment, the rioters are seemingly in the service of the devil.[14]

This reversal of sacrifice and sacrilege has two climaxes – the first is the murder of Abram Franklin, the young, disabled Black man we met at the beginning of the novel, and the second is the death of Will and Francesca. Franklin is dragged from his sick bed into the street, beaten, hanged, and then burned to death. Even out of this dreadful moment, though, Dickinson draws the lessons of white radical sentimentalism we've seen in other points of the novel. As Franklin is at his last,

Radical Sentimentalism and Black Death 121

his dying face was turned towards his mother, – the eyes dim with the veil that falls between time and eternity, seeking her eyes with their latest glance, — the voice, not weak, but clear and thrilling even in death, cried for her ear, "Be of good cheer, mother! they may kill the body, but cannot touch the soul!" and even with the words the great soul walked with God. (263)

It does not take a deep engagement with *Uncle Tom's Cabin* to see the resonances between Abe's death and Tom's. In response to Legree's threats of violence, Tom assures him "'Mas'r,' ... I know ye can do dreadful things; but,' – he stretched himself upward and clasped his hands, – 'but, after ye've killed the body, there an't no more ye can do. And O, there's all ETERNITY to come, after that!'" (330). Similarly, at his death Tom invokes the power of the soul to transcend bodily pain and sanctify suffering. At the moment of his death, Tom exclaims, "*Heaven has come!* I've got the victory! – the Lord Jesus has given it to me! Glory be to His name!" (364). By aligning Abram Franklin with Uncle Tom, Dickinson operationalizes white sentiment to make Black suffering a prerequisite for readerly sympathy even if (or perhaps because) it ends in death.

Dickinson's use of the novel genre, especially as a white Northern woman, seems to envelop (or even entrap) her in the narrative conventions of sentimentality in more ways than one. As with the death of Jim earlier in the novel, and the patriotic sacrifice of his arm that Robert makes, *What Answer?* is incapable of embodying the clear political vision that Dickinson articulates in her speeches, essays, letters, and other writings. Rather, she toggles between the radical commitment to white loss as a promissory note for Black empowerment and the sentimental deployment of saintly Black (self-)sacrifice. As Kyla Schuller has observed,

> [s]entimentalism stimulates the moral virtuosity and emotional release of the sympathizer and her affective attachment to the nation-state at the expense of the chosen targets of her sympathy, typically those barred from the status of the individuated Human. (2)

We can see the tension between these two different narrative and political strategies in the deaths of Abram Franklin, on the one hand, and that of Will Surrey, on the other, both at the hands of the rioters. Unlike Franklin's sentimental death that proves his nobility and worthiness for a citizenship he will never achieve, Will's demise follows the script laid out by the tenets of white self-sacrifice. After taking down Abram's charred body, he tries to take Franklin's mother back to his own home. Almost there, they run into another group of rioters. As he helps Mrs. Franklin into the home of "a friendly black face" (264), Will is pulled back into the crowd, and in "an instant . . . a thousand forms surrounded him, disarmed him, overcame him, and beat him down" (265).

Will's dying moments reinforce the message of the novel. For Dickinson, the rioters are simply another kind of Confederate Army, "Northern rebels" rather than Southern ones. As soon as Francesca hears of a one-armed blond officer taken down by the mob, she rushes out to find him. Held in her arms, Will "stirred; the eyes unclosed to meet hers, a gleam of divine love shining through their fading fire, the battered, stiffened arm lifted, as to fold her in the old familiar caress. 'Darling – die – to make – free' – came in gasps from the sweet yet whitening lips" (267).

Will sees the loss of his life as the price to pay for Black freedom, and Dickinson is explicit in telling readers that Black enslavement in the South and white racism in the North were the causes of his death: "prejudice, living and active, had now thus brought death and desolation" (269). Strikingly, Francesca dies of a broken heart with Will in her arms, but the novel does not make clear whether it is the loss of Will that kills her or the virulence of the racism she has witnessed. Is the "awful but sublime sight" of both of their faces, "radiant as with some celestial fire, and beatified as reflecting the smile of God," more connected to Abram Franklin's Christ-like sacrifice of his life, or Will's?

This question is, to my mind, the stickiest thing about *What Answer?* The linkage between sentiment and antislavery was a major strategy that required the representation of enslaved people as supplicants at best and objects of violence at worst.[15] While Dickinson mostly avoided this trope in her speeches, invoking both enslaved and free Black people as full persons and deserving of US citizenship, it proved a soft place for her to land when tackling the unfamiliar genre of the novel. Dickinson herself provided little commentary on writing the novel in her letters, so we're forced to speculate on the disjuncture between her onstage persona as an abolitionist, antiracist firebrand and her adoption as a novelist of the figure of the suffering, self-sacrificing Black character, whose pain redeems white sympathies.

Given that Dickinson was perennially cash-strapped, supporting her family back in Philadelphia as well as herself, she might have seen *What Answer?* as a potential money-maker, earning above and beyond what her speeches, with their large but limited audiences, could bring. Robert Ercildoune's education and urbanity required an equal measure of suffering and loss to render him sympathetic to a white audience, used to a character like Stowe's George Harris, whose claim to personhood was matched by the torture visited upon him by his enslaver (the branded letter "H" burned into his right hand, for example).

The Threat to Black Citizenship and the Fourteenth Amendment 123

In addition, the fact that *What Answer?* was her only novel, even as she continued her speaking and writing career, suggests the struggle she may have had with adapting to the genre. While female-authored novels spanned a number of subgenres – sensationalist, adventure, "highly wrought" – before the juggernaut of *Uncle Tom's Cabin* appeared, there were few models for antislavery and/or antiracist long-form fiction written by white women.[16] The template provided by sentimental abolitionism shaped her otherwise radical sensibilities.[17] In many ways, I am describing the effects of what Pierre Bourdieu has called "habitus" – the way that social and cultural arrangements (of class, race, gender, and the like) are enacted by individual people, whether they are aware of it or not. Dickinson's inability to shuck off the conventions of racial sentimentalism strikes me as a kind of habitus: the ways that white women were expected to and expected themselves to write fiction about Blackness.

At the same time, Dickinson does not relinquish her radical bona fides. As I show in the next section, her rage at what she saw as Andrew Johnson's betrayal of the promise of Reconstruction and the consequent urgency for the passage of the Fourteenth Amendment informs both this passage as well as the final pages of *What Answer?* The novel's primary conviction that white sacrifice was the prerequisite black liberation was put to the test by Johnson's version of Reconstruction, which was at its height as she was beginning to write *What Answer?* and was finally fulfilled by the passage of the Amendment by the Thirty-Ninth Congress, securing – or so she believed – the Black citizenship for which the losses of the war paid.

"This isn't 1860 but 1865": The Threat to Black Citizenship and the Urgency of the Fourteenth Amendment

The final scenes of the novel enact Dickinson's fears about presidential Reconstruction and the urgency for the passage of the Fourteenth Amendment (indeed, Andrew Johnson almost never used the word "Reconstruction," preferring "restoration" – that is, a reestablishment of the status quo ante as much as possible). Former antislavery activists had had high hopes for Johnson when he first ascended to the presidency, believing that he shared their values in terms of Black citizenship, enfranchisement, and structural equality. After Johnson's inauguration, longtime radical abolitionist Gerrit Smith wrote to the new president, declaring, "I know your history – and I honor and love you. I know your sufferings and perils at the hands of the rebels" (qtd. in Levine 53). And in an 1865 *New*

124   1860 or 1865? Amending the National Body

York Times article about radical agitation for Black male suffrage, veteran abolitionist Wendell Phillips praised Johnson as

> one of the ablest men south of Mason and Dixon's line ... He is naturally our leader, and the ablest champion of this question [of black suffrage].... He knew the danger of caste and classes, and fully recognizes the necessity of calling the negro into the arena of civil life as the guarantee of the Union. ("Negro Suffrage" 8)

However, soon into his term as president, Johnson offered lenient terms to all Confederates except the highest echelon either politically or financially, issuing an Amnesty Proclamation that pardoned all of those who swore loyalty to the Union and authorized them to form new local, regional, and state governments. This offered a clean slate to the hundreds of former Confederates and empowered them to hold state legislative office. Ex-Confederate officers wasted no time in forming new, all-white governments or in passing a raft of laws governing the status and rights of their Black inhabitants. The results of this were the infamous Black Codes, which put severe limits on freedpeople in the former Confederate states and in some cases returned them to a state near to slavery.[18]

For white radicals, this was disaster, and threatened to render the sacrifices of the war pointless. Republicans worried that "all arbitrary and unequal discrimination in regard to any laws, even laws regulating the right to vote, tended to ultimately corrupt the polity" and were horrified by the damage presidential Reconstruction could do so soon after the end of the war (W. Nelson 113). As a response Dickinson drafted a coruscating speech condemning Johnson.[19] Written in November 1865, seven months after Lincoln's assassination and six months after Johnson began offering pardons to Confederate collaborators, the speech radiates anger and contempt.

Starting with Lincoln's death, Dickinson traces the initial hope in and eventual disillusionment of Republicans and radicals with Johnson:[20]

> Seven months ago, a man standing on the grave of a martyred President stepped to his place and assumed his power. A nation bound [?][21] to the earth with unutterable grief, listened through its sobs, and watched through its tears, while this man gave to the world a promise of his future career. ("Draft of Speech" n.p.)

In this speech we see Dickinson's rhetorical power. She picks up on the concept of "promise" and through anaphora hammers at the ways in which Johnson has betrayed the potential of Reconstruction.

> A promise to annihilate rebellion – uproot treason, and bring to strife – judgment – serious and leading [?] traitors ... A promise to maintain the

The Threat to Black Citizenship and the Fourteenth Amendment 125

> policy of his illustrious predecessor, which was to bestow ... suffrage on the masses of loyal blacks ... A promise that loyalty should be honored and treason made odious ... A promise that merit should be rewarded without regard to color. A promise that traitors should take back hand [?] in the new union ... and that loyal men whether white or black should alone control its destinee [*sic*]. A promise that the cause of the people should be upheld against their oppressor, against the spirit of caste, aristocracy and slavery ... I charge this man with the breaking of every promise, the non-fulfillment of every pledge – the falsifying of every declaration he at that time made. (n.p.)

In this extended passage we see most of the concepts behind *What Answer?*: the loyalty of Black soldiers and the implicit repayment of the sacrifices of war with the equal citizenship of African Americans. Certainly, Dickinson wasn't alone in her censure toward Johnson. During debates about the Fourteenth Amendment, Congressman Elihu B. Washburne (R-IL) condemned him in equally harsh terms, claiming that Johnson's "whole career as President has been marked by a wicked disregard of all the obligations of public duty and by a degree of perfidy and treachery and turpitude unheard of in the histories of a free people" (qtd. in Aynes 64). It's striking, too, that both Washburne and Dickinson focus on the idea that Johnson has not simply done wrong, but that he has broken promises and shirked his obligations as president. As Dickinson thunders, "I charge him with betrayal of trust.... I charge him as an enemy alike of his party, his country and his God" ("Draft of Speech" n.p.). If the war was in part a transaction in which white loss was traded for Black freedom and, by extension, citizenship, Johnson has, in the name of the American people, abandoned his side of the deal by allowing the South to regain political power and effectively reenslave freed African Americans.

In *What Answer?* Dickinson translates her anger at Johnson and her commitment to Black citizenship into a scene at a voting booth in 1865 New York. In the final chapter of the novel, Will Surrey's old friend Tom Russell and Robert Ercildoune go to the polls. Robert worries that his vote will be refused, but Tom scoffs at his concerns – "'Nonsense! This isn't 1860 but 1865. It is after the war now – come'" (296). As it turns out, Robert is correct in his fears. The white poll officials are hostile to him from the beginning, to Tom's puzzlement.

> "Courage, man! What ails you?" whispered Russell, as he felt his comrade tremble; "it's a ballot in place of a bayonet, and all for the same cause; lay it down."
> Robert put out his hand.
> "Challenge the vote!" "Challenge the vote!" "No niggers here!" sounded from all sides. (297)

126   1860 or 1865? Amending the National Body

As Ercildoune's ballot is refused and "fluttered to the ground," he turns Russell's statement into a question: "'1860 or 1865? – is the war ended?'"(297). As she does earlier in the novel, Dickinson translates the challenges freed people faced in the South in the wake of presidential Reconstruction to the scene of New York, the site of Will Surrey's racist parents, Abram Franklin's white supremacist coworkers, and the violent mobs of the Draft Riots. For Dickinson, even more is at stake in the securing of Black citizenship promised by the Fourteenth Amendment – it guarantees equality for African Americans north and south.

This was hardly a controversial issue for supporters of the Amendment, who "all agreed that race was not a legitimate reason to treat people differently in respect to their civil rights" (W. Nelson 89). While "equality" was in the years before the war "a vague, perhaps even an empty idea . . . it was the very emptiness and vagueness of the concept that made it so useful and popular. Equality could mean anything" (W. Nelson 21). The Civil War changed all of that. Like the equally slippery category of "citizenship" before the passage of the Amendment, "equality" needed to be pinned down, defined, made specific, when millions of African Americans around the country occupied a liminal position, neither enslaved nor exactly entitled to civil rights (and in many northern states explicitly excluded from the franchise, either completely or based on property ownership).

For Dickinson, civil and political equality was the sine qua non of the task of Reconstruction, because of all the sacrifices that had been made. As David A. J. Richards argues, "the theorists of radical antislavery drew the . . . inference [from the Constitution] that blacks must be fully included in the term of national citizenship that extended equal protection of basic rights to all" (152), and the Fourteenth Amendment definitively granted the reality of this citizenship. In the final page of *What Answer?*, as Robert Ercildoune walks dejectedly away from the polling place that has refused him, Dickinson makes the transaction that the Union took on explicit:

> Among the living is a vast army: black and white – shattered, and maimed, and blind: and these say, "Here we stand, shattered and maimed, that the body politic might be perfect! blind forever, that the glorious sun of liberty might shine abroad throughout the land, for all people through all coming time."
>
> And the dead speak too. From their crowded graves come voices of thrilling and persistent pathos, whispering, "Finish the work that has fallen from our nerveless hands. Let no weight of tyranny, nor taint of oppression, nor stain of wrong, cumber the soil, nor darken the land we died to save." (298)

In this passage, Dickinson classes together different kinds of permanent loss: of life and of limb. But both were offered up for the same reason. The "shattered and maimed" were injured not to save the Union but to create a more perfect one, in which liberty and equality are key. It is here that we see the logic of the Fourteenth Amendment, in which what was only implicit in the Constitution must be made explicit. It might be 1865 in the novel, but in the absence of meaningful legislative change, Black civil rights can be refused as easily as Robert Ercildoune's ballot, his amputated arm no guarantee for his access to the ballot box.

In fact, as *What Answer?* was being published, the Fourteenth Amendment was ratified by enough states to be included in the Constitution. Followed by the Fifteenth Amendment, which explicitly gave Black men the right to vote, this document was designed to serve as a permanent basis for the racial equality that Dickinson and her radical cohorts believed was in the future. However, as she found out seven years later in her tour of the Reconstruction South, this was far from the case.

"They *hate! hate! hate!* us": Dickinson's Southern Tour

Dickinson's tour south took place as the sparks of the Panic of 1873 had turned into flames, which were fanned further by the election of 1874, flipping congressional control from 198 to 88 in favor of Republicans to 169 to 109 for Democrats. The murderous violence at the polls in Alabama and campaign of terror in Mississippi had contributed to the shifting balance, and, as Eric Foner puts it, "Congressional Republicans had little stomach for further intervention in Southern affairs" (556). Certainly, Dickinson herself had not expected overnight change, arguing in 1867 that "there is nothing like patience in this matter, for the crimes of a century are not to be repaired in a day" ("Breakers Ahead" 5). But she was not prepared for the intense antipathy toward the North in general and Reconstruction in particular that she experienced on her trip south.

Given the reversals of many of the achievements of Reconstruction by the mid-1870s, it is surprising that Dickinson thought she would be positively received in a speaking tour of the South. Her tour was planned for April 1875, in which she traveled to Richmond, Petersburg, and Norfolk in Virginia, through North and South Carolina and Georgia, and ending in Nashville. There were financial reasons for her to expand her usual circuit, however: with the crash of 1873 the lyceum crowds shrank, and Dickinson saw the tour as an opportunity both to find a new audience and to gather material for a set of lectures for the following year.

128   1860 or 1865? Amending the National Body

Ironically, she set off for her tour just after the signing of the Civil Rights Act of 1875, which guaranteed equal access to public accommodations.

As J. Matthew Gallman points out in his introduction to the letters that Dickinson wrote that formed the basis for *A Tour of Reconstruction*, Dickinson had a talent "for asking important questions about what she saw, and for seeking out black and white Southerners across the spectrum to discuss the issues of the day" (15). At the same time, she had no inclination toward sympathizing with Confederate nostalgia. In Sara C. VanderHaagen and Angela G. Ray's words, she "wrote of her travels in the voice of a Unionist Pilgrim, paying homage at sites of valor and sites of suffering; and she wrote in the voice of a Unionist critic, gathering detailed evidence of Union heroism and Confederate barbarism" (358). Her anger at the Confederacy was undimmed, and she was astounded by the revanchism that she encountered throughout the South.

Most striking to Dickinson was the unapologetic nostalgia she found for Robert E. Lee and the Confederacy more generally across the South but especially in Richmond. On her visit to the state legislature she sat in on a session whose

> chief work was a series of laudations of General Lee – that he was the greatest, wisest, best, most humane, most christian like soldier and states-man the world had *ever* seen . . . I doubt whether in the hottest days of the war wilder eulogies of Lee and more hot bitterness towards his opponents was ever displayed. (*Tour of Reconstruction* 39)

The state house was filled with portraits of "Lee, Lee, Lee in every shape and form" (41), and Dickinson noticed the irony of "six or seven colored members of this legislature" who "must have had a good time of it," as their colleagues disavowed the very changes that brought them to Richmond in the first place (which is not to say that white lawmakers did not need their Black counterparts, who "had their revenge whenever a bill was pending that needed their votes, by seeing these bitter enemies of theirs run to, and button hole, and entreat of them as tho' they had been 'men and brethren'" [39–40]).

Dickinson may have been able to express humor about the hypocrisy of white racism, but she was also disgusted by the sight of the "colored convicts, in their striped prison dress," who were maintaining the grounds – and who far outnumbered their lawmaker counterparts – a sight she found "degrading" (41). She was also enraged by the hagiographic treatment of Lee that she encountered, seething with bitter anger in her letters home:

It is reasonable to say that in the estimation of multitudes here, this speaker of solemn oaths, this renegade to his flag, this false soldier, this traitorous citizen, this butcher and murderer, under whose command were enacted the horrors of Libby Prison and Belle Isle, – is absolutely above God Almighty, and in the estimation of the rest of them, second only to Him alone. (41)

Ultimately, Dickinson was profoundly disheartened by what she found in Virginia, not least the intense hatred of the North that she encountered. "Body and soul, root and branch, through and through they *hate! hate! hate!* us" (40) and indeed "hate the Republic and Republican institutions far more than they could have hated under any condition the negroes. They love State Sovereignty far better than they ever loved slavery" (45). Similarly, she found in North Carolina that the people she met would "not merely assert, but assert with full belief that they are not only a 'brave, chivalrous and sensitive people' ... but that literally and truly, – they are the superiors of *all* the rest of the world in mind, body, and estate" (67).

This attitude is a far cry from the acknowledgment of loss that Dickinson believed underwrote the establishment of Black citizenship. For most of the white Southerners that she met, despite – or perhaps because of – their material poverty and the widespread reminders of destruction and defeat, there was a concerted refusal to acknowledge any alteration of circumstance or reckoning with the meanings of the losses suffered during the war. The claim to cultural superiority and the veneration of Lee, whom Dickinson saw as a symbol of the sins of the Confederacy, operated in inverse proportion to white Southerners' willingness to welcome freedpeople into the republic. That is to say, the insistence that the war *changed nothing*, that the South maintained wholeness "in mind, body, and estate," was the converse of the insistence of Black inferiority, just as the radical Republican embrace of loss and injury was the prerequisite for an embrace of Black citizenship.

For Dickinson, this mechanism was most clearly illustrated by two visits: one to the previous headquarters of Jefferson Davis and the other to the studio of the sculptor Edward Virginius Valentine. Davis's "Confederate White House" in the middle of Richmond, a "big, roomy handsome house, with [a] pretty garden and [a] big, pillared back portico," had undergone a radical change. From the keystone of the Confederacy, the house had been repurposed into a school for freedpeople. As Dickinson observed, "Where once was the head and front of the effort to reduce these people to a hopeless beastiality [*sic*], is now a school to elevate them to a *real* humanity" (41). Vanity had been transformed into utility, arrogance into humility, a symbol of white supremacy into a place of Black uplift. Confederate loss was not denied, but rather lent toward empowering Black education and thereby an informed Black citizenry: an acknowledgment of the changes all around Richmond, Virginia, and the South.

By contrast, Valentine's studio seemed to be conceptually frozen in time, celebrating both Confederate honor and white supremacy. Valentine was responsible for the most prominent statues of Robert E. Lee, and his studio was a gathering place for the artistic and social elite of postwar Richmond. Dickinson noted the grandeur of Valentine's most famous piece, a posthumous sculpture of a recumbent Lee, at "rest after warfare," which she called "very elaborate and fine," but was less impressed by his other work (44) (Figure 3.1).

Most offensive to her was a sculpture Valentine titled *Knowledge Is Power* – "A negro boy, dirty, ragged, forlorn, with great splay fat and clumsy head fallen to one side, mouth gaping and eyes closed in sound sleep, with an open book lying on his knee" (44) (Figure 3.2). One might see this piece as a direct response to the transformation of Davis's headquarters into a school for freedpeople: it denies African American capacity for education and extends the racist trope of Black laziness and stupidity.

It is also of a pair with the recumbent Robert E. Lee. In many ways, these pieces seem the exact opposites of each other: one a reverent celebration, the other a cruel parody; one an invocation and evocation of classical artistic tradition, the other hearkening to vernacular minstrelsy.

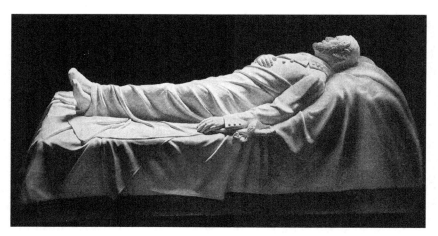

Figure 3.1 Edward V. Valentine, *Recumbent Statue of Robert E. Lee* (1870).

Figure 3.2 Edward V. Valentine, *Knowledge Is Power* (1868).
Courtesy of the Valentine, Richmond, VA.

While the sculpture of Lee has him lying down, either asleep or in death, the "negro boy" is sitting up, although both their heads turn to the side. *Knowledge Is Power* is executed in plaster, an inexpensive and popular medium, whereas the Lee statue is carved out of a single piece of high-quality marble. At the same time, they both represent a refusal of loss, of change, of alteration of any kind. Lee is always, already, and eternally heroic, part of a sculptural tradition that extends from Julius Caesar to George Washington to Lee himself. The "negro boy" can be nothing but lazy and incapable of refinement, a waste of educational efforts and resources. It's no coincidence that both figures are asleep, in a kind of stasis around which change may happen but which cannot change itself.

Interestingly, the further south Dickinson traveled, the more signs of the successes of the radical changes Reconstruction had wrought appeared. A paradigmatic moment occurs in her visit to the grounds of the military prison at Salisbury, North Carolina. Unlike Libby Prison in Richmond, which had been returned to its previous usage as a tobacco warehouse, with only a small sign indicating its use during the war, the Salisbury prison was maintained by a superintendent who was a Union veteran.

132   1860 or 1865? Amending the National Body

At the prison, the narrative that Dickinson understood the war to have created was in full view. The superintendent was "a fair haired, fair faced, one armed, noble looking fellow. – 'This is as it should be,' thought I, as I looked at his right stump, limp and empty" (86). The prison, itself a tribute to suffering and loss, is overseen by a living monument to the costs of the war. Dickinson comments on the appropriateness of an amputee guarding over the place where so many Union soldiers sickened and died in the fight for Black freedom, similar to the amputees who often took up places as agents of the Freedmen's Bureau.

This freedom was fully exemplified during her trip to South Carolina, especially Charleston, which had been a center of the international and then later domestic slave trade. Due to the large numbers of previously enslaved people in the state, even in 1875, as Reconstruction was being dismantled, African Americans maintained political and social prominence in South Carolina. In Columbia she noticed

> It is curious to see the number of colored people of all shades, men and women, slaves ten years ago, who are not only well and elegantly dressed, but who carry themselves – not with the peacock shirt you often see in these people, – but with real – dignity and air of command, – a great many of them have held, or do hold office, and the effect of that thing is seen in the negroes all through the state. (99)

For Dickinson, South Carolina was the symbol of true Reconstruction, not just a transformation in social and political systems, but the remaking of the meanings of blackness from enslavement to citizenship, from degradation to dignity. If, as David Blight argues, "the great challenge of Reconstruction was to determine just how defeated the South was, and to establish how free the emancipated slaves were," South Carolina seemed to have met and overcome that challenge (44). Not only were freedpeople protected by the law; they were agents of it.

Of course, Dickinson could not have known that the South Carolina she witnessed was doomed to destruction, and the stubborn desire to reestablish the racial status quo ante would triumph in the post–Civil War South. At the same time, the intense antipathy against the Union that she encountered on her Southern tour made clear that in most of the region the framework of Reconstruction had not affected the larger cultural attachment to white supremacy and the belief in Southern superiority. The faith that *What Answer?* evinces in structural change through both individual transformation (like that of Jim Given) and political reconstruction via the Fourteenth Amendment was severely shaken by her experiences of 1875.

Dickinson was also troubled by the trivialization of the value of the vote itself. As she wrote in her 1875 book *A Paying Investment*, despite the struggles of freed people to gain citizenship and the franchise, "[i]t is a horrible thing, the way that men talk of this duty of citizenship as a work of small worth, of slight dignity, of insignificant moment" (25). The struggles of only a few years ago had been eclipsed by politicking and cynicism.

This combination of the rolling back of Reconstruction and the horse-trading of Gilded Age politics transformed the political scene from the hard-driving radicalism of the Thirty-Ninth Congress to a more quietist, reconciliation-oriented legislative environment. The heroic amputees of *What Answer?* and *A Tour of Reconstruction* lost their glamour, and, as we'll see, were increasingly denigrated and degraded as Reconstruction itself was systematically and violently dismantled.

CHAPTER 4

"I don't care a rag for 'the Union as it was'"
Amputation, the Past, and the Work of the Freedmen's Bureau

> If the old Slaveholders are to retain in the reconstructed States the old supremacy, are to dictate measures, without any check, are to domineer after the old fashion, this gift of freedom to the black will be only a cruel mockery.
> —Horace Greeley, *New York Tribune*, June 14, 1865

> We must bury a thousand fathoms deep all those ideas and feelings that prompted those cruel laws against teaching these people and must quicken our diligence to see that the means of light and knowledge are placed within the reach of every one of them.
> —Thomas Settle, March 1867

If, as I have argued, amputation was a powerful trope for the potential of radical change in the years after the Civil War, no institution was staffed by more veteran amputees or represented the radical possibilities of Reconstruction more than the Freedmen's Bureau. Although it was hamstrung from the beginning and was in danger of dissolution more than once during its seven-year run from 1865 to 1872, the Bureau sparked the imagination of white radicals who saw in it an instrument for deep and lasting change as much as a clearinghouse for the needs of freedpeople. Officially called the Bureau of Refugees, Freedmen and Abandoned Lands, the Bureau's brief was both broad and deep; it was responsible for

> providing food, clothing, and medical care for thousands of freedpeople and white refugees; managing abandoned and confiscated lands that had fallen into the hands of occupying forces; working with freed communities and northern philanthropic agencies to open schools for African Americans; helping freedpeople to secure justice in the courts and setting up its own judicial tribunals where they could not; formalizing marriages and assisting freedpeople to trace missing family members; and, above all, supervising the establishment of free labor relations in the former free states. (Harrison 206)

134

In addition to these, although it was not officially part of the initial charge, the Bureau took on the massive task of providing education for the mostly illiterate population of freedpeople,

The Freedmen's Bureau was officially established in March 1865, as the outcome of the Civil War was becoming increasingly clear (although it would not officially end for a couple of months). Overseen by General Oliver Otis Howard, it was imagined as a short-term initiative to process the millions of soon-to-be emancipated enslaved people and equip them for freedom. Initially, it provided mostly material services – food, clothing, housing – since previously enslaved people had little in the way of personal property either on their backs or over their heads. Many who had left the farms, plantations, and households in which they had been enslaved were homeless, and even those who stayed where they had been born were now functionally unemployed, their previous labor conditions having been eradicated with nothing to replace them.[1]

For many radical Republicans, the Freedmen's Bureau represented the kind of federally initiated program that could transform the South, providing not just physical resources but also education, initiation into the world of politics, and inclusion in all elements of civil society.[2] The migration of hundreds of white women and men from the North and members of free Black communities north and south to teach in schools funded by the Bureau shows how central education – from basic literacy to more advanced knowledge – was to the imaginations of the "friends of the freeman." And newly emancipated communities embraced the project of self-determination through education.

In this chapter, I focus in particular on the Freedmen's Bureau and what it meant to white radicals, and how the imagery and reality of amputation appear again and again in both fictional and historical discussions of the Bureau. The Freedmen's Bureau's vision was to provide material and moral support for the new world in which formerly enslaved people found themselves. The Bureau is, in many ways, the limit case for irrevocable change, especially in its education campaign. Unlike the distribution of lands, which could be and, in the case of the territory initially awarded by William T. Sherman to freedpeople, were reclaimed for white ownership under Andrew Johnson, literacy cannot be rescinded. Education was an abstract possession whose ownership was invisible but profoundly empowering for freedpeople. And the Bureau represented the kind of reparative project that narratives of amputation gestured toward: the creation of a newly constituted nation, divested of its white supremacist past, fitting itself to a new reality.

136   Amputation, the Past, and the Freedmen's Bureau

Having himself lost an arm in the Civil War, Oliver Howard is a fascinating figure in all this, by turns energized and frustrated by the work of the Bureau, shocked by and incredulous of the violent responses from white Southerners, and inspired and irritated by the Bureau's clients. My main focus, though, is Albion Tourgée's 1880 *Bricks without Straw*, a novel written shortly after the end of Reconstruction, which has been brought back into the scholarly conversation by the indefatigable Carolyn Karcher. In his commitment to Black liberation and his deep faith in and activism for Reconstruction, Tourgée is, in Karcher's words, "an ideal lens through which to examine relations between progressive whites and African Americans" in the years after the Civil War (Tourgée, *Bricks without Straw* xi). For Tourgée, himself seriously wounded in the war, it was appropriate that the Bureau be staffed by amputees, whose visible sacrifice and commitment to permanent change in political, economic, and social relations were literally worn on their (empty) sleeves.

I also enter into conversation with Lydia Maria Child's textbook, *The Freedman's Book*, which she designed to be used in Bureau schools. Child's book functions as the other side of the coin from Howard's autobiography and Tourgée's novel. Howard's and Tourgée's experiences with injury and loss during the war led them to identify the work of Freedmen's Bureau with the necessity for white bodily loss in recompense for the violence of slavery against Black bodies and Black subjectivity, and a rejection of a white supremacist past in favor of an interracial, antiracist present and future. As an observer of the war – perforce as a woman – rather than an active participant in it, Child focuses on a narratable, notable Black past, and sees the Freedmen's Bureau as an engine for producing a present oriented toward Black wholeness of body, family, and sense of self. This (re)constitution of a usable Black history does exactly the reparative work that Howard and Tourgée imagine the Bureau achieving: the progress for which amputation is the price. In addition, while Howard had a bird's-eye view of the Bureau, and *Bricks* describes the local work of agents and schools, the task of the *Freedman's Book* is to intervene directly into the educational mission of the Bureau, and act as a virtual interlocutor with freedpeople, one on one.

Tourgée, Howard, and Child saw Reconstruction in general and the Freedmen's Bureau in particular as intervening not only in freedpeople's lives but also in white and Black Americans' relationship with the history of slavery, the challenge of the present moment, and the promise of an egalitarian future, which the Bureau and the white radicals who supported it would help midwife into existence. As white radicals immersed in the experience of the Reconstruction South, Tourgée and Howard saw Southern nostalgia for the antebellum past as a threat to real change. Opposing appeals to "the Union as it was," they argued against any representation of the pre-emancipation South that minimized the horrors of slavery.

Child's involvement with the Bureau was more distant and at the same time more intimate, since she hoped that freedpeople would hold *The Freedmen's Book* in their hands and read – and absorb the message of – her work. Focusing on the needs of her Black readers, she celebrated a heroic African American past that her readers had been deprived of knowledge of. For Child, the Bureau schools were a vehicle for racial pride and self-determination for newly emancipated adults and children.

The Freedmen's Bureau was one of the major sites of contestation between those who imagined and worked for radical change in the postwar South and those who yearned for (and were willing to violently reinstate) the systems made possible by chattel slavery. Its various projects were designed to establish racial equity in education, politics, work, and association, projects that were undermined almost from their inception. And it was entwined, historically, narratively, and metaphorically, with the phenomenon of amputation.

Shattering "the whole previously existing social system": Amputating the Antebellum Past

While Howard and Tourgée led quite different lives, one at the heart of the Reconstruction efforts (and later a central figure in the destruction of Indigenous peoples in the American West), the other a passionate antiracist whose connections to Black liberation efforts involved him in some of the most important legal battles against segregation, they were both radicalized by their experiences of fighting and being wounded in the Civil War. It's not surprising that amputation appears again and again in representations of the Freedmen's Bureau, given that both Howard and Tourgée's political development was accompanied by serious injury and witnessing the injuries of others. Howard himself had lost an arm at the Battle of Fair Oaks, and Freedmen's Bureau agents in *Bricks without Straw* are either amputees or otherwise disabled.

Tourgée came to his allegiance toward formerly enslaved people during his time in the Union Army, whereas Howard traced his empathy with Black Americans back to his own childhood in Maine. When he was six, his father "befriended a little negro lad and brought him to our house"

138   Amputation, the Past, and the Freedmen's Bureau

(v. 1, 12). Quite where the elder Howard found this boy and how he convinced the boy's parents to let him move in with the Howard family is never explained, nor is this boy ever named – surprising, given the fact that he lived with the Howards for four years. It's clear, though, that in Howard's narrative the child lived as an equal in the family – Howard describes himself and his siblings playing, eating, and learning with him – and he "believed it a providential circumstance that I had that early experience with a negro lad, for it relieved me from that feeling of prejudice which would have hindered me from doing the work for freedom which, years afterward, was committed to my charge" (v. 1, 12–13). It is hard to trace the accuracy of this account – the vagueness with which it is narrated might strike the reader as suspicious. But at the very least, Howard's desire to include this nameless "negro lad" in the story of his own growing up shows the importance to him of constructing a solid autobiographical rationale for his commitment to Black independence and equality.

However, Howard's passion for transforming the Union into a nation without slavery was sparked by the trauma and loss he witnessed and experienced firsthand at Fair Oaks and later in almost every major engagement: after a short convalescence to recover from his loss of an arm, he returned to duty in August 1862, in time to fight at Antietam, Fredericksburg, Chancellorsville, and eventually Gettysburg, before joining William T. Sherman's march to the sea. Although Howard was profoundly committed to the Union cause, and worked his way up to the rank of general over the course of the war, he was not a booster for war itself, seeing it as a series of wounds both in the bodies of the men fighting and in the soul of the nation itself. A veteran of many brutal battles, Howard rejected the criticism that writing about war glamorizes it, focusing in his autobiography on the shock, sorrow, and distress he and others felt on the battlefield. It is one thing to imagine war, he argued, but

> it is another thing to see our comrades there upon the ground with their darkened faces and swollen forms; another thing to watch the countenances of friends and companions but lately in the bloom of health, now disfigured, torn, and writhing in death; and not less affecting to a sensitive heart to behold a multitude of strangers prone and weak, pierced with wounds, or showing broken looks and every sign of suppressed suffering, waiting for . . . the relief of the surgeon's knife or death. (v. 2, 441)

Howard's characterization of the "surgeon's knife" as a relief maps onto his own experience of amputation. Wounded in the right forearm while

Amputating the Antebellum Past 139

approaching the front lines at Fair Oaks, he pushed forward. Later in the battle, "though I was not then aware of it, I had been wounded again, my right elbow having been shattered by a rifle shot" (v. 1, 247). His arm was destroyed by this second shot, as "the last ball had passed through the elbow joint and crushed the bones into small fragments," an injury typical of the work of the minié ball (v. 1, 249).

After it became clear that his arm could not be saved, and infection threatened, the surgeon, Dr. Palmer, "kindly told me that my arm had better come off. 'All right, go ahead,' I said. 'Happy to lose only my arm'" (v. 1, 250). In contrast to many later (and mostly inaccurate) representations of the scene of amputation as excruciatingly painful in the absence of anesthetic, Howard remembers his own surgery as painless due to "a mixture of chloroform and gas ... When I woke I was surprised to find the heavy burden was gone" (v. 1, 250).[3]

Howard's relief after his amputation is echoed by his later commitment to transforming the South in the wake of the Civil War. The reimagining of his place on the battlefield and in the world aligns with his increasing conviction that slavery itself was a kind of shattered limb of the nation that had to be excised. This belief is played out in a speech he gave in Springfield, Massachusetts, after the Bureau's first year. Responding to former enslavers' "glowing accounts of the blessedness of slavery in its prosperous and patriarchal days ... [and] curses [toward] that freedom which he believes to be the occasion of so much restlessness and suffering," Howard repudiates any nostalgia for the past (v. 2, 314).[4] "But you and I know," he declares, "that the real cause of the desolation and suffering is *war*, brought on and continued in the interest and from the love of slavery" (v. 2, 314).[5] Itself a "heavy burden," this longing for the old ways not only maintains the fiction of slavery as intrinsic to the regional identity of the South and the economic health of the nation, but acts as a roadblock to Black emancipation. The more white Southerners (and perhaps members of his white Northern audience as well) hold onto nostalgia for the antebellum Union, the more difficult it will be to maintain the work of Reconstruction. As Howard explains, "the rights of the freedman, which are not yet secured to him, are the direct reverse of the wrongs committed against him" (v. 2, 315). Howard's argument elides the four years of conflict that shifted the nation from one that permitted slavery to one that abolished it. I would argue that for Howard, the losses of the Civil War, not least the loss of his own arm, are the unspoken conduit from one to the other. If the rights of the formerly enslaved were "the direct reverse" of the "wrongs committed against him," the vehicle for (and, to a certain

140 Amputation, the Past, and the Freedmen's Bureau

extent, the engine of) that reversal is the devastation wrought by the war. For Howard, Black civil and human rights were at their root reparations for the physical, political, psychological, and economic harm done to enslaved people, a gain that grew out of and reflected, even if they did not make up for, the massive "wrongs" of slavery and discrimination – rights that required sacrifice and loss by white Americans to secure.

At the same time, Howard imagined Reconstruction not just as healing the injury done to formerly enslaved people but also as remaking and revolutionizing the lives of poor white Southerners. He saw the massive and rapid changes brought on by the end of the war as world-changing for all Americans, north and south. For Howard, the collapse of the Confederacy and the attendant result of "making emancipation an actual, universal fact, was like an earthquake. It shook and shattered the whole previously existing social system" v. 2, 363–4). Strikingly, Howard uses the same word – "shattered" – that he used to describe the injury to his arm at Fair Oaks. The shattering of the entire social and economic system that was infused by slavery from root to branch is metonymically linked to the change in his own body, as though his own injury makes way for and is the forerunner to the larger act of breakage. Both represent the necessity of moving forward in new, as yet unknown ways. And, as he found, "the Bureau constantly stirred up all social life where its operations touched the field" (v. 2, 423). The work of the Bureau was to destabilize, recombine, and reconstruct the racial and class hierarchies in the locations in which it operated.

This dislocation was, for Howard, indispensable. In a direct critique of aristocratic Southerners for whom the losses during the war signified only their social, economic, and political demotion, Howard argued that only with the deep and slashing changes of war and Reconstruction that were necessary to secure emancipation could the sociopolitical fabric of the South be rewoven and white and Black working people be brought together to learn and coexist. After all, he argued, the cutting off of slavery and the remaking of the nation in its absence brought new advances to the South that no one could have imagined: "it is a wonderful thing to recall that North Carolina had never before that time [i.e., 1865, with Union army occupation and the enforcement of racial equality] a free school system even for white pupils . . . The death of slavery unfolded the wings of knowledge for both white and Black" (vol. 2, 338).

Howard's celebration of integrated, free public education invokes not just human but divine (or semi-divine) agency. The angel of knowledge unfolds its wings to embrace the people marginalized by slavery: enslaved

Bricks without Straw *and the Drama of Radical Reconstruction* 141

people, of course, but also poor whites whom Reconstruction could help understand that their interests lay in identifying with their emancipated Black counterparts, not the plantation-owning Southern oligarchy.

"It was most fortunate and providential that the Confederacy had failed": *Bricks without Straw* and the Drama of Radical Reconstruction

In many ways, despite his Northern birth, Albion Tourgée embodied Howard's hope for an alliance between emancipated Black and rural white citizens. He was born and raised in rural Ohio, and after his mother's death was moved to Massachusetts to attend school and live with an uncle. Tourgée was wounded by a bullet to the back at the first battle of Bull Run in 1862, held as a prisoner of war in Virginia for the first six months of 1863, and then fought at Chickamauga and Chattanooga. His fighting experience alongside Black troops radicalized him,[6] and when, after the war, he was admitted to the Ohio bar he and his family moved to North Carolina both for the warmer climate to help his back injury and to support African American citizens. He was largely responsible for the justice-oriented new constitution of North Carolina, which ended property qualification for jury service, outlawed corporal punishment, established popular election of all state officials, mandated free public education, and affirmed equal voting rights for all (male) citizens. As first a lawyer and then a district court judge, Tourgée had a front seat to the successes of Reconstruction as well as the violent resistance by many white residents. He was a productive and celebrated author, writing three novels in the course of ten years. Although he made his living as a writer after the release of *A Fool's Errand*, his first published novel, and again with *Bricks without Straw*, Tourgée did not completely abandon the law and in the early 1890s was lead attorney for Homer Plessy in the landmark segregation case.

Bricks without Straw is remarkable in many ways, not least in its representation of Red Wing, a self-sustaining Black-owned Southern community, built on land bought by the novel's Black protagonist, Nimbus. Strikingly, at the novel's beginning, Nimbus raises the specter of amputation in his desire to buy the land, introducing the reader to Tourgée's intertwining of lost limbs and the promise of Black self-determination. Nimbus announces his desire to buy the land in the Red Wing section of town, which he sees as "jest de berry place we wants, an' I'm boun' to hev it ef it takes a leg" (140).

142 Amputation, the Past, and the Freedmen's Bureau

Here Nimbus is enacting the logic of the Civil War itself, in which the loss of limbs is the necessary prerequisite to ensuring Black emancipation. However, for him, amputation is only imaginary, since his losses due to slavery – of his liberty, of bodily integrity, of a claim to family or property – have already been tallied in Tourgée's imaginary balance sheet. For the white male protagonist of the novel, however, amputation is very real. Hesden Le Moyne, the scion of the leading family in town, is a Union sympathizer but is pressured to join the Confederate Army to prove that he is not a traitor to the South. Despite his antipathy to the Confederate cause, he fights valiantly and loses his left arm in battle. This loss does not endear the Confederacy to him. Quite the opposite: Hesden returns from the war "with a bitterer hate for war and a sturdier dislike for the causes which had culminated in the struggle than he had when it began" (247).

Hesden's amputation does not align him with the South. In fact, by making him an amputee, Tourgée implicitly places Hesden in the company of the local branch of the Freedmen's Bureau, which was run by agents "chosen from among the wounded veteran officers of our army. Almost every one of them had won honor with the loss of limb or health" (157). In this formulation, the work of transforming freed slaves is best suited to amputees, who embody the promise of the postwar period. Defending the Bureau against accusations that it was populated by "corrupt and unprincipled agents of undefined power" (158), Tourgée points to their altered bodies as proof positive of their commitment to honesty, fairness, and Black liberty:

> It must be said that this [claim of corruption] cannot be true; that thousands of men selected from the officers of our citizen-soldiery by the unanswerable certificate of disabling wounds ... a class of men in physical, intellectual, and moral power and attainments far superior to the average of the American people – it may be said that such could not have become all at once infamously bad. (158)[7]

The Bureau agents' injuries are more than the inevitable damage done by military conflict. In Tourgée's formulation, they are an "unanswerable certificate" – a kind of proof of purchase of African American civil rights, or a diploma of graduation from the slave economy to a nation organized around liberty. Tourgée's use of the modifier "unanswerable" intensifies the power of this visible proof. It cannot be debated or argued away, answered as in a verbal disagreement. But "answer" here can also mean responded to in kind, matched, or equaled. Implicitly, Tourgée is drawing a contrast between the wounds of a Union soldier, who struggled for the

Bricks without Straw *and the Drama of Radical Reconstruction* 143

Union's new dispensation, and those of his Confederate counterpart. Their injuries may look the same – a lost arm, leg, hand, eye, and the like – but the latter does not "answer" the former. The Bureau agent's loss speaks a different language, makes a different claim, based on a logic of radical transformation; the Confederate veteran's injury is a certificate of a very different kind, supporting a superannuated system of violence, tyranny, and duress.

Tourgée was partially correct about the composition of Bureau agents, if not their motivations. Many were selected from the Veteran's Reserve Corps, a unit of men disabled by the war but still able to function in a bureaucratic (and occasionally military) capacity (Cimbala, *Under the Guardianship* 53). As Paul Cimbala shows, for many amputee veterans, the Bureau represented a reliable and sustainable income as much as or more than a tool to gain justice and equality for freedpeople (53–4). And amputees *were* disproportionately represented in the ranks of the Freedmen's Bureau. In Georgia alone, almost half of the Assistant Bureau Commissioners or Assistant Inspector Generals (the regional directors of the Bureau) had lost limbs or hands. Moreover, it is striking how many of the amputee Bureau employees were outspoken supporters of Reconstruction, from agents up to regional commissioners. Edward Wild, for example, had lost an arm and was injured in the other hand. A radical, even vengeful, proponent of Reconstruction, he was described by a contemporary as "a *splendid man, heart and soul* in the cause" (Cimbala 51). Similarly, John Randolph Lewis, who had lost an arm up to the shoulder in the Wilderness campaign of 1864, was appointed assistant inspector general. Unlike the career soldiers in their sixties who had held leadership positions in the Georgia Bureau, Lewis was thirty-two when he was appointed, and full of radical energy. He believed that "the schools established and the school-houses built and freedmen educated are the seed sown in this land of oppression that shall spring up soldiers strong and mighty to resist the oppressor and strive for their rights" (qtd. in Cimbala 11).

Lewis's image of seeds transforming into soldiers alludes to the myth of Cadmus, the founder of Thebes. According to the myth, Cadmus killed a dragon who was guarding a spring that he needed to water his cows. On the advice of Athena, he buried the dragon's teeth in the ground. Immediately, the teeth transformed into armed soldiers – *Spartoi* (which means "the sown") – who threatened to attack him. Cadmus threw a jewel (sometimes translated as "stone") among the soldiers, who then fought among themselves to claim it. Ultimately, all but five were killed, who joined Cadmus to build the citadel of Thebes.

144   Amputation, the Past, and the Freedmen's Bureau

This recasting of the schools, schoolhouses, and educated freedpeople as the seeds that rise up as soldiers is a fascinating rereading of the myth. First of all, the internecine battle among the Spartoi is transformed into the Civil War itself, in which soldiers from the same nation turned on each other. At the same time, the Spartoi are also the educated and empowered freedpeople who are now fully armed to fight against their previous enslavers and white supremacy generally. In this reworking of the myth, the dragon's teeth do double narrative duty: first as the losses of the war through death and amputation and second as the seeds of a newly "armed" and radicalized free Black population. Through his subtle reworking of the Cadmus myth, Lewis aligns white loss with Black empowerment.

In this vision of the Freedmen's Bureau, then, the loss that Lewis himself suffered in the amputation of his arm leads almost directly to the schoolhouses supported by the Freedmen's Bureau: the severed arms, legs, hands, and feet are buried in pits from which spring up radicalized Union veterans, who, in turn, sow schools that germinate into autonomous and self-determining freedpeople. Like Howard and Tourgée, Lewis imaginatively aligns the physical loss of bodily integrity on the part of Union soldiers with the possibilities of politically and educationally self-sustaining free Black people and communities.

Tourgée was actively involved in the work of the Freedmen's Bureau in Greensboro, and while the Bureau agents and the task of teaching formerly enslaved people make up only a small part of *Bricks without Straw*, the trope of the amputee warrior for Black self-determination infuses the novel. Tourgée returns again and again to the amputated bodies of Union soldiers and sympathizers as the agents of reparation and justice for Black citizens. But this justice is not just the work of white radicals and sympathetic Northerners like the female protagonist of the novel, Mollie Ainslie, a young woman who comes south after the wartime death of her brother, to work as a schoolteacher in Red Wing. It is struggled for by Black characters, who lay claim to the rights accorded them by the Thirteenth, Fourteenth, and Fifteenth Amendments. When Nimbus takes a complaint to the Bureau against Desmit, the man who had enslaved him before the war and was suing him for encouraging a friend to leave his employ, his case is heard by "a captain of the United States infantry, [who] was a man of about forty-five years of age, grave and serious of look, with an empty sleeve folded decorously over his breast. His calm blue eyes, refined face, and serious air gave him the appearance of a minister" (160).[8] The captain decides that forcing employees to remain in a job because of

Bricks without Straw *and the Drama of Radical Reconstruction*   145

exploitive contracts runs counter to the emancipation amendments, and finds for Nimbus.

This unnamed officer combines military heroism, physical suffering, dignity, and spiritual purity. His "empty sleeve" not just is a sign of his bravery and loss, but also provides another mode of expression for his calmness and refinement: it is "decorously" folded, imbued with serious-ness and gentility. The empty sleeve also seems to intensify his "serious air," which "gave him the appearance of a minister," as though his physical sacrifice in war analogizes to the spiritual commitment to service shared by clergy. Nimbus himself links his new rights with national transformation, and "was glad that there was a law for him – a law that put him on the level with his old master – and meditated gratefully, as he rode home, on what the nation had wrought" (155).

The agent's decision in favor of Nimbus intensifies the white towns-people's already powerful opposition to the Bureau. In Tourgée's narra-tion, at the core of white Southern resistance to Black equality are both racism and a mistaken belief in Southern superiority overall, the belief that they had been "in all things utterly innocent and guileless" (156). Unlike their pro-Union counterparts, Southerners regard the damage and losses they have sustained as disabling the possibility that the nation could return to its former condition, whose disappearance they mourn: they experience injury without a vision of redemption (or, rather, they regard the virtual reenslavement of Black citizens *as* redemption). As Tourgée argues, they see Reconstruction as a vindictive punishment, "done solely and purposely to injure the master, to punish the rebel, and to further cripple and impoverish the South" (320). Given Tourgée's use of injury and disability as tropes for remaking the nation along egalitarian, antiracist lines, it is hard not to see the use of "injure" and "cripple" here as undergirding the novel's condemnation of white supremacy: not only do white Southerners not accept Black humanity and dignity, but they appropriate the very terms, the bodily sacrifices that underwrite a reconstructed Union.

For Tourgée, then, the error that white Southerners commit is not just a refusal to see that slavery was wrong, or that formerly enslaved people deserve human and civil rights (although he certainly believes both those principles). Rather, it's that they fundamentally misunderstand the mean-ing of the damage done by the war itself, both to the nation and to the bodies of the soldiers who fought in it. For them, injury is another reason for resentment and holding onto the past, instead of looking forward into the future. Moreover, they wholly ignore the centuries-long injury done to

146 Amputation, the Past, and the Freedmen's Bureau

the people they enslaved, whom they left totally impoverished and saw as their right to punish.

Over the course of the novel, Hesden's growing refusal to celebrate the past and investment in an egalitarian future gives his physical injury greater meaning. He becomes increasingly convinced of the need for this work of remaking and rebuilding. A Ku Klux Klan raid on Red Wing intensifies Hesden's antipathy toward the South, aligning him with the Black citizens of the area.[9] As well as being characterized by the brutal violence typical of Klan attacks, this incident is marked by an attack on the disabled preacher Eliab Hill. Eliab's disability is significant – his legs have been withered by illness, and before Mollie Ainsley comes to Red Wing he has been the sole teacher for the community. Equally importantly, he supports Black self-reliance and self-determination.

The Klan raid culminates with the (implicit) rape of Lugena, Nimbus's wife, and an attack on Eliab. Given that the loss of the use of a limb by white characters in *Bricks without Straw* signifies the promise of progressive change, it is significant that the violence toward Eliab is a cruel parody of the healing of his disability and of amputation of a leg:

> There was a fall upon the cabin floor – the grating sound of a body swiftly drawn along its surface, and one of the masked marauders rushed out dragging by the foot the preacher of the Gospel of Peace. The withered leg was straightened. The weaken sinews were torn asunder, and as his captor dragged him out into the light and flung the burden away, the limb dropped, lax and nerveless to the ground. (276)

In this passage, Eliab's body is resected – "the withered leg was straightened" – and dissected – "the limb dropped" – by Klan aggression. The attackers pervert the logic of bodily loss in the service of racist violence, which transforms Hesden's relationship to the community of Red Wing and the work of Reconstruction. Up until this moment Hesden had subscribed to the efficacy of Reconstruction and the efforts of the Bureau, but within a pragmatic, legalistic frame in which Black rights existed because of the power of the federal government to secure and enforce them, not for intrinsic constitutional, ethical, or justice-oriented reasons. After the attack, however, he

> had begun to question – God forgive him, if it felt like sacrilege – he had begun to question whether the South might not have been wrong – might not still be wrong – wrong in the principle and practice of slavery, wrong in the theory and fact of secession and rebellion, wrong in the hypothesis of

Bricks without Straw *and the Drama of Radical Reconstruction* 147

hate on the part of the conquerors, wrong in the assumption of exceptional and unapproachable excellence (291).

Given the logic of the novel, and its representation of amputation as a result of the inequities of the slave system as well as a conduit to undoing those inequities, it's not surprising that Hesden, the sole amputee protagonist in the text, becomes increasingly disillusioned with the South's claim to superiority and opposed to the exercise of white supremacy via the violence of slavery or of Klan vigilantism. Hesden's body becomes the nexus of the various antiracist, Black emancipation impulses of the other characters in the novel. He links Mollie Ainsley, the northern schoolteacher who comes to teach at the Black school and with whom he falls in love; Jordan Jackson, a white Southern radical whom he shelters and hides; Nimbus; and Eliab Hill. As the switch point between white radicalism and Black self-determination, his lost arm the sign of his allegiance to the Union, Hesden ends up believing that "it was most fortunate and providential that the Confederacy had failed" (319). By extension, he recognizes the bodily loss suffered by Confederate troops as not doing the work it should have – representing a microcosm of the larger defeat of the South. Ultimately, he sees Southern resistance to Reconstruction as a rejection of American identity *tout court*: "there was nothing his class could gain [through Reconstruction] except a share in the ultimate glory and success of an enlarged and solidified nation" (322). Whereas the amputated Freedmen's Bureau agents give meaning and a kind of nobility to self-sacrifice, to have lost so much and yet still believe in the Confederate cause is not just disloyal – it is to squander the opportunity to participate in the rebuilt nation's "ultimate glory and success."

Such a commitment to a newly constituted nation requires the abandonment of any nostalgia for the white supremacist, slave economy past: past political systems, past racial hierarchies, past bodies. Hesden "regarded the experiment of reconstruction, as he believed, with calm, unprejudiced sincerity; he had buried the past, and looked only to the future" (377). As I've argued, amputation forces readers of *Bricks without Straw* to focus on the present and move beyond the past, in recognition that the past of the intact body is irrecoverable. And the past of an ostensibly intact nation – held together by the ligaments of slavery – was diseased from the very beginning. In this way, the past of a South organized around the enslavement and exploitation of Black Americans is buried, just as Hesden's lost arm is, on a Civil War battlefield, or in a pile of other dismembered limbs: discarded in favor of a future that puts Black self-determination at its core.

148   Amputation, the Past, and the Freedmen's Bureau

This echoes Tourgée's own goals for Reconstruction. He rejected the goal simply of preserving the Union, avowing, "I don't care a rag for '*the Union as it was.*' I want and fight for the *Union better* than '*it was*'" (qtd. in Karcher, "Introduction" to *Bricks without Straw* 8).

Tourgée's radical declaration of an emancipated future was, if we credit Oliver Otis Howard, a common belief among Northerners a few years into the Civil War. In the early days, when the war was more theoretical than actual, "military operations were influenced very much in the interest of slavery by purely political considerations. Plans were modified by the endeavor not so much to conquer an enemy under arms, as to restore the Union or preserve the Union" (191). By 1862, according to Howard, this had changed, and "the majority [of Northerners] evidently inclin[ed] to the belief that 'the Union as it was' could never be restored" (202).

The phrase "the Union was it was," which characterized the retrospective narratives of Tourgée and Howard, was also part of political speech during the Civil War, doing important imaginative work.[10] Although Lincoln famously refused to see the Confederacy as a separate or seceded government and insisted that the Union was simply putting down an insurrection, the phrase "the Union as it was" when uttered in 1862 or 1863 suggests a sharp break with the recent past, relegating a Union economically and socially defined by its inextricability from slavery, and grammatically as something that has already disappeared, to the past. The question then was what would or should replace "the Union as it was."

In part, Howard saw this shift from the desire to patch up a fractured nation to reconstructing the nation without slavery as a response to the refusal of slave-owners, even those who were Union sympathizers, to step away from – let alone repudiate – slavery or abandon the Confederacy. They were "too ardent, too determined, too well prepared in plan and purpose to accept any sort of compromise. They had no patience whatever with the Unionists and half-Unionists among themselves" (193). In other words, it became increasingly difficult for Unionists to hope for a reunited nation when Confederates so clearly had no interest in reconciliation and insisted in living in a past characterized by dehumanization and injustice.

What led Unionists, from Lincoln on down, to imagine that the Confederacy would be interested in restoring or preserving "the Union as it was" is, from the vantage point of the twenty-first century, mysterious, and the fact that they maintained the fantasy of achieving this goal for an entire year is itself something of a feat. Indeed, I would argue that the abandonment of this hope had little to do with a political reorientation. And it was hardly supported by any Union victories. The year 1862 was a

Bricks without Straw *and the Drama of Radical Reconstruction* 149

bloody and horrifying one for the federals: it saw the battles of Shiloh, Antietam, Fair Oaks (where Howard lost his arm), and the second battle of Bull Run, all of which were the sites of immense Union Army loss, with deaths in the hundreds of thousands. Instead, that loss itself was an engine for this political repositioning of the ostensible motivation for the Union's military engagement.

Howard is specific in pinpointing the exact moment when national sentiment shifted from the mission to restore the Union to a commitment to abolish slavery and refuse any kind of reconciliation that included the continuation of the slave economy: April 1862. Given that the battle of Shiloh, the most bloody of the war so far, with over 1,700 killed and five times as many wounded, took place in the first week of April, this coincidence is more than just suggestive. While it would not be until after Antietam, when Matthew Brady's crew of photographers brought the realities of the war's slaughter to his studio in New York in October 1862, that Northern civilians saw with their own eyes evidence of loss and destruction, the shock of Shiloh was still considerable. During the weeks after the battle, debates raged over how many Union soldiers had been killed or wounded, whether the Union Army had been surprised by Confederate forces or were expecting them, and the meaning of the death of Confederate General Albert Sidney Johnston (who was killed by a single shot to the head). Although an official account of the battle and the estimated numbers of the dead took a while to find their way into the public discourse, Shiloh was a topic of discussion in newspapers and other periodicals long after the fighting itself ended.

Shiloh represented a decisive break for the Union side through its violence and how, as Howard suggests, Northerners recognized that the Confederacy was determined to destroy the North in order to maintain and extend slavery. In part, this was because Shiloh was so thoroughly reported on in print and in images. In his thorough narrative of the battle from its beginnings to its aftermath, Larry Daniel cites dozens of journalists reporting on Shiloh from newspapers as far as Cincinnati, Indianapolis, Chicago, and New York. While reporters often hung around military encampments, they were rarely present during actual battles, and descended on the field shortly afterward. They reported fields covered with dead men and horses, the stench of decomposing bodies, and the piles of amputated limbs around the field hospitals. Stories began appearing within the same week of the battle and continued for more than ten days, reporting on the horrors of the battlefield.

150 Amputation, the Past, and the Freedmen's Bureau

Moreover, news traveled quickly via telegraph and letters. One of those letters, from "W.W.W.," a member of the Fifteenth US Infantry who was part of the Union engagement at Shiloh, was published that same year.[11] The writer's regiment arrived at Savannah, the Harden County, Tennessee, county seat, across the Tennessee River from Shiloh, on the second day of the battle, and received faulty information about the Union Army's progress: they were told that Grant's forces "defeat[ed] and completely rout[ed]" the Confederate troops "after a desperate fight of fifteen hours duration" (2). In fact, nothing could have been further from the truth. W.W.W. quickly learned that "Grant's force was then defeated and panic-stricken ... and ... the morrow would introduce us to scenes of carnage the mere imagination of which sickens the heart" (2). Nearby buildings were filled with the wounded and "through the windows, the sash of which were removed to give air to the injured, we could see the surgeons plying their horrid profession. The atmosphere was that of a vast dissecting room" (2).

Taking a ferry over the river, W.W.W.'s regiment arrived at Pittsburg Landing, a main mooring point in Shiloh.[12] As they marched into battle, they were assaulted by "a shower of grape, canister, spherical case, rifle balls &c ... every tree and sapling [still] bears the marks of shot" (6). After a charge at the cannoneers, they found "every horse in each piece and caisson lay dead in his harness, and the ground was covered with the killed and dying" (7).

At the end of the letter, W.W.W. reports that he heard that "our loss in killed and wounded will not fall short of nine thousand men" – in fact, a fairly accurate estimate of the casualties (8). "From what I have seen myself, I give the fullest credence to his statement," posits W.W.W. "On the evening of the engagement, the dead were everywhere. There has never been such carnage on this continent.... How any of us escaped is more than I can imagine" (8).

Certainly, it's impossible to know how many people read this pamphlet-letter. But given that the letter itself was dated April 14, and with several deliveries per day and a railway mail system that had been operating for almost a decade, it's conceivable that any family member of a man who fought at Shiloh could have received news within a few days.[13] Shiloh marked a shift in awareness about the war, the massive losses it had begun to incur, and, if we are to believe Howard, a transition in Northern understanding of what the war and its sacrifices were *for*. Over 1,700 men lost their lives, but thousands lost limbs in the "vast dissecting room" surgeons had set up across the river in Savannah. Whether he was correct

Lydia Maria Child's The Freedmen's Book 151

or not, it's not surprising, then, that Howard pinpoints within the month of Shiloh the change in national sentiment away from an investment in going back to "the Union as it was" and toward a commitment to end slavery and create a radically new vision of the nation.

"I have prepared this book expressly for you": Lydia Maria Child's *The Freedmen's Book* and the Reparations of Black History

While white Reconstruction supporters like Howard and Tourgée actively resisted returning to the past, and invested their energies in pushing forward into an egalitarian future, some Black and white radicals simultaneously looked to the past to invoke Black achievement. Lydia Maria Child, a white feminist activist who had engaged any number of progressive causes, from indigenous land rights to antislavery to female suffrage, included historical Black figures in her *Freedmen's Book*, published in 1865 to be distributed among freedpeople's schools.[14] As a sort of complement to the amputated body of the pro-Reconstruction white soldier and Bureau agent, Child focuses on the intact, functioning, even heroic Black body, invoking great figures from Black history and reprinting texts by Black authors.

It is hard to overemphasize how radically different *The Freedmen's Book* was from its mainstream counterparts. As Saidiya Hartman has shown, many textbooks written for the new schools were not interested in empowering the newly freed as much as inculcating them with "correct" Christian values about "labor, conduct, consumption, hygiene, marriage, home decorating, chastity, and prayer" (128). In addition, more mainstream textbooks for freedpeople echoed the Christian-centered paternalism of organizations like the American Tract Society (ATS) and American Missionary Association (AMA), which produced and distributed the bulk of primers and readers for Bureau schools.

Books like *John Freedman and His Family* and *Plain Counsels for Freedman*, both published by the ATS, functioned as textbooks for new readers and also as guides to appropriate behavior by newly freed people. As Hartman observes, these books "focused primarily on rules of conduct that would enable the freed to overcome the degradation of slavery and meet the challenges of freedom ... Most important in the panorama of virtues imparted by these texts was the willingness to endure hardships, which alone guaranteed success, upward mobility, and the privileges of citizenship" (128–9). It seems redundant to point out the ironies of this

Amputation, the Past, and the Freedmen's Bureau

emphasis by these books: after all, if slavery taught anything, it was the endurance of hardship.

Most striking, as Hartman points out, these mainstream textbooks presented emancipation as a result of the sacrifice of white soldiers, who gave their lives for the abolition of slavery. As *Advice to Freedmen,* another ATS volume, put it, "With treasure and precious blood your freedom has been purchased. Let these sufferings and sacrifices never be forgotten when you remember that you are not now a slave but free" (qtd. in Hartman 130). The argument of these textbooks was the inverse of the logic of Tourgée and Howard, for whom the suffering and loss of limbs by white soldiers were appropriate payment for the expropriation of Black labor and personhood. The message by mainstream textbooks was not only that formerly enslaved people should be grateful for their emancipation, but that they actually owed a debt to white Union soldiers and were interpellated into a discourse "that ... effaced the enormity of the injuries of the past, entailed the erasure of history, and placed the onus of the past onto the shoulders of the individual" (Hartman 132).

By contrast, Child approached the task of educating and socializing freedpeople from the same perspective as Tourgée and Howard, although with a different starting point: liberty and education were formerly enslaved people's due for the losses they suffered from the beginnings of slavery to the present of white violence. Rather than focusing on the losses of white soldiers, Child saw education as a reparative project that made the changes that these representations of amputation called for. Moreover, for Child, schools for freedpeople were a mode of reparation that could be undertaken by women, who had not been able to sacrifice their own bodies during the war (although they had surely offered up family members, friends, and spouses).

Education had been a major goal of the Bureau from the very beginning, since the vast majority of newly emancipated people were wholly illiterate, and like its mainstream equivalents, *The Freedmen's Book* served double duty as a reader and a literacy primer. White radicals were inspired by the schools on the South Carolina Sea Islands, which had been in existence since their liberation by the Union Army in 1861. The "Port Royal Experiment," in which formerly enslaved people organized to work the plantations of their former enslavers, also included schools for adults and children. As Oliver Howard reported, in a letter home, "I found the children [in Port Royal] sparkling with intelligence.... One school bears the look of our best New England schools; the order, the reading, the arithmetic, and the singing strike you with wonder" (98). As a radical and a

Lydia Maria Child's The Freedmen's Book   153

writer, then, Child felt compelled to join in this experiment in education by assembling a volume that both empowered and educated former slaves.

Throughout *The Freedmen's Book*, Child condemns enslavement and presents knowledge of Black achievement as part of the reparative work of Reconstruction: an essential part of the national remaking that Tourgée and Howard gesture toward. The excerpts in *The Freedmen's Book* are organized roughly chronologically, starting in the eighteenth century with profiles of Ignatius Sancho and Benjamin Banneker, and ending in Child's present day, telling the story of John Brown, reprinting the Emancipation Proclamation, and publishing contemporary poems by Frances E. W. Harper. Child's volume was unusual among textbooks for freedpeople in that it featured short biographies of Black luminaries and writers, and included selections written by Black authors – selections that were noted with an asterisk for easy identification by their readers. Rather than instructing her readers to see education as a gift or a favor done for them by white philanthropists, Child acknowledges that she is fashioning one part of a larger effort at reparations for the losses of slavery. The achievements of the Black subjects of each profile are pieces in what she sees as the plan to help formerly enslaved people foster a sense of dignity and pride in themselves as Black people. As she tells her readers, "I have prepared this book expressly for you, with the hope that those of you who can read will read it aloud to others, and that all of you will derive fresh strength and courage from this true record of what colored men have accomplished, under great disadvantages" (Child, *Freedmen's Book*, "Preface," n.p.). For Child, education in Black history and culture provides the missing element of the amputated personhood experienced by enslaved people. If during the time of slavery enslaved people were counted as three fifths of a person, Child implicitly hopes to contribute to the reconstitution of the two fifths that Black people were denied: self-determination, a sense of their own history, and pride in their collective achievements that for her are the prerequisites of full Black citizenship.

Child is from the beginning explicit about the abusive and expropriating power of enslavement: in the short biography of Ignatius Sancho, for example, she narrates the coming to America of his "father and mother [who] were stolen from Africa" (2). Similarly, she challenges the legitimacy of the language, and indeed of the very mechanisms, of chattel slavery, pointing out that the man "who took possession of the little orphan . . ., *claimed to be* his master" (2, emphasis added).

Child underlines her disgust for enslavement and her support for Black authorship and self-determination at every turn. In her short essay in *The*

Freedmen's Book, "The Beginning and Progress of Emancipation in the British West Indies," she contextualizes the international slave trade with refreshing clarity: "Nothing has ever been done in this world more wicked and cruel than the slave-trade on the coast of Africa" (124). Like Tourgée, she draws a bright line between the past and present, and encourages her readers to do the same. Integrating feminist analysis into her discussion of the wrongs of slavery, she identifies domestic violence, especially violence toward and among children, as part of the legacy of slavery, which

> in every way fosters violence. Slave-children, being in the habit of seeing a great deal of beating, early on form the habit of kicking and banging each other when they are angry, and of abusing poor helpless animals intrusted to their care. On all such occasions parents should say to them, "those are the ways of Slavery. We expect better things of free children." (225)

As the quotation above shows, part of that mission was to protect the bodies of free children from the violence they had been helpless to resist during slavery. Protection of this kind required a sharp distinction between past, present, and future, all embodied in formerly enslaved children, who have absorbed past practices of slavery and are playing them out in the present, but must be instructed to build a different kind of future, free of violence and coercion. In this short essay, Child insists on relegating slavery to the past, to older generations who unconsciously reproduced the structures of violence that undergirded the system of slavery, and to their white enslavers who initiated this cycle of violence in the first place.

At the same time, she realizes that without deliberate and conscious intervention, the past lingers, with old, destructive assumptions about Black humanity retaining their salience for both Black and white Americans. By absorbing the lessons of *The Freedmen's Book*, formerly enslaved parents are instructing themselves (and perhaps their own parents, and ideally their white neighbors) as much as their children that violence is a legacy of slavery and must be affirmatively repudiated in order to construct new Black selves in the reconstructed nation. The present of emancipation must not forget the past, for fear that they repeat it, but also so as to fashion a liberated future.

Several of the excerpts in *The Freedmen's Book* manipulate chronology and its relationship to slavery in this way. One fascinating example is "Emancipation in the District of Columbia, April 16, 1862," an excerpt from a longer poem by James Madison Bell.[15] In two of the excerpt's stanzas, Bell describes a capital city the day after emancipation, a day the poem looks forward to:

Lydia Maria Child's The Freedmen's Book

The slaver's pen, the auction-block
The gory lash of cruelty,
No more this nation's pride shall mock;
No more, within those ten miles square,
Shall men be bought and women sold[.] (244–5)

The time frame of the poem is unusual: Bell both describes the recent past of slavery in the nation's capital and at the same time represents it as existing in a future past/present in which slavery will have no longer existed. Its tone is anticipatory: "no more *shall*" rather than "no more *are*." In the chronology of the *Freedmen's Book*, "Emancipation in the District of Columbia" occupies several points in time simultaneously: the present of the book, in which all enslaved people have been emancipated; the past of Washington, where the "slaver's pen, the auction block" were everyday parts of the built environment; and the time of "no more," when slavery shall have been abolished in the nation's capital, which is already in the reader's past.

Another way that Child distinguished the past of enslavement from the present of emancipation was to demonstrate how even under slavery, African Americans had a cogent claim to citizenship, to humanity. She quotes at length from Frederick Douglass's "What to the Slave Is the Fourth of July," under the heading "A Pertinent Question":

> Is it not astonishing that while we are ploughing, planting, and reaping, using all kinds of mechanical tools, erecting houses and constructing bridges, building ships, working in metals of brass, iron, and copper, silver and gold; that while we are reading, writing, and ciphering, acting as clerks, merchants, and secretaries, having among us lawyers, doctors, ministers, poets, authors, editors, orators, and teachers; that while all are engaged in all manner of enterprises common to other men, digging gold in California, capturing the whale in the Pacific, breeding sheep and cattle on the hillside; living, moving, acting, thinking, planning; living in families as husbands, wives, and children, and above all, worshipping the Christian's God, and looking hopefull for immortal life beyond the grave; – is it not astonishing, I say, that we are called upon to prove that we are *men*?" (93)

In this quotation, Child points to the physical, intellectual, and emotional labor of Black people enslaved and free, and the existential amputation of their humanity by the institution of chattel slavery. In many ways, the verb structure of this passage works in partnership with the excerpt from Bell. Written in the present tense, the passage implicitly distinguishes between the past of slavery, in which Douglass's argument was no less true, but had no opportunity to prove itself, and the present of freedom, in which these skills can combine to create a new kind of Black identity, one defined by physical, intellectual, and spiritual productivity. In the context of *The Freedman's Book*, this passage from Douglass is transformed from a cry of protest to a claim for humanity to a kind of guidebook to freedpeople as to the many paths their lives could now take. The past amputation of humanity cannot be redressed, but the possibilities of emancipation redefine what the work of Black bodies might signify and how white society might engage with Black workers, intellectuals, and artists.

I would argue, too, that Child's use of a rough chronology in the materials of the *Freedman's Book* encourages its readers to simultaneously value a previously devalued (if even visible) Black past, fully inhabit an emancipated present, and look to the promise of the future. Unlike Tourgée, for whom the work of the Freedmen's Bureau reminds white Southerners of a past signified by the permanently damaged bodies of agents so as to prevent them from indulging in nostalgia, Child invokes a valuable Black past to inspire the present and make possible visions of an empowered future. By focusing on the past achievements of African Americans as well as the profound losses, Child represents a kind of usable past for her Black readers that focuses on the reconstitution and reconstruction of Black personhood, and shows how African Americans in the past survived and even excelled within the seemingly unbreakable binds/bonds of slavery.

It was essential to Child, then, that schools for freedpeople, and the texts that were taught in these schools, continually reinforce the integrity of Black identity, the self-ownership of Black bodies, and the wholeness of the Black family.[16] In *Bricks without Straw*, Tourgée's narrator observes that the insistence on this integrity was to Southerners among the most galling of the aftershocks of the "earthquake" of emancipation: "Perhaps the most outrageous and debasing of all the acts of the Bureau, in the eyes of those who love to term themselves 'the South,' was the fact that its officers and agents, first of all, allowed the colored man to be sworn in opposition to and in contradiction of the word of a white man" (159). Child implicitly and explicitly threads this wholeness of Black subjectivity, instantiated in the spoken and written word, throughout *The Freedman's Book*.

Certainly, not all educators in Bureau schools subscribed to these principles.[17] However, at their best they lay at the root of the work of the American Missionary Association, which sent hundreds of Black and white teachers south. AMA leaders recognized that "the feeling of prejudice, extensively existing in this country against the people of color," was

Lydia Maria Child's The Freedmen's Book   157

"both wicked in itself and a great barrier in the way of their elevation" (qtd. in Blum 55). Furthermore, despite the often paternalistic attitudes of their educational materials, the AMA kept as close as possible to its policy that "no person who yields to that prejudice, or suffers himself to be influenced thereby, ought to be appointed or sustained among [the Bureau's] officers, teachers, or agents" (qtd. in Blum 55).

Even with her commitment to Black empowerment and full person-hood, Child would have been mistaken to believe that *The Freedmen's Book* would solve deep-rooted problems of Black poverty. The work of repar-ation through education was often fitful, usually due to a shortage of resources. Schools (which is to say the Bureau) had to provide all supplies – spelling books, primers, slates, arithmetic textbooks, chalk, as well as chairs, desks, even buildings – because freedpeople could not afford to fund them.[18] In addition, schools occasionally had attendance troubles due to the many and often competing demands on students' time. A school in Crossroad, Maryland, experienced a serious drop in enrollment, which a member of the board explained had occurred because "Persons have been busy with their crops, and good many, have not good and sufficient clothing for their children (for the Winter)" (*District of Columbia Education* n.p.). At the same time, Black and white correspondents with the Bureau commented on the "beauty," "happiness," and "delight" of both teachers and students. In 1868, Rev. Alexander Posey of Romney, West Virginia, expresses "sorrow to say that our coulard school in romney stoped on the first day of September" because of reduced resources. He notes that "the children are all in a very beautiful way of learning ... Mrs. Quinn is a very good teacher and takes great delight in teaching the coulard children" (*District of Columbia Education* n.p.). Similarly, C. W. Sharp writes to James Kimball, DC Superintendent of Education, from Charleston, West Virginia, that "I never saw [a school] more industrious, and making better progress, and certainly never a happier one" (*District of Columbia Education* n.p.).[19]

This happiness was to be short-lived. Even as African Americans were finding their way to schools and polls, to literacy and even elected office, the backlash against formerly enslaved people claiming their freedom was violent and omnipresent.[20] In every report of the Bureau, in every region, are records of murders, rapes, whippings, beatings, shootings, lynchings attempted and actual, as well as the exploitation of Black workers by planters and employers more generally. As Oliver Howard observed, "the reports of murders, assaults, and outrages of every description were so numerous and so full of horrible details, that at times one was inclined to believe the whole white population engaged in a war of extermination against the Blacks" (v. 2, 370).[21]

As he realized later, though, the goal was not genocide (although it may have often felt that way), but a desire to reconstitute "the Union as it was." Howard recognized that white Southerners were, in many ways, playing a long game, waiting for the opportunity to turn back the clock on emancipation and racial equality. In the form of the Ku Klux Klan and other white vigilante groups, "the main object from first to last was somehow to regain and maintain over the negro that ascendancy which slavery gave, and which was being lost by emancipation, education, and suffrage" (v. 2, 375). This extreme violence is a kind of bitter repetition compulsion, a white supremacist melancholia, in which the lost object of slavery is replayed by white Southerners within the new context of emancipation. If for O. O Howard, and in *Bricks without Straw*, amputation and loss provide a language for accounting for the damage slavery did to African Americans and imagining a reconstituted, reconstructed nation forged in the context of that language, the viciousness with which the gains of Reconstruction were clawed back through damage to Black bodies is a kind of inverse: reparations to white Southerners for the losses they believed that Black liberation visited upon them.

At the same time, texts like Lydia Maria Child's *Freedmen's Book* offered what Pierre Bourdieu has called "embodied cultural capital": something that can take time and effort to accumulate and is inalienable once assimilated into the self. In Child's model, this embodied cultural capital is not simply a possession but rather a process of reconstitution and reconstruction of the self through knowledge of Black history and the embodiment of Black citizenship. The reader of *The Freedmen's Book*, whether Black or white, picks up the work that the radical vision of amputation lays out: not the "Union as it was" but the Union as it can be.

CHAPTER 5

Shaking Hands
Manual Politics and the End of Reconstruction

So far I have been writing as though lost body parts are interchangeable: to lose an arm, a leg, a hand, a foot is all part of the larger category of the amputated limb. In this chapter, as we approach the wholesale dismantling of Reconstruction, I want to focus on hands. If lost limbs operate metaphorically in the Civil War imaginary, hands function doubly or triply so. They are always already signs of connection or repudiation, of utility and uselessness.

Hands, after all, are what distinguish us from other animals – the opposable thumb that makes possible writing, touching, connecting, and also holding and firing a gun. They are, in Janet Zandy's words, "microcosms of the whole human," revealing work done, lives lived (xi). Hands "bind us together and set us against each other" (Radman xiv). Our hands are essential to our sense of ourselves in the world, our proprioception: they "help define a pragmatic area around the body that has significance for movement, action, attention, and accomplishing tasks" (Gallagher 214). Losing a hand profoundly alters one's relationship to the physical world, especially if it is the dominant hand. People who are right-handed and lose their right hand have to reorganize their brains to have the left hand take the right's place, something that William Oland Bourne was aware of when he formed the "Left Armed Corps" and organized his left-handed penmanship competitions. Even more surprising, loss of feeling in the hands affects the entire nervous system, reducing proprioception to such an extent that patients must reestablish how they judge distance or even move their bodies through space (see Gallagher).

Hands connect us to ourselves neurologically and to others affectively. As Wolff-Michael Roth has argued, "in touch I relate to the other, but this other relates to me. It is through the self-relation to the other that I come to be myself" (47). Touch also connects us to the world around us, the materiality of the world, and is inextricable from "verification, the connotations of tangibility being solid, foundational, undeceiving" (Paterson 2).[1]

159

160 Manual Politics and the End of Reconstruction

In this chapter, I take the uniqueness of hands seriously, both their literal and metaphorical meanings. Unlike other body parts, hands play several roles simultaneously: the hand is "an organ of cognition and exploration in its own right" (Tallis 28); it feels and "sees" shapes and textures independent of the eye.[2] Unlike the eye, "the hand is not a neutral observer, but an instrument of value" (Radman x). Hands interact with the objects and people they encounter; there is minimal separation between the hand and what it holds. The actions of hands can be both instrumental and figurative at the same time. As Jacqueline Francis observes:

> [T]he raised hand represents greeting, welcome, or farewell. It admonishes or blesses; it is a defense against a blow, a deferential homage to someone or something; a refusal or another form of negation.... Two hands raised may protect or prophesy; they may express joy, excitement, or attainment, or fear, despair, or supplication. (121)

Descriptions of hands tend to include lengthy lists – they serve so many purposes, can mean so many things. Hands can communicate affection and tenderness and/or deal violence and pain. They can generate language and also demand that language stop. The multiplicity of the hand is captured by Raymond Tallis in his description of

> [t]his hand – the professor of grasping, seizing, pulling, plucking, picking, pinching, pressing, patting, poking, prodding, fumbling, squeezing, crushing, throttling, punching rubbing, scratching, groping, stroking, caressing, fingering, drumming, shaping, lifting, flicking, catching, throwing, and much else besides – ... the master tool of human life. (22)

Intrinsic to the hand is the ineffability of touch: a hand touching something is also being touched. Unlike vision, in which the roles of subject and object can be clearly distinguished (I can look at something without being looked at by it), touch confuses those roles, even between a person and an inanimate object. To hold something – especially someone else's hand – is also to be touched by it.

In this chapter, I explore a variety of different hands, both attached to and detached from bodies, both present and absent. In all these representations, amputation is either actively portrayed or implicitly haunts the stories these hands tell. Given the centrality and materiality of touch, my discussion of the representation of hands is not only verbal but also visual – I interrogate how hands are not just imagined in text but also imaged in drawings and cartoons. I begin with a discussion of the representation of hands in some of the drawings Thomas Nast made about the politics around Reconstruction – an unusual set of images given the larger corpus of his work. Then I move from images of interacting hands to actual shaking hands during the twenty-fifth anniversary of the battle of Gettysburg, which brought together veterans of both the Army of the Potomac and the Army of Northern Virginia in 1888. Throughout the proceedings, newspapers reported on the copious handshakes that accompanied the encounters of these former enemies as signs of national reunification even as Reconstruction was being systematically dismantled.

I end the chapter with an extended reading of *A Hazard of New Fortunes*, by William Dean Howells. Usually read as a story that allegorizes the shift of literary and economic power from Boston to New York, for my purposes *Hazard* is especially interesting because of a secondary character, Berthold Landau, a German 1848-er who lost his hand in the Civil War. Overlaid by a North-South romance, *Hazard*'s ambivalence toward Landau and Howells's decision to kill him off is another sign of the abandonment of white commitment to Black freedom. Lindau's radicalism is exchanged for a bourgeois romanticization of prewar enslavement, a shift that characterizes the transformation in discourse among white Americans, especially those in the North, about racialization in the 1880s and 1890s.

"The Equality of Man before the Law": Thomas Nast's Disembodied Hands

Thomas Nast is best known for his campaign against Tammany Hall and "Boss" William M. Tweed in the 1870s, but he was deeply invested in abolition and Reconstruction in his earlier work. He was a good fit for *Harper's Weekly* magazine, where he started working in 1859: although "never an official organ of the Republican Party, [*Harper's*] evolved into a highly influential advocate of Republican principles during the war" (Jarman 157). While he was hardly free of white racist views of Black people, Nast was committed to the idea that they "deserved freedom, education, employment, and dignity, and he expressed these thoughts in his drawings" (Halloran 81).

The child of German immigrants, Nast embraced the idea of the Union and the struggle for Black emancipation. As his biographer, Fiona Deans Halloran, argues, Nast was "radicalized" by the violence of the Draft Riots, especially their focus on the destruction of Black New York institutions such as the Colored Orphans' Asylum. In Halloran's narrative, once he was "[c]onfronted with the violent opposition to Republican policies, black freedom, and the effort to save the Union, Nast responded by cementing his commitment to the ideals of the Union" (89).

162   Manual Politics and the End of Reconstruction

Nast's drawings tended to be detailed and busy, layering text on top of images of individuals and objects. One prime example of this is his cartoon "Andrew Johnson's Reconstruction and How It Works," which appeared in *Harper's* in September 1866 (Figure 5.1). The focal point of the cartoon is Johnson as Iago, lying to Othello, here portrayed by a Black veteran, complete with sling on his left arm. But the cartoon itself is populated by several other images that surround this central pair, including Johnson as a snake charmer playing his pipe for Democratic Copperheads, scenes of Black people being attacked by white citizens in the Memphis riot earlier that year, a representation of the New Orleans race massacre later the same summer, and copious written commentary.

A few of Nast's cartoons stand out, though, for their comparative simplicity and the focus on their central figure: an interaction between two hands. These hands are disembodied and dominate the field of the drawings. They represent a moment in which power is bestowed, challenged, or acceded to in relation to Black citizenship and freedom. And, I would argue, they connect to white radical discourse about abolition and Reconstruction through their implicit use of the trope of amputation. The hands are, one might say, cousins of their amputated counterparts – they emerge from a similar origin, although they follow a different direction. These hands do not gesture toward a body from which they came; they exist independently of a body. But they participate in the same discourse of Black liberation as the amputated limbs in previous chapters.[3]

Nast first used the image of two hands in gestural conversation in an 1875 cartoon entitled "To Thine Own Self Be True" (Figure 5.2). Originally published in *Harper's Weekly* and later widely reproduced both in black and white and in color, the image represents two hands – one of Columbia, the female embodiment of the United States, and one of a Black man. Columbia's hand holds a sheaf of papers, tied by a red ribbon, on which is inscribed the message of the Civil Rights Act of 1875:

> The Equality of Men before the Law. Civil Rights Bill. It is the duty of the Government in its dealings with the people to mete out equal and exact justice to all, or whatever nativity, race, color, or persuasion, religious or political. Signed by the President U. S. Grant.

The Black hand, dressed in a jacket and cuffed shirt, reaches out for the document. This hand almost grasps the papers, but is a little short, reaching out for them without yet touching them. The drawing is of the moment at which the nation hands African Americans their rights under this new bill and they are just about to receive equal treatment under the

Figure 5.1　Thomas Nast, "Andrew Johnson's Reconstruction and How It Works." *Harper's Weekly*, September 1, 1866.

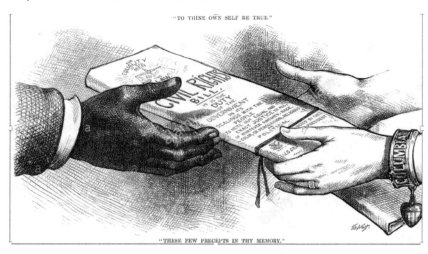

Figure 5.2 Thomas Nast, "To Thine Own Self Be True." *Harper's Weekly*, April 24, 1875.

law. The two hands are on an equal horizontal plane, a radical statement in and of itself, visually insisting on racial equity between white and Black Americans. At the same time, the act of transferring these rights into Black hands is in suspended animation – just about to happen but not yet achieved. The negative space between the Black hand and the document is pregnant with anticipation – once this transition to being invested with the full rights of citizenship is completed, the promise of Reconstruction will be realized.

This image can be usefully contrasted with Thomas Ball's much-discussed Emancipation Memorial, installed the following year, which represents a very different relationship between Black Americans and a representative of the United States (Figure 5.3). In this sculpture, Abraham Lincoln towers over a mostly nude, kneeling man, granting him liberty with an outstretched arm. His other hand is on the Emancipation Proclamation, which lies on a plinth whose top is roughly on the same level as the newly emancipated man's head. While the man's crouch suggests that he might be in the act of rising up to standing, the hierarchy of the sculpture is clear – Lincoln is the superior, bestowing the emancipation of which the kneeling man is the grateful beneficiary. As Kirk Savage has shown, this arrangement of Lincoln and emancipated man was not new to Ball. Several prominent sculptors of the time had experimented with representing emancipation through the image of a grateful

Figure 5.3　Thomas Ball, *Emancipation Memorial* (1879).

freedperson (sometimes male, sometimes female) kneeling at Lincoln's feet. In these images, "Lincoln is the benevolent white authority who mediates between God and the lowly slave, while the recipient of that kindness represents a thankful, though undeveloped race" (74).

　　Nast's drawing is both radical and radically different from this image of the relationship between Black and white. There are striking aesthetic and structural distinctions between the two. First, in Nast's drawing the Black person's hand is classed as bourgeois: he wears a blue jacket and crisp white-cuffed shirt, whereas in Ball's statue the kneeling man is naked except for a loincloth. Second, he is ready and anticipating taking hold of his rights on his own terms. An additional detail implicitly cements the idea that Columbia and her Black counterpart are on equal standing: each of their thumbs casts a parallel shadow upon the text of the bill, pointing toward the other's shadow, creating another potential connection between them.

　　The cooperation and cross-racial collaboration between these two hands contrasts strongly with two later images Nast made of hands interacting. In a January 27, 1877, cartoon "Compromise – Indeed!" (Figure 5.4).

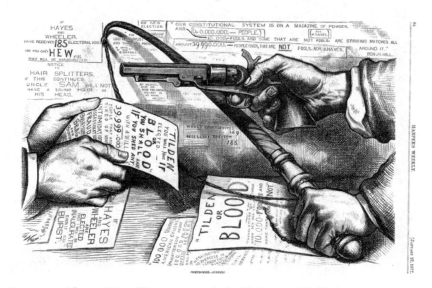

Figure 5.4   Thomas Nast, "Compromise – Indeed!" *Harper's Weekly*, January 27, 1877.

Nast embodies the interparty conflict between Democrat Samuel Tilden and Republican Rutherford Hayes, whose close race for the presidency ultimately led to the compromise that withdrew the last Union troops from the South. *Harper's* published this cartoon the day after Congress created an Election Commission to sort out the complications of the 1876 election and to hammer out a compromise.

For Nast, however, any hope of compromise was threatened by the possibility of Democratic strong-arming and the fear that Republican gains in Reconstruction would be undone, a fear that was hardly misplaced.

The drawing features two sets of hands across a table from each other. One, the avatar of the Republican Party, holds a handbill as if to read it, whose emphatic headline reads "TILDEN you will have if elected, or BLOOD you shall have if you shed any with a will." The other set of hands holds a pistol and a bullwhip, threatening to draw the very blood that the handbill threatens. By contrast with "To Thine Own Self Be True," "Compromise – Indeed!" is jam-packed with textual detail. Every spare inch of the cartoon not occupied by these hands is filled with reproductions of handbills name-checking Tilden, Hayes, and Abram Hewitt, Tilden's campaign manager. But the focus of the drawing is the gun and the whip, which point directly at the other hand and take up the center of the image.

While there is nothing explicitly racialized about this image, we can see the signs of slavery, emancipation, and backlash everywhere. The whip itself carries with it the implications of enslavement – narratives and photographic images of the whipping of enslaved people were omnipresent before the war, and the fact that the whip is held by a Democrat whose party opposes Reconstruction strengthens that association.[4] The whip also refers back to a prior Nast cartoon, "The Same Snap – 'Reform' Slavery," published earlier that year, in which another disembodied hand wields a whip whose handle is labeled "Bulldozer," suggesting that Democrats will bulldoze over the gains of Reconstruction if given a chance (Figure 5.5).

Figure 5.5   Thomas Nast, "The Same Snap – 'Reform Slavery.'" *Harper's Weekly*, December 30, 1876.

And at the end of the snapping whip is "1861 1876," implicitly arguing that Democrats in Congress see themselves as continuing the Civil War by other means, and attempting to reenslave African Americans.

In "Compromise – Indeed!," then, Nast indicates that if Democrats take the presidency, newly freed Black people could be returned to the violence of slavery. In this image the legacy of enslavement and the fate of Reconstruction are everywhere even as they are nowhere to be seen within the image itself.

Nast produced a follow-up image to "Compromise – Indeed!" three weeks later, featuring the same two hands in quite a different (although somewhat ambiguous) relationship. In "A Truce – Not a Compromise," the bullwhip is gone. The hand of the government (indicated by the "US" cufflinks) holds down the Democratic Party hand, resting it on top of the gun, which lies on the table inert (Figure 5.6). The threat has dissipated. However, it still lingers in many ways. The handbills surrounding the two hands are more violent than before, revealing both the high stakes and the fragility of this truce. The sentence "Tilden you shall have if elected, or blood you shall have" is reduced down to an even more basic threat

Figure 5.6   Thomas Nast, "A Truce – Not a Compromise." *Harpers Weekly*, February 17, 1877.

"TILDEN or BLOOD." Similar sentiments show up on other handbills: "Tilden or Fight," "Are you ready for civil war?," and "The Bloody Age of the United States of America."

Nast captioned this cartoon "A truce – not a compromise, but a chance for high-toned gentlemen to retire gracefully from their very civil declarations of war." It is hard to read this as anything but ironic, given this drawing and the one that preceded it. After all, threats of civil war are not civil – the threats of violence in "A Compromise – Indeed!" are hardly those of a gentleman (not least because the sleeve out of which the hand emerges is that of a workman's shirt, not the elegantly cuffed sleeve of its Republican counterpart: the conflict here is not just of party but also of class). And the threats of "Tilden or Blood" have intensified in the face of this compromise.

Moreover, faintly carved into the wall above the cuff of the Democratic hand are the letters "KKK" and a skull, as though to permanently remind readers of the connection between the Southern Democrats and vigilante justice against freedpeople. And, I would argue, the indelibility of the inscription does not augur well for the results of this compromise – the Klan hovers over the scene threatening even more violence and degradation. Rather than representing a cessation of hostility from the Democrats toward the US government and the project of Reconstruction, then, Nast suggests that the truce is not just fragile, but possibly counterproductive.

In all of these drawings, Nast utilizes hands either to represent or to invoke the precarious position of freedpeople and the threat posed by Democratic control of Congress and potentially the presidency. Disembodied hands are no longer simply the signs of the sacrifice of Union soldiers in the struggle for Black self-determination. Rather, they are inextricable from the political developments of the post–Civil War nation. These hands (re-)enact what is at stake in Reconstruction: the risk that Confederate and/or Democratic power will (re-)assert itself over the nation, reinaugurating the oppression of Black people or the destruction of the promise of liberty and the defense of the formerly enslaved. In these cartoons, Nast offers two alternatives: a peaceful granting of civil rights to Black Americans, or the potentially violent and racist rise of the Democratic party to power, not just in Congress but to the presidency.

In fact, Hayes won the election (or at least was endowed with it after intense negotiation), but the conditions inherent in that compromise loosened the reins on white supremacy. Nast was more prescient than he knew with the faint inclusion of the KKK in "A Truce – Not a Compromise." The Compromise of 1877 was one of the most

170 Manual Politics and the End of Reconstruction

consequential steps in the North's abandonment of not just the formerly enslaved, but all Black and many poor white people in the South. The compromise at stake was the withdrawal of the last vestiges of US troops from the Southern states, allowing Democrats to complete their campaign of violence and intimidation against Black citizens, especially at the ballot box. As Eric Foner has documented, almost all of the advances of Reconstruction – free public education, a fair judicial system, attempts at equal employment, Black franchise and service on juries – were reversed over the following years, as active state and interpersonal discrimination against African Americans became the rule.

"Our great standing army of volunteer mendicants": Hands and Handouts

Hands do not just give and/or hold, as the hands in Nast's cartoons do. They can also be held out to beg. One of the most debated legacies of the war was the rationale for the government handout: pensions for veterans of the Union Army, now represented by the veteran's advocacy organization, the Grand Army of the Republic. As former soldiers aged, they made more claims for federal support, as those who through their sacrifice had saved the nation. Eventually, veterans receiving pensions were not just soldiers disabled by their service but aging men who had fought in the war.

Over time, veterans' pensions took up a larger and larger proportion of the federal budget. James Marten shows that by the 1890s there were over three quarters of a million former soldiers claiming pension benefits (200). Pensions quickly became politicized, with Republicans arguing for generous benefits for all veterans and Democrats claiming that only men disabled by the war were deserving (of course, "disabled" was a broad umbrella; men not only lost limbs, sight, hearing, or brain function but often suffered from other kinds of sequelae more difficult to see but often just as damaging: disrupted digestive systems, ongoing headaches, and what we would now diagnose as post-traumatic stress disorder). When in 1888 Grover Cleveland vetoed a bill that would expand pension benefits, the *Chicago Tribune* condemned veterans as "our great standing army of volunteer medicants" made up of "the claim agents, the demagogues, the dead-beats . . . deserters and coffee coolers and bounty jumpers" (qtd. in Marten 202). "It will be a happy day for the republic," the *Tribune* concluded, "when the last beggar of the Grand Army humbug is securely planted" (203).

One publication that maintained a harsh critique of the pension system was *Puck*, a successful humor magazine. Founded as a German-language

Hands and Handouts 171

publication in 1871, it expanded into English in 1877. *Puck* was at best skeptical of the pension system and featured several cartoons that targeted both the federal pension administration and the veterans who were, to the magazine's mind, feeding at the federal trough.

An attack on handouts becomes explicit in a December 20, 1882, cartoon that was featured in full color on the front page of the magazine (Figure 5.7). Titled "The Insatiable Glutton," this cartoon by Friedrich Graetz depicts a white veteran of the war literally feeding on federal money.[5] Sprouting from the man's body are multiple plump arms, each jacket cuff labeled with the fabricated or corrupt recipients of pension aid: "Bogus Grandma," "Bogus Grandpa," "Bogus Orphan," "Bogus Invalid,"

Figure 5.7 Friedrich Graetz, "Insatiable Glutton." *Puck*, December 30 1882.

as well as four arms labeled "agent" (pension agents advocated for veterans' benefits and were accused – not always wrongly – of exaggerating their clients' needs to pad their own commissions) and half a dozen unlabeled arms, all digging in with spoons to a bowl, identified as "US Treasury," filled with coins.

This cartoon is a harsh indictment of what Graetz, or at least *Puck's* editors, saw as rampant corruption and abuse of the pension system. I'd like to pause a little in looking at it, though, since Graetz's powerful image of the dozens of grasping hands connects us not just to Nast's disembodied hands bestowing civil rights or threatening armed conflict over an election, but even further back to the piles of dismembered limbs of Chapter 2. As I argued there, the heaps of anonymous limbs signified the irreparable damage of the war as well as the potential for a nation in which bodies could coexist regardless of race. The "rejected members," in Whitman's words, separated not just limb from body but the prewar from the postwar nation.

In Graetz's cartoon, however, we have a surfeit of limbs, almost all of which are carefully identified by type. No longer are we in the "butcher's shambles" of Whitman, witnessing the separation of men from their body parts. Rather, it is as though all of those limbs – or arms, at least – have returned to testify against the former soldier. The inert arms of the amputee have taken on new life and been sutured back, in excess, onto the veteran's body. It's interesting, too, that the figure in the cartoon, although a veteran who would have been at least in his late thirties up to mid-fifties by 1882, is represented as a corpulent young man with thick arms and pudgy fingers, grasping spoons to feed himself with government dollars. The debate around pensions from the anti-pension perspective doesn't just deny the necessary losses of the war; it overcompensates for them, generating hypertrophied arms and hands shoving money into a distended mouth. Moreover, rather than acknowledging that Civil War veterans were an often disabled and certainly aging segment of the population, Graetz intensifies the message of outrage by (mis)representing the archetypal pensioner as young and hearty, with a vast appetite.

I find this image fascinating, compelling, and disturbing. I cannot look at it without seeing its ghostly, ghastly doppelganger, the mounds of dismembered limbs of battlefields and hospitals. The plump hands multiply and multiply, some having no apparent source of origin in the veteran's body but seemingly autochthonous, growing up out of the plane of the cartoon itself. The multiple arms are almost force-feeding the grotesquely wide mouth, which cannot even swallow all that it is fed, as coins tumble back down into the bowl. Is the veteran accepting a pension against his will, implicitly repudiating his need for government benefits? Here the disembodied limb, the principal signifier for heroic loss, the mark of sympathy with the cause of enslaved and later freed people in the texts I've looked at so far, is not a sacrifice for the greater good but a gluttonous hoarder, competing with its likenesses to scoop up government largesse. Indeed, these multiplying hands want to take more than the mouth can handle.

Intrinsic to this image is the notion of insatiability, that nothing is ever enough. Here loss has been written out of the equation. The arms are not a symbol of sacrifice and bloodshed on behalf of the Union and the enslaved people at the crux of the war. The identity of soldier or veteran has been replaced by that of pensioner, whose purpose is to gobble up national resources via corruption or outright fraud.

Most importantly, these are hands that take, that grasp. They are hands with a single purpose – to feed the insatiable mouth. Toward the end of the century, however, Union veterans' hands were finding another use: to shake the hands of their Confederate counterparts at various reunions at Civil War battlegrounds. As 1888 rolled around, the Grand Army of the Republic began to organize nostalgic commemorations of the twenty-fifth anniversary of some of the watershed battles of 1863, as the war slowly moved in the Union's favor. The most significant of these was the twenty-fifth reunion of veterans of Gettysburg, held on in the first week of July 1888.[6]

Shaking Hands over the Bloody Chasm: Reunification at Gettysburg, 1888

The 1888 Gettysburg reunion was sponsored by the Society of the Army of the Potomac (SAP), which had organized its own reunion the previous year. By July 1, 1888, roughly 30,000 people assembled in Gettysburg to observe the twenty-fifth anniversary of the three-day battle. The crowd was predominantly Union veterans and their families; while some former Confederate soldiers and several generals attended, and the SAP had resolved to invite the veterans of the Confederate Army of Northern Virginia, they had not spread the word through the South far enough in advance to gain a large showing.[7]

While attendees started gathering at the end of June, and many stayed through July 4, the main event was on July 2: a grand procession, followed by speeches by officers from both sides. These speeches bear close

174   Manual Politics and the End of Reconstruction

attention, but equally as interesting is the rhetoric that surrounded the more casual encounters among veterans and between regular soldiers and officers from the Union and Confederate forces. Characteristic is this description of a chance July 1 meeting on Cemetery Hill between four New York Militia veterans and their counterparts from the Louisiana regiment nicknamed the Tigers. As the New Yorkers were describing the scene to their wives and children, they were overheard by the Louisianans, who approached them. Once both sets of men realized that they were erstwhile opponents, "the [Louisiana] veterans made a forward dash and such a shaking of hands was never before seen on the top of East Cemetery Hill" ("On Gettysburg Field"). The perspective of this story shifts quickly from a Union narration of events to an experience shared between the two sides, their opposite causes dissolved in manly fellowship.

Newspapers reporting on the reunion returned again and again to the image of middle-aged veterans of North and South meeting and shaking hands. As the *New York Times* noted, "When a Northern veteran met a veteran from the South, the former simply extended a hand to find it grasped hard" ("United at Gettysburg"). The shaking of hands is, as Raymond Tallis observes, "an underwritten earnest of sincerity, of authenticity, commitment and probity" (115). Handshakes bring strangers together, they cement deals, and they certify a horizontal, egalitarian relationship between the two participants. It is, in Tallis's words, "a mark of fraternalism, actual or potential" (115). These repeated handshakes at the Gettysburg reunion are also a kind of interpellation of comradeship, a sign that the participants have gone from being enemies to becoming, if not friends, at least brothers-in-arms.

Handshakes at the reunion were both horizontal and vertical (or at least diagonal). One of the most popular stories, which was reprinted in papers from Pennsylvania to as far north as Brattleboro, Vermont, described a meeting between James Longstreet, a general from the Army of Northern Virginia, and an amputee member of the Grand Army of the Republic:

> A one-legged veteran hobbled on his crutches up to the General, and, grasping his hand, said: "General, I fought against you at Round Top. I lost a wing there, but I'm proud to meet you here." General Longstreet's face beamed with satisfaction as he grasped the extended hand. ("Sunday at Gettysburg")

This mutual grasping follows a convoluted logic. First, how can Longstreet grasp the veteran's hand, when the man has already grasped Longstreet's hand? Second, this gesture substitutes the handshake for the loss: the joining of Union and Confederate hands implicitly rewrites the story of Gettysburg. Where the loss reminds readers of the sacrifices of the war and, implicitly, of the gains that the war achieved, the handshake glosses over why the veteran might have been fighting in the first place. Again and again we see the handshake rendering the realities of the war invisible, even irrelevant, prioritizing reunification between white men over the liberation of Black Americans. Interesting, too, is the veteran's claim of being "proud" to meet General Longstreet. It is as though the glamour of Longstreet, the representative of the Lost Cause, somehow rubs off on the veteran, erasing the differences between them.

The grasping of hands is repeated at every level of the military: between ordinary veterans, between veterans and officers, and between officers. A similar, although somewhat more tense, scene had played out the previous day between Longstreet and his Union counterpart General Daniel E. Sickles, who were staying at the same hotel. Longstreet had been eating dinner with some of his comrades when Sickles entered. Sickles hesitated, seeing his former opponent. However,

> Longstreet caught sight of him. Pushing his chair to the rear, the Southerner reached out his right hand. It was quickly grasped by Sickles, around whose shoulder Longstreet threw his disengaged arm. They were friends in a moment. ("It's Again a Tented Field")

Longstreet shook hands again with his former enemies at the ceremony on July 2, and with General Hiram Berdan, former commander of Union sharpshooters on July 3 ("Gettysburg Field"), and I found any number of reports of hands being shaken between Union and Confederate soldiers, with hands being mostly offered by Northern veterans and then "grasped" by their Southern counterparts. Indeed, the *Philadelphia Inquirer* explicitly contrasted the hands that twenty-five years earlier had held weapons with the shaking hands of the present day. Thousands of men traveled back to Gettysburg, "not to meet again in deadly conflict but to **Shake Hands over the Bloody Chasm**" (bold type in the original).[8]

What is this bloody chasm? Of course, in its original coinage, it referred to the enormous gap between the Union and the Confederacy that caused a brutal and carnage-filled war. Thomas Nast invoked this version of the chasm in a September 21, 1872, cartoon satirizing Liberal Republican presidential candidate Horace Greeley, whose plea "let us clasp hands across the bloody chasm" is savaged.

In the cartoon (Figure 5.8), Nast places Greeley, in whose pocket is a small sheaf of papers entitled "What I Know about Shaking Hands over

Figure 5.8   Thomas Nast, "Let Us Clasp Hands over the Bloody Chasm." *Harper's Weekly*, September 21, 1872.

the Bloodiest Chasm," on a wooden platform on one side of a fence made of sharpened logs – the so-called dead line that marked the limits of the camp beyond which prisoners could not go, on pain of death.[9] To the right of the fence is a sign that reads "Andersonville Prison. Who Ever Entered Here Left Hope Behind," emblazoned with a skull and crossbones. Greeley stretches his hand over the fence, gesturing across a field barren except for row after row of gravestones punctuated only by the figures of mourners – the remnants of Andersonville, in which almost a third of Union prisoners of war died.[10] At the other end of the enormous graveyard is a barely visible figure of another person reaching out his hand.

Clearly, only five years after the end of the war, Nast was tapping into a powerful resistance on the part of many Northerners to stretching their hands out to their erstwhile opponents. It's no coincidence that Greeley stands on a "pigeon roost" – the platforms from which prison guards shot at men who violated the dead line; in the imaginary of the cartoon, by suggesting that Americans extend a hand to the South Greeley is reenacting the horrors of Andersonville. The memories of bloody battles and the brutalities of the war prisons at Andersonville and, to a lesser extent, Belle Isle were too vivid to be obviated by any urge toward reconciliation.

Indeed, Nast suggests in his cartoon that any effort to reach out to former Confederates is to do so literally over the dead bodies of Union soldiers tortured and starved to death.

By 1888, not only did these scruples no longer obtain, but scenes of reconciliation were foregrounded. Considering that Union veterans at the reunion outnumbered their Confederate counterparts one hundred to one, these handshakes could not have been very common, unless the same Southerners were shaking hands with multiple veterans of the Army of the Potomac. News reports, as well as the members of the officer class who were given the platform to address the crowd, focused on reconciliation and unity in ways that many of the veterans themselves would not have. Given the massive rollbacks of Reconstruction, I would argue that rather than the white victims of Gettysburg, the bodies of the formerly enslaved are now relegated to the bloody chasm, over which the reconciled white men shake hands, banishing questions of enslavement and liberation.[11]

Despite the official line of the Grand Army of the Republic and the ideology that pervaded the 1888 reunion, however, M. Keith Harris has argued at length that the majority of Civil War veterans were not keen to forget the causes or results of the Civil War. Despite the national urge toward reconciliation, they often balked: "In their reluctance to forget, veterans from both sides of the Potomac undermined the broader reconciliatory message tacitly – often explicitly – endorsed by the nation" (1). Just as we saw in the Introduction that Union soldiers consciously linked their own corporeal losses to the cause of emancipation, Harris shows that "veterans did not calculatingly contribute to historical amnesia along racial lines in the name of reconciliation" (6). Indeed, only a year after the twenty-fifth anniversary of Gettysburg, Charles E. Fuller, speaking on the battlefield to a group of fellow veterans, expressed quite different sentiments from those recorded in the newspaper accounts I quote above: "Never forget that we fought for Freedom and Union, and they for Slavery and Disunion; and that we stood for the right and they for the wrong" (qtd. in Harris 90).

This version of the battle, and the war more generally, was muted during the 1888 reunion. By the account reported in both local and national press, the reunion's purpose was not to provide former Union soldiers with a taste of their former victory, nor to commemorate the struggle for emancipation, nor to revisit the site at which the Civil War finally turned in the North's favor. Rather – and despite the much smaller number of CSA veterans at the event and, as Harris points out, "[r]arely did veterans meet face to face with their former enemies when revisiting wartime memories" (9) – it is for these men to join their hands together to connect over the blood-soaked abyss of secession itself, to mend the schism, and reunite the nation. The material reality of the battle dissolves into the "bloody chasm"; in the words of the *Philadelphia Inquirer*, "the hosannas of peace and fraternal greetings today compare most strangely with the steadily increasing angry roar of musketry that marked the 2d of July 1863" ("Victories of Peace"). Or, as Sickles declared in his speech on July 2, "Today, there are no victors, no vanquished. As Americans we may all claim a common share in the glories of this battlefield" ("United at Gettysburg").

Just as white radicals' acknowledgment and embrace of the losses incurred by the war was a way of clearing space for the antiracist work of Reconstruction, this multiplication of shaking hands erased both the realities of war and the hard – and, by 1888, unfinished and unraveling – work of rebuilding a new nation with Black freedpeople as full participants. Speakers from both Union and Confederate sides rhetorically elided the actual political events of the years between the war and the reunion. The hands of the veteran in Graetz's cartoon are no longer grasping for money from the federal trough – now they are grasping for the hands of their former enemies, forming a bridge over the disintegrating ground of Reconstruction.

Indeed, we might see in the image of shaking hands a different kind of revision of the dismembered limbs of the actual battlefield at Gettysburg twenty-five years earlier. The disembodied hands floating over the erstwhile pit of death and destruction are not signs of an irremediable break in the nation's story – a story in which enslavement plays a central role. Instead, they are bloodless, covering over the "bloody chasm," erasing the realities of who won and who lost the battle, what losses were sustained over three days, and what gains – primarily the end of slavery – were imagined to have been garnered from the battle and the war itself. As David Blight has argued, "the national reunion required a cessation of talk about causation and consequence, and therefore about race" (191).

To believe that there are "no victors, no vanquished" at Gettysburg, but only Americans who "may all claim a common share in the glories of this battlefield" argues against Lincoln's own interpretation of Gettysburg as the harbinger of "a new birth of freedom" for enslaved Americans in particular and the nation more generally. Indeed, I would argue that Sickles's "Americans" are defined by the fact of war itself – that the battle has become a kind of aesthetic, depoliticized artifact instead of a step on the ladder toward freedom. Gettysburg is disarticulated from its historical realities – not least that it turned the war toward Union victory – and by redefining it as only a place of military engagement between "Americans" (half of whom, after all, did not identify as such at the time), Sickles evacuates it of the meaning it was accorded at the moment it was fought and won by Union troops.

In their speeches, general after general metaphorically shakes hands over the bloody chasm. Most remarkably, as the earlier quotation suggests, Sickles entirely rewrites history to erase both the post-1862 consensus that the war was over the abolition of slavery, and the recent past of Reconstruction. He represents the war as a crucible for all soldiers and for the nation itself to remake itself through American (which is to say white) sacrifice:

> The war of 1861–5 was our heroic age. It demonstrated the vitality of republican institutions. It illustrated the martial spirit and resources and genius of the American soldier and sailor.... We fought until the furnace of war melted all our discords and molded us in one homogenous Nation. ("United at Gettysburg")

Of course, Sickles is wrong in almost every way here. The war's result was a more *heterogeneous* citizenry, Black and white, not a "more homogenous Nation." The very "discords" he points to were not simply sectional divisions but profound disagreements about the role of African-descended people in the United States, people who are rendered invisible by this compressing of history. Moreover, does "the American soldier and sailor" include or exclude the members of the Confederate Army? The Black recruits to Union regiments? These questions are implicitly answered by John P. Gordon, a commander of the Army of Northern Virginia, who also spoke at the ceremony on July 2. Like Sickles, Gordon focuses on the similarities between Union and Confederate soldiers and their work in reunifying the nation (not that there is any mention of why it was divided in the first place):

> We join you in setting apart this spot as an enduring monument of peace, brotherhood and perpetual union. I repeat the thought with additional emphasis, with a singleness of heart and of purpose, in the name of our common country and of universal human liberty, and by the blood of our fallen brothers we unite in solemn consecration of these battle-hallowed hills as holy eternal pledge of fidelity to the life, freedom and unity of this country. ("Gettysburg: A Continuation of the Celebration Yesterday")

Most noticeable here is the proliferation of synonyms for indivisibility: "join," "union," "singleness," "common," "universal," "unite," and

180   Manual Politics and the End of Reconstruction

"unity": seven words in two sentences (one admittedly fairly long). The unity of clasped hands is expanded to other parts of the body – "heart" and "blood" – and then to the whole country. Or, rather, the whole white country. For, as we've seen, the fantasy of wholeness is the fantasy of Black exclusion, so that Gordon can equate the elision of the story of Reconstruction with the "eternal pledge of fidelity to the life, freedom and unity of this country." Coming at a moment when the Black vote was already being suppressed and the Southern states were poised to impose Jim Crow laws throughout the region, Gordon's claim that the fields at Gettysburg are the sinecure of freedom rings particularly hollow.

In addition, Gordon's consecrating of the battlefields at Gettysburg implicitly invokes while it actively undermines Lincoln's act of consecration twenty-five years earlier. As Lincoln said in the Gettysburg Address, the only people who could consecrate the grounds of Gettysburg were the dead themselves and the "unfinished work" of liberty for which they fought and died. The handshakes that surround Sickles's and Gordon's speeches gesture toward the "last measure of devotion" of the dead, but in fact rewrite the story of liberation and sacrifice that Lincoln tells in the Gettysburg Address.

The 1888 reunion at Gettysburg came at a peculiar moment. African American lawmakers still served in local, regional, and national legislatures and in other elected offices, and the tsunami of segregation legislation had not yet swept the South. But we can see these shaking hands and the rhetoric that surrounded them as a portent of what was to come. The hands of white veterans were not just shaking over the bloody chasm of a battle whose carnage was especially brutal; they were cementing a pledge to forget the reasons for which the war was actually fought, and the Black Americans whose freedom was being steadily eroded.[12]

Ironically, Thomas Nast had foreseen some elements of this outcome twenty-four years prior, in his cartoon, "Compromise with the South: Dedicated to the Chicago Convention," which was published in *Harper's Weekly* on September 3, 1864 (Figure 5.9). Nast's cartoon comments on the Democratic party convention of that year, held in Chicago, in which the party negotiated a cease-fire with the Confederacy if their candidate George McLellan were to win the presidential election. There are marked differences between the cartoon, though, and the hearty handshakes of the Gettysburg reunion.

Nast's cartoon imagines a disastrous union between North and South: the centerpiece of the image is a gravestone dedicated to the "Memory of our Union Heroes who died in a Useless War," flanked by a Union and a

Figure 5.9 Thomas Nast, "Compromise with the South: Dedicated to the Chicago Convention." *Harper's Weekly* on September 3, 1864.

Confederate soldier shaking hands over it. The Northern soldier's head is bowed in shame and defeat; he leans on crutches, and his right leg is amputated above the knee. His hand is limp, almost grabbed by his Confederate counterpart. By contrast, the representative of the South stands tall, his chest puffed out in pride. The lower part of the Confederate soldier's body is surrounded by phallic substitutes – the sword hanging from his belt, the baton in his hand, the pistol that resembles an enormous erect penis pointing directly at his crotch. By contrast, the Union soldier's virility, represented by the sword on the grave mound, is snapped in two and beneath the Confederate's foot. At the gravestone the figure of Columbia weeps. And to behind the Confederate soldier kneels a Black family – a man, a woman, and a baby, remanded to permanent slavery.

In many ways, Nast was right about the fate of Black Americans if their well-being was left up to the Southern states. But he could not have predicted the terms under which Union and Confederate veterans would be shaking hands two and a half decades later. Rather than a scene of humiliation on the one side and victory on the other, the Gettysburg reunion recast the battle, and the war, as a shared victory for white veterans

182   Manual Politics and the End of Reconstruction

to claim the country as their own, sidelining the fragile gains made by freedpeople over the previous twenty years. These handshakes were not reluctant or forced, as is the handshake Nast's amputee Union soldier is forced into, but eager and fraternal, forging a new order of white nationhood.

"And what's the use of our ever fighting about anything in America?": *A Hazard of New Fortunes* and the Death of Reconstruction

I end this chapter by returning to the trope of amputation: a hand lost in the Civil War. Berthold Lindau, a German immigrant who lost a hand in the war, may be a minor character in William Dean Howells's 1890 novel *A Hazard of New Fortunes*, but he is the lightning rod for the implicit rewriting of the story of the antebellum period, the war, and Reconstruction, and his death toward the end of the novel provides an alibi for a disavowal of the impetus for the war itself.[13] Lindau's radicalism, a combined product of the European socialism of 1848, the abolitionist antiracism of the 1860s and '70s, and the anticapitalism of the Gilded Age, is redefined as irrational and even destructive in the context of post-Reconstruction, 1880s Gilded Age New York.

Intrinsic to this repudiation is a reworking of the notions of past, present, and future. Howells draws the reader's attention to this as Basil March, the main protagonist of the novel whose move from Boston to serve as the editor of a new magazine in New York sets the narrative in motion, takes the southbound train to set off on his new life:

> "So you see [he comments to his wife Isabel] how the foreground next the train rushes from us and the background keeps abreast of us, while the middle distance seems stationary?... There ought to be something literary in it; retreating past, and advancing future, and deceitfully permanent present." (35)

For March, and in *Hazard*, modernity requires the past always to retreat and the present to deceive not just in its fiction of permanence but also (and perhaps more importantly) in its substitution for the past. In *Hazard* the past is always in the process of being erased and rewritten even as the present subtly rearranges itself to accommodate the revised past and a future that enshrines that fictional past by materializing it in the present. This reworking of time is most evident in the character of Colonel Woodburn, a proudly unreconstructed Southern veteran of the Civil War, who moves to New York in part to peddle his narrative of an

A Hazard of New Fortunes *and Reconstruction* 183

idealized pastoral antebellum South replete with patriarchal enslavers and the contented enslaved.

Ironically, although Lindau looks forward to a socialist future and Woodburn is invested in a fictionalized past, the novel confuses, or even reverses, these phenomena, representing Woodburn as the voice of the future and Lindau as hopelessly mired in a utopian past.[14] This is in part because the novel conflates the past with the "deceitfully permanent present" and the future. When Woodburn suggests a series of articles about "responsible slavery," but laments that they would "hardly be acceptable to your commercialized society" (175), the magazine's publisher, Fulkerson agrees that "as a practical thing" the articles might not be a success, "'but as something retrospective, speculative, I believe it would make a hit'" (175). Fulkerson's musings make inextricable the past of slavery and the future of white supremacy in his pairing of two otherwise incompatible adjectives, "retrospective" and "speculative." If something looks back to the past, it cannot at the same time speculate about the future, unless this particular past is redefined *as* the future. Woodburn's anticapitalist pastoral representation of slavery as, at its best, "the mild patriarchalism of the divine intention" (152) is, in fact, the wave of the future for how Northern urbanites understood it from the late nineteenth century onward.[15]

This romanticization of the antebellum South is not limited to Woodburn. The Marches also participate in what had increasingly become the dominant narrative of the slavery. By the 1880s, as David Blight has shown, "the old-time plantation Negro became the voice through which a transforming revolution in race relations and the remaking of the republic dissolved into fantasy and took a long holiday in the public imagination" (221). The Marches unselfconsciously participate in this fantasy. After an interaction with a Black doorman during their lengthy apartment hunt, Isabel comments, "'I don't wonder they [white Southerners] wanted to own them [slaves].... If I had such a creature, nothing but death should part us, and I should no more think of giving him his *freedom* –'" (40). When Basil responds that "'we couldn't afford it,'" although whether he means to own a slave or to free one, is not clear, Isabel responds, "'It's true. I *am* in love with the whole race. I never saw one of them that didn't have perfectly angelic manners'"(42).

Lindau's radicalism disturbs the Marches' sense of themselves as on the right side of history, despite (or perhaps because of) Isabel's plantation-style "love" for "the whole race."[16] On the one hand, March sees Lindau as "the best and kindest man I ever saw, the most high-minded, the most generous. He lost a hand in the war that helped to save us and keep us possible, and that stump of his is character enough for me" (130). And Isabel March recognizes in principle that she should respect Lindau because of his amputation due to her "sense of his claim upon her sympathy and gratitude ... as a hero who had suffered for her country. Her theory was that his mutilation must not be ignored, but must be kept in mind as a monument for his sacrifice" (253). But ultimately, she finds him too radical, too outré, and, most importantly, too unwilling to stay in the past where she thinks he belongs: "what she really could not reconcile herself to was the violence of Lindau's sentiments concerning the whole political and social fabric" – his insistence that "American democracy [was] a shuffling evasion" or the Senate "a rich man's club" (253–4).

As Joseph Darda has argued, Lindau's arguments are too uncomfortably close to the truth. *A Hazard of New Fortunes* has trouble making up its mind about the validity of Lindau's radicalism, on the one hand, and the Marches' bourgeois complaisance, on the other. Certainly, they want (or they think they want) to honor his sacrifice, but not at the cost of recognizing the horrors of the world in which they live. Darda observes that "the sight of poor or disabled ex-soldiers reminded citizens of the precariousness of life in the United States, challenging the idea that success is fair recompense for bootstrap determination and, on the other hand, failure the result of idleness" (212).

Lindau challenges this easy opposition, since he chooses his failure – or at least what March reads as failure. When he comes across Lindau at his local haunt, a down-at-the-heels Italian restaurant downtown, March wonders at how far, to March's mind, Lindau has fallen:

> was this all that sweet, unselfish nature could come to? What a homeless old age at that meager Italian *table d'hôte*, with that tall glass of beer for a half-hour's oblivion! That shabby dress, that pathetic mutilation! He must have a pension, twelve dollars a month, or eighteen, from a grateful country. But what else did he eke out with? (83)

In fact, Lindau has refused a pension "'begause I would sgorn to dake money from a gofernment that I ton't pelief in anymore'" (276). For him, the past loss of his hand does not justify taking money from a state that still oppresses and exploits, indeed, that oppresses and exploits more than it did when the war was at its end. Lindau himself connects his lost hand not just to his commitment to abolition but also to the present gap between rich and poor that widened during the Gilded Age and to the possibility of a socialist future. Indeed, he denies that the loss of his hand is for the national benefit of elites and laments what freedom has brought:

A Hazard of New Fortunes *and Reconstruction*   185

"Do you think I knowingly gave my hand to save this oligarchy of traders and tricksters, this aristocracy of railroad wreckers and stock gamblers and mine slave drivers and mill serf owners? No; I gave it to the slave; the slave – Ha! Ha! Ha! whom I helped unshackle to the common liberty of hunger and cold." (167)

In this passage Lindau merges the past and the present, connecting his past commitment to antislavery with his present anticapitalism (ironically, he and Col. Woodburn are both serious anticapitalists but for very different reasons). His lost hand points toward not the past battle against slavery but the present and future struggle for workers' rights and political and economic equity. While the Marches consign the war and the cause of Black liberation to a vanished past that made the present moment possible, Lindau sees a direct connection between his radicalism twenty-five years earlier and his current campaign against robber baron capital. Moreover, he recognizes that times have changed from the early days of Reconstruction to the current moment, rife as it is with both racial and economic inequality. As Lindau says vis-à-vis refusing his pension,

"when the time gome dat dis iss a vree gountry again, then I dake a bension again for my woundts; but I would *sdarfe* before I dake a pension now from a rebublic dat is bought ap by monobolies andt ron by drusts and gompanies and railroadts andt oil gompanies!" (277)

While March is made profoundly uncomfortable by Lindau's refusal to disarticulate the past and the present, he also has trouble disagreeing with the argument. After a disastrous dinner party attended by March, the magazine's publisher Fulkerson, Lindau (who is translating articles for the magazine), and Dryfoos, the magazine's nouveau riche owner, Dryfoos calls Lindau "'a red-mouthed labor agitator'" who wants to "'ruin the country'" (301). Not only does March defend Lindau as someone who "'had once done his best to save the country,'" he skates dangerously close to Lindau's political logic:

"We could print a dozen articles praising the slavery it's impossible to have back, and it wouldn't hurt us. But if we printed one paper against the slavery which Lindau claims still exists, some people would call us bad names, and the counting room would begin to feel it." (310)

But for Basil March, ultimately this rhetoric is "tasteless," unfit for the world he wants to live in, in which "it was enough to provide well for his family; to have cultivated tastes and to gratify them to the extent of his means; to be rather distinguished, even, in the simplification of his desires" (24).

186 Manual Politics and the End of Reconstruction

March's bourgeois simplicity is at odds with Lindau's radical self-denial. In this, the gesture of Lindau's amputated hand is one of repudiation: of his task being done, of living with comfort in an uncomfortable world, even of a pension (we can think here of Lindau's absent, refusing hand as the diametric opposite of Gaetz's multiplying grabbing hands). Indeed, Lindau *chooses* to live on the Lower East Side rather than, as March assumes, having no other options, so as to live among the poor. Again, he puts himself squarely in the present: "'you must zee [poverty] all the dtime – zee it, hear it, smell it, dtaste it – or you forget it ... I was begoming a ploated aristocrat'" (165). These moments in the novel that are given over to Lindau's political views disrupt the calculation that *Hazard* struggles to establish, in which the slavery of the past effortlessly becomes the white supremacy of the present and future, and the radicalism of the present is cast back among the political relics of the past. But March resists that disruption. Ultimately, his "fantasies are less about honoring Lindau for Lindau's sake than about rehabilitating and silencing Lindau for his own personal relief" (Darda 213).

This conflict that March feels between his own desire for bourgeois comfort and his sense of obligation toward Lindau both for his past friendship and for Lindau's sacrifice in the war seems impossible to resolve. The very existence of Lindau as a character in the novel, however caricatured by his German accent and socialist fervor, unsettles the novel's insistence on the events of the Civil War and Reconstruction as artifacts of the past, and the twin phenomena of industrial capital (embodied by Dryfoos) and white Southern revanchism (represented by Woodburn) as the waves of the future. The only way to reconcile this fissure in the temporal narrative that March – and the novel – wants to tell is either to acknowledge Lindau's version of the relationship between past, present, and utopian future or to erase it and, by association, him.

It's no surprise that Howells chooses the latter path. And this road is eased for him by the character of Conrad Dryfoos, the idealistic son of the magazine's capitalist father. Where Lindau lives among the poor, lives *as* an impoverished man, Conrad is in the model of a bourgeois reformer who goes downtown to do good works. When he suggests that March's proposed series of sketches of life in New York might "do some good," and March agrees that he might "get something quite attractive out of it," Conrad argues for the series as an instrument of empathy and uplift:

> "If you can make the comfortable people understand how the uncomfortable people live, it will be a very good thing Mr. March. Sometimes it seems

A Hazard of New Fortunes *and Reconstruction*   187

to me that the only trouble is that we don't know one another well enough; and the first thing to do is this." (128)

This kind of approach to the problems of poverty and exploitation runs exactly counter to Lindau's philosophy. Indeed, it hearkens back to an earlier mode of aid to the poor, rooted in evangelical Protestant sentimentality.[17] We don't exactly know what it is that Conrad does when he is downtown in the tenements visiting the poor, but it would not be beyond the realm of imagination to identify him with mid-nineteenth-century tract visitors, who hoped to bring religious and moral uplift to an immiserated population.[18] The kind of discomfort Conrad suggests the comfortable submit themselves to is a moral, ethical, aesthetic kind of discomfort, not a material one. And once they feel this discomfort, it's not clear what the "comfortable people" are supposed to do with it to make actual change. Moreover, the Civil War itself proved that "the only trouble" was *not* that "we don't know one another well enough." It was represented, after all, as a war of brother against brother, friend against friend – a conflict between people who knew each other well but divided down ideological and regional lines.

Unlike Lindau, Conrad has not suffered meaningful loss, nor does he imagine actual sacrifice to help the poor of New York. His desire to help the poor is based in religious faith (he wanted to be a minister but his father put a stop to it), not political commitment. In the words of the artist Beaton, Conrad "goes among friendless people" (234), as a kind of missionary, trying to change one person's life at a time. As the novel observes,

> His ideals were of a virginal vagueness; faces, voices, gestures had filled his fancy at times, but almost passionately; and the sensation that he now indulged was a kind of worship, ardent, but reverent and exalted. The brutal experiences of the world make us forget that there are such natures in it, and that they seem to come up out of the lowly earth as well as down from the high heaven. In the heart of this man well on toward thirty there had never been left the stain of a base thought; not that suggestion and conjecture had not visited him, but that he had not entertained them, or in any-wise made them his. In a Catholic age and country, he would have been one of those monks who are sainted after death for the angelic purity of their lives, and whose names are invoked by believers in moments of trial. (303)

Once again, Conrad is identified with a (feminized) outdated sentimentalism, not to mention an archaic Catholic Church. He is untouched by the "brutal experiences of the world," cordoned off from the realities of the present. While Conrad is saintly, and wants to build "'the kingdom of heaven upon this earth, as well as in the skies'" (304), Lindau by contrast, is firmly of this world. The loss of his hand is a sign of his materiality, his being made of flesh and blood. Lindau's ideas are not of "virginal vagueness"; rather, he believes that the change that needs to be made is structural, a complete overhaul of economic and social relations akin to that attempted by Reconstruction, but for all working and poor people.

The apex of the differences between Conrad and Lindau comes in the context of a streetcar drivers' strike, which Conrad initially calls "foolish," given the other options for public transport in New York. He does in principle support the strikers' claims to underpayment and feels for them: "'I believe they have a righteous cause, though they go the wrong way to help themselves'" (365). A chance meeting with Margaret Vance, an equally saintly (and wealthy, although better connected) young woman with whom Conrad is secretly in love, strengthens his resolve. In their discussion of the strike, Margaret echoes both Conrad's sympathy for the strikers and his sense that he should personally intervene in their situation:

> "Don't you think that if someone went among them and tried to make them see how perfectly hopeless it was to resist the companies and drive off the new men [i.e., scabs], he might do some good?" (366)

Conrad is wholly convinced by this argument and strides off toward a streetcar line, where he encounters "a tumult of shouting, cursing, struggling men" (368). In the melee, Conrad sees both strikers throwing bricks and stones, and policemen clubbing the strikers: "the blows on their skulls sounded as if they had fallen on stone; the rioters ran in all directions" (368). On the sidelines is Lindau, berating the police, one of whom "whirled his club, and the old man threw his left arm up to shield his head. Conrad recognized Lindau, and now he saw the empty sleeve dangle in the air, over the stump of the wrist" (368). At that very moment, Conrad is shot in the chest (by whom it isn't clear) and killed.

This climactic scene (although not the end of the novel, which goes on for another thirty pages) is a kind of confrontation between Lindau's method and Conrad's, and between past and present. Lindau links the police violence to the power of corporations, asking, "[W]hy don't you co and glub [club] the bresidents that insoalt your laws, and gick your Boart of Arpidration out of toors?" (368). At the same time he accuses them of corruption: "Glup the strikers – they cot no friendts! They cot no money to pribe you, to dreat you!" (368). As Lindau is being beaten by the police, Conrad drops dead beside him, without a word. His last impulse before he falls is to defend Lindau in the same terms he was initially described by March: "He was going to say to the policeman, 'Don't' strike him! He's an old soldier! You see he has no hand!'" (368), but he is unable to speak,

Here Conrad returns us again to the image of Lindau as an artifact of the past even as Lindau is embroiled in that present moment. It's not surprising that Howells kills Conrad off, given his own well-documented (not least by himself) distaste for the sentimentalism of the previous generation and his embrace of the present moment as the ideal subject of American literature. But it is ironic that Conrad, a young man of not even thirty, invokes the past, both in his own ideological and idealistic world view and in how he imagines Lindau, while Lindau, at least in his sixties, embraces that very moment of conflict that Conrad wants to disrupt. In the end, they both suffer the same fate: Lindau's left arm is so badly injured that it must be amputated, and shortly afterward he dies.

While Conrad Dryfoos's death is represented in the novel as "tragic happenstance, distinctly the chance of life and death," as March frames it (380), Lindau's is represented as ambiguous at best. It occurs offstage – the last time we see him, Howells's description runs counter to the persona Lindau constructed for himself: "Lindau's grand, patriarchal head, fore-shortened to their view, lay white upon the pillow, and his broad white beard flowed out over the sheet, which heaved with those long last breaths" (386). Lindau, who in life gave of himself to break down hierarchies, is here described as a patriarch, and his dying body is aestheticized. Most importantly, the sign of his final sacrifice, the loss of his arm, is hidden from view. The hand that is visible is clasped by Margaret Vance, who kneels by his side, praying – what feels like grace to her but is a betrayal of his own atheism. In death, then, Lindau is transformed from amputee radical to shrouded patriarch, from activist atheist to the subject of prayer – like the losses of the Civil War he is contained, whitened, domesticated, and made palatable for a late nineteenth-century white readership.

But only so palatable. When Tom March asks his father, "I suppose, Papa, that Mr. Lindau dies in a bad cause?" March responds:

> "Why, yes . . ., he died in the cause of disorder; he was trying to obstruct the law. No doubt there was a wrong there, an inconsistency and an injustice he felt keenly, but it could not be reached in his way without greater wrong." (392)

Lindau's dying for a "bad cause" – the uprising of the overworked and underpaid – is particularly striking, given that only pages earlier March characterizes Conrad as having "died in a good cause" as "a peacemaker"

(375). Of course, that is not how or why he dies. Rather, the "cause" for which he dies – ostensibly stepping in to help Lindau – is represented as a kind of emblem of the past simultaneously created by and memorialized in the present. It is an image of the past that sentimentalizes the costs of amputation rather than seeing its connection to the current moment, and the kinds of disfranchisement that Lindau opposes with his body.

March's response to Tom is also a repudiation of Lindau's raison d'être – his radical ideology and methodology. This kind of conservatism masquerading as rationality leads Tom to a conclusion that implicitly disavows the work of the Civil War: "'And what's the use of or our ever fighting about anything in America?'" (392). What indeed? Especially since Tom's follow-up to this thought is "'I always thought we could vote anything we wanted,'" as though the vote was equally and fairly distributed (392). In this exchange, March erases the role that violence did play in liberating the enslaved and in actually granting the votes that by the time the novel appeared in 1890 were being eroded by law, custom, and vigilantism.

In this interaction, Tom replaces Lindau's lost hand, the result of the fighting that *did* have a use, with the hand that writes on a ballot. As we saw in *What Answer?*, that hand's whiteness is enforced with violence both north and south. More importantly, though, Tom and his father throw up their hands in the sight of real action to make change, action in which Lindau has participated in the past and the present.

Decades after the fighting stopped, veterans' hands stood, in many ways, for the meanings of the Civil War. For Democrats, they were plunged deep into the public trough, using the past fact of their service to defraud present government funds. For radicals (of a sort) like Thomas Nast, they were still engaged in the complicated work of Reconstruction and political struggle, fending off (increasingly in vain) the depredations of Southern home rule and national white vigilante justice.[19]

It's Howells, though, who most accurately prophesies what will happen to the veteran's hand, whether amputated, morphed, or multiplied. It will die, alongside the possibility of radical change, in the "bad cause" of social equality.

Conclusion
Eloquent Emptiness

On August 17, 2017, in response to the removal of statues commemorating Confederate forces in the Civil War (both leaders and ordinary soldiers), then-President Donald Trump tweeted, "Sad to see the history and culture of our great country being ripped apart with the removal of our beautiful statues and monuments . . . the beauty that is being taken out of our cities, towns and parks will be greatly missed and never able to be comparably replaced!" (Alexander).

In many ways, Trump was more correct than he knew. While the country was not being ripped apart, something was being excised, amputated, that could not be replaced, at least not in the same way. The removal of Confederate monuments, starting in 2017 and continuing to the current moment, was part of a movement that was galvanized by anti-Black violence (the murder by white supremacist Dylann Roof of nine members of the Emmanuel AME Church in Charleston, South Carolina, in June 2015, the "Unite the Right" white supremacist rally and march of August 2017, and the killing by white Minneapolis police officer Derek Chauvin of George Floyd in May 2020). But that movement, which crystallized in large part – although not exclusively – around the banner of Black Lives Matter, was not merely reactive. It recognized the political power of subtraction and absence, a process that began a few years earlier, with Bree Newsome Bass's removal of the Confederate battle flag from outside the South Carolina state house. As Erin L. Thompson observed in an interview with the *New York Times* in June 2020, the call to removal Confederate monuments was "attacking symbols of a hateful past as part of fighting for a peaceful future" (Bromwich).

Objections to removing these monuments also invoked the relationship between past and future often, claiming that only in the presence of this "hateful past" could Americans (which implicitly meant white Americans) truly understand the history of what the sculptures commemorated. Brandon Walker, writing in a signed editorial in the Brigham Young

University *Scroll* on June 26, 2020, argued that a racially just future depended on retaining the monuments: "In order to change the future for all, we must first look at the mistakes of the past and learn valuable lessons. We learn through what we see. That which we cannot see, we often don't remember." Similarly, in a June 11, 2017, editorial in the *Atlanta Journal-Constitution*, responding to New Orleans Mayor Mitch Landrieu's official removal of the city's statue of Robert E. Lee, Barry D. Wood claimed that "[t]he campaign to cleanse the South of Confederate monuments is itself a whitewashing of history" for two reasons. First, the installation of the Lee statue was viewed at the time as a national rather than sectional event, "attended by Union veterans [who] joined with those who served under Lee . . . The theme was reconciliation and national unity." Second, Wood argued that agitating for the removal of Confederate statuary was itself a sign of bad faith and denied the fact of "the sad reality . . . that both North and South were racist in the latter 19th century" (Wood).

In more explicitly right-wing media, the critique became sharper. In the "conservative and libertarian" blog *Bacon's Rebellion*, based in Virginia, the removal of Confederate monuments in Richmond sparked a column by Jock Yellott, a lawyer who had successfully sued the City of Richmond in 2017 to forestall statue removal. Yellott struck a melancholic tone in his column, entitled "The Battle over History Never Ceases." Focusing on the absence of the statues that formerly towered over Richmond's Monument Avenue and other civic spaces, he lamented that "[i]n the parks the emptiness itself is eloquent, speaks in a sad way." Much like Walker and Wood, Yellott advocated for the pedagogical value of Confederate statuary, but to quite a different purpose: "The space should be contextualized as a cautionary tale, of what happens when the censorious Woke censor history" (Yellott n.p.).

Similarly, in the religiously oriented (although ecumenical) journal *First Things*, Wilfred M. McClay, a historian at the University of Oklahoma, sees the removal of statues as an unalloyed wrong, "acts of unmitigated hate, a blind and abstract hatred devoid of any impulse of charity toward others." Not considering how the installation of these statues might have itself been an act devoid of any impulse of charity toward African Americans, especially the formerly enslaved, McClay focuses on the trauma of absence, in which "[t]earing [a statue] down leaves only an empty place."

These arguments all take different tacks, from the most conciliatory (we need Confederate monuments so we can remember how terrible the past

Conclusion 193

was) to the more challenging (hypocritical Northerners shouldn't be let off the hook so easily for nineteenth-century white racism) to the outraged (the absence of the statues reminds us of the tyranny of "wokeness" and is itself an act of hatred). But they all make similar rhetorical moves about the relationship of absence to past, to present, and to future. For Walker, Wood, and Yellott, these monuments are about the Civil War itself rather than the circumstances of their installation (indeed, Wood complains that Landrieu's "action dishonors the 289,000 dead Confederate soldiers" and their descendants), let alone the accretion of history that has orbited around them over the course of the twentieth and twenty-first centuries or what they signify in the present. The past that these writers invoke is one shrouded in sentiment and the residuum of the discourse of the Lost Cause, a discourse that the creators and initial funders of these monuments hoped to cement with the installation of commemorative sculpture.

Of course, these appeals to the importance of history are themselves profoundly ahistorical. After all, the bulk of Confederate monuments, especially those in shared public spaces rather than cemeteries, were erected between 1910 and 1920, not immediately after the war. Moreover, Confederate monuments communicated in metal and stone white supremacy's will to rewrite the past in order to secure the future. As Cassandra Jackson shows, they constituted a "plan for the future" (192). One example she cites in Clarendon, South Carolina, is inscribed "Unconquered in defeat; Undismayed in divine faith; Undiscouraged in hope for the future; Untiring in rebuilding" (193). This is the post-Reconstruction manifesto in a nutshell, the direct inverse of the rhetoric of amputation I have been exploring throughout this book: loss is not loss, the past is the future, rebuilding is not Reconstruction.

Contemporary support for maintaining Confederate statuary has used this unspoken manifesto as a launching pad, especially in white suprema-cist circles. As Danielle Christmas argues, for white nationalists, the past as represented by these monuments is a sinecure for the future, and removal is a harbinger of "white cultural and biological erasure" (106). What she calls "heritage politics" may be "dressed up in the cloak of regional pride and southern sentimentality" but is in fact underwritten by fear: "what is the future of history if eliminating Confederate monuments is one step on a path to exterminating white people?" (107).

By saying the quiet part out loud, white nationalists actually get close to the heart of what is at stake in amputating Confederate statuary from the shared landscape: not the extermination of white people, but a step toward the destruction of whiteness as it now exists, a legacy of slavery and Jim

194 Conclusion

Crow. Confederate monuments aimed not just to threaten Black autonomy – although that was certainly part of the plan – but to *normalize* white domination and the rewriting of history. In Brook Thomas's words, "a monument exists in the present. The significance of a public monument that people see every day is not confined to the moment of its dedication" (23). Or as J. David Maxson observes in his analysis of the New Orleans removals, "the all-but-inescapable repetitiveness of traversing beneath Jim Crow–era monuments served to engrain Lost Cause memorial attitudes into the fabric of everyday movement in New Orleans" (52).[1] Public disassembling of these memorials resists that normalization, and "collective faith in the longevity of messages transmitted by memorial architecture is challenged by the sensational demolition of prominent monuments" (Maxson 50).

These messages were forged into the very material of Confederate statuary. We can remember Anna Dickinson's experience in the Virginia statehouse in Richmond in 1875: portraits of "Lee, Lee, Lee in every shape and form" (*A Tour* 41), as though the Black legislators serving Virginia had no purchase on the history of the Civil War and what came before it.[2] Richmond was an exception, however: most Confederate memorials erected in the years directly after the war were limited to cemeteries and battlefields. As Kirk Savage points out, this "symbolically placed distance between [Southerners'] daily lives and the lost cause. Memorial activities thereby helped the South assimilate the fact of defeat without repudiating the defeated" (45).

While Robert E. Lee was already the subject of statuary in the 1880s,[3] the death of Jefferson Davis in 1889 inaugurated a new phase in Confederate memory, not least because, as we have seen in Chapter 5, white Americans nationally were increasingly focused on sectional reconciliation. The apotheosis of both Lee and Davis in the national imaginary allowed Southerners "the resurrection of memories of the past that ... could be cherished without disloyalty to a reunited nation" (G. Foster 96). Indeed, a muscular appreciation of the values of the "Old South" seemed to be a prerequisite to national belonging across the nation.

Organizations like the Sons of Confederate Veterans and especially the United Daughters of the Confederacy embarked on a decades-long campaign to install memorial statuary throughout the South (including in Arlington Cemetery) as "vindication for the Confederate generation" (Cox 3). But the UDC in particular imagined their mission as pointed toward the future as much as the past, to instill Confederate values "among future generations of white southerners," spearheading the funding, construction,

Conclusion 195

and installation of Confederate monuments as well as exerting increasing control over Southern history textbooks, to create a 360-degree revisionist history for white children in the region (Cox 32).[4]

The UDC had an enormous reach and made Confederate monuments "a centerpiece of the Lost Cause movement" (O'Connell 1481). But while they provided the funding and impetus for erecting Confederate memorials, the UDC needed public buy-in, which was more available at some sites than others. It is no coincidence that the presence of a public Confederate statue tracks with the historic and ongoing wealth disparity between Black and white in any given Southern county: the greater the gap, the more likely it is that the county has a monument (O'Connell 1497). Moreover, these monuments were implicitly (and sometimes explicitly) agents of what Koritha Mitchell has called "know-your-place aggression" toward African Americans (2). Heather O'Connell tracked the histories of the hundreds of Confederate monuments throughout the South and found that more than a third were constructed in the decade from 1900 to 1910, with another 20 percent installed between 1910 and 1920, a period that coincided with increased repression of Black people in the South.[5] As she observed, "the racial hierarchy of a county is among the most dominant factors explaining Confederate monument construction" during these years (1480). While the majority were erected in the Southeast, over the years, and especially in the 1950s onward, the location of these monuments moved west toward Texas, and "the concentration of enslaved people in 1860 [was] the strongest explanatory factor [for selection of a site], second only to the presence of a UDC chapter" (1491).

This is a thick and chunky stew of anti-Black racism, white supremacy, nostalgia for the antebellum period, and denial/romanticization of enslavement, all of the factors that characterized the post-Reconstruction period. It also gestures toward the fantasy of a certain kind of wholeness, in which white Southern mythology has national purchase, and the racialized and social positionality of white and Black Americans is seen as, in effect, uninterrupted from the days of enslavement to the moment in which these monuments were erected, and on into the future. Such a fantasy explains why Confederate statuary was still being installed in the 1960s (and in fact in higher numbers than the previous two decades), as a way to symbolically beat back the change wrought by the Civil Rights Movement.

This logic was especially acute in the context of statues of Robert E. Lee, whose reputation as a nonideological military genius who fought for the Confederacy out of sectional loyalty rather than political affiliation made him both the object of the greatest post-Reconstruction worship and the easiest figure to bring together Northern and Southern whites at the cost of African American freedoms. As Kirk Savage argues, "the legitimation of Lee after the war helped re-establish old lines of [white] racial sympathy ... If Lee was no longer traitor, no longer 'other,' otherness was left to reside in the emancipated slaves and their descendants who did not forget that the Confederacy with Lee at its head had fought to keep them in bondage" (132).

The fantasy of uninterrupted wholeness that Reconstruction radicals countered, and that became ascendant after 1880, the fantasy that nothing had changed from the past nor need change in the future, was undeniably disrupted by the movement to bring down Confederate memorials: both the Confederate battle flag and then the monuments themselves. We can see Bree Newsome Bass's physical removal of the Confederate flag from its perch in front of the South Carolina capitol building as a symbolic amputation of the normalization of white supremacist imagery, and the sight of the empty flagpole as itself telling a story of resistance to anti-Black racism (see Mzezwa). As with the trope of the amputee, absence has radical resonances, insisting on loss as the first step in the process of political reparation toward Black Americans in general and Black Southerners in particular.

It is this absence that Jock Yellott laments in his *Bacon's Rebellion* blog post. For Yellott, "the emptiness itself is eloquent, speaks in a sad way." And for him it is sad – a symbol of active resistance to white supremacist historiography and the normalization of the suppression of African Americans. I would argue, however, that this emptiness is eloquent in productive, generative ways: that the amputation of Civil War monuments from public space acknowledges the sins of the past and the exigencies of the present, and opens up the possibility for a different kind of future, one that refuses quotidian reminders of white dominance.

Lisa M. Perhamus and Clarence Joldersma, educational philosophers, zero in on this potential in their analysis of the meanings of the removal of Confederate monuments. For them, the damage to or removal or destruction of a monument interrupts white supremacy's presence, and "this interruption is a form of anti-racist critical public pedagogy" (1316). Physically pulling down statues or covering them in graffiti is a productive practice that educates viewers in ways of seeing that run counter to the visual narrative that the statues themselves communicate. That is, the absence of a statue is not the same as the statue's never having been there: its amputation from the civic landscape tells the story of resistance to white supremacist versions of history that come down from organizations like the

Conclusion 197

United Daughters of the Confederacy, who were often behind the installation of the monument in the first place.

New Orleans was the first major Southern city to take down Confederate monuments: the city authorized removal of four statues between April 26 and May 19, 2017. Unlike the removals in Memphis and Richmond, these actions were taken before (and in part led to) the "Unite the Right" rally in Charlottesville on August 11 and 12 of the same year. Although there had been an ongoing debate for decades in New Orleans, spearheaded by Black leadership, to decommission Confederate monuments, the murders in the Emmanuel AME church in 2015 created the conditions of possibility to enact change.

Take 'Em Down Nola (TEDN), a Black-led, multiracial organization that had been active since 2015, was the public face of the movement to remove Confederate monuments (as well as a statue of Andrew Jackson) from the streets of New Orleans. The group took a broad socialist, antiracist, antihomophobic, and feminist stance, and rooted its politics in the "demand that the city government finally begin the real work of reckoning with the WHOLE truth of white supremacy in New Orleans" (www.takeemdownnola.org/why-it-matters). The New Orleans city council voted 6-1 in favor of removing four monuments, including one that commemorated the 1874 Battle of Liberty Place, initiated by a mob led by the White League (and that resulted in the violent overthrow of the administration of then-governor William Pitt Kellogg, although he was reinstated by President Grant a few days later).[6]

The formal removal of the monuments, marked by a speech by then-mayor Mitch Landrieu, was followed several days later by a ceremonial "Second Line to Bury White Supremacy" organized by TEDN: an enactment of a funerary ritual that in part defines New Orleans. As J. David Maxson, who has written in detail about the event, says, "New Orleans' communities of color have historically used mock funerals, brass band music, and public parades to resist structures of white supremacy by performatively reclaiming urban space and promoting local practices of memory" (59), and jazz funerals, which parade down city streets replete with a band (the first line) and a line of followers (the second line), are a major element of this history of resistance. Most importantly for my analysis, second lines are funeral processions without the presence of the corpse.

The Second Line to Bury White Supremacy used the occasion of symbolic and material amputation and subtraction to engage a recognition of the past, an understanding of the present, and an aspiration for the future. Crucially, the Second Line began in Congo Square, the locale most associated with Black New Orleanians' African heritage, processed around the former sites of Confederate monuments, and ended at the former site of a statue of Robert E. Lee. The absence of these monuments was the point of the second line: just as routine funeral second lines note the passing of a life with the body in absentia, this procession celebrated the subtraction of these images from civic space. Moreover, this second line articulated a future in which white supremacy would be excised from the body politic. As J. David Maxson observes, "Take 'Em Down Nola argued that white supremacist monuments . . . are inherently violent and that Lost Cause practices of memory must be replaced, but not forgotten" (59).

A few months later, another antiracist organization, Take 'Em Down 901 in Memphis (901 is the Memphis area code), won a similar victory with the removal of the statues of Nathan Bedford Forrest, a lieutenant general in the Confederate Army best known as the founder of the Ku Klux Klan in the 1870s, and Jefferson Davis. Both statues were erected for explicitly white supremacist purposes: the Forrest monument was installed in 1904, just over a decade after Ida B. Wells published her exposé of an 1892 lynching in the city, which resulted in the offices of her newspaper, the *Free Speech*, being ransacked and burned down. The Davis statue was set up in 1964, in the midst of major civil rights organizing in the city.

Beginning in June 2017, Take 'Em Down 901 held weekly protests in the park that housed the Forrest statue. Because a Tennessee statute, the Tennessee Heritage Protection Act of 2013 (revised in 2016), forbade Memphis from removing any historical monuments, the city sold the parks in which both statues stood to nonprofit organizations, which, as private groups, were not bound by the law (Morris). On December 20, 2017, at 9:01 pm, the Forrest and Davis statues were lifted by cranes off their pedestals (Figure C.1).

This image, captured by CBS news, is emblematic of the discursive – even kinetic – power of the removal of Confederate monuments. The space between the statue of Jefferson Davis, bound by yellow cords and raised by machinery, and the pedestal on which it once stood vibrates with energy. We witness the moment of amputation, the moment in which loss is rendered vibrant, generative, and reparative.

Through these narratives we can see that amputation as a trope for antiracist radicalism endures to the present day. However, rather than affecting the bodies of Northern soldiers, this amputation is directed at the sources of enslavement and oppression: the symbols of the

Conclusion

Figure C.1 Robert E. Lee statue being removed in Memphis, TN.
Courtesy of CBS News.

Confederacy itself. It's no coincidence, I would argue, that so many images exist of the bare pedestals from which these monuments have been removed.

The most photographed image is the one shown in Figure C.2, taken by Steve Helber of the Associated Press. It shows the elaborate pedestal that once supported the statue of Robert E. Lee on Monument Avenue in Richmond, Virginia.[7] The pedestal resembles the stump of a limb, the space above it evoking the former presence of the statue. But this stump does not just speak for itself. It has been written on hundreds, maybe thousands, of times by demonstrators with slogans such as "How Much More Blood?," "Fuck Racism Stop White/Supremacy," "Justice for Floyd," and "Black Lives Matter" (as well as more pedestrian graffiti).

These inscriptions act as a palimpsest: one can still see the ornate curlicues and other sculptural details underneath the slogans, which creates a layered history of post-Reconstruction, post–Civil Rights, and post–Black Lives Matter Richmond, the ongoing struggle between white supremacy and antiracism. Much like during Reconstruction, they capture the possibility of a moment in which voices against anti-Black racism came to the fore, challenging disparate and disproportional state power over

Figure C.2 Steve Helber, "Pedestal that once held a statue of Robert E. Lee, Richmond, VA."
The Associated Press.

Black bodies. And like an amputated limb, these statues cannot be put back together again. The empty pedestals articulate a complex past that moves far beyond claims to "history" and "heritage," and invoke a polyphonic multiracial present.

Of course, this raises a pressing and vexing question: What of the future? The backlash to Black Lives Matter has been swift, and in many states even teaching about the past that brought these statues into being is prohibited. Despite – or, more likely, because of – Take 'Em Down 901's successes, Tennessee's SB263 forbids teaching any material that might make a student "feel discomfort, guilt, anguish, or another form of psychological distress solely because of the individual's race or sex," as though any negative feeling about the white supremacy that has characterized the United States since its inception trumps the pedagogical value of learning a full and complicated history of the nation. Moreover, this language calls into being an unperturbed nation, untroubled by its racist past, dedicated at all costs to leave white Americans, especially children, unruffled by the divisions, ruptures, violences, and struggles for justice that have characterized US history. These kinds of laws are a soft echo of the

Conclusion 201

inexorable drag away from Reconstruction-era reform and the ultimate instantiation of Lost Cause historiography throughout not just the South, but the whole nation.

Even with their faults and lacunae, nineteenth-century radicals like Thaddeus Stevens, Anna Dickinson, and Albion Tourgée provide historical examples of how white activists can work in cross-racial coalitions and support Black-led activism dedicated to antiracist justice. I would hope that we can avoid the depredations of the post-Reconstruction romance of the Lost Cause and regroup to fight back against the seemingly evergreen fantasy of national wholeness that always comes at the cost of Black lives. A more perfect union is not one that is free of fracturing or loss, after all. It is one that recognizes the generative power that emerges out of the excision of the infection of white supremacy, a nation that maintains an expansive view of past, present, and future: an amputation nation.

Notes

Introduction

1 See, for example, Megan Kate Nelson, *Ruin Nation*; Miller, *Empty Sleeves*; Jordan, "'Living Monuments.'"

2 And it's still used as a metaphor today. In his 2021 book, *Failed Promise: Reconstruction, Frederick Douglass, and the Impeachment of Andrew Johnson*, Robert S. Levine characterizes Johnson's goal as President "to restore the ex-Confederate states to the national body" (xiv). This was exactly what radical Reconstructionists wanted to avoid, insisting that the amputation of enslavement was essential to the rebuilding of a new kind of nation, what Eric Foner has called a "second founding."

3 Following Cody Marrs, I would argue that abolitionists both Black and white saw Reconstruction as of a piece with their activism in the prewar years and support for Union forces during the Civil War (even those, like William Lloyd Garrison and Wendell Phillips, who had previously denounced the nation as irrevocably marked by slavery). For them, the war was not "a triumphal end point and moral cleansing of the republic" and Reconstruction was "part of the Long Civil War and the struggle for emancipation out of which it evolved" (Marrs 414).

4 For a few of the many discussions of the significance of "cripping" as a political, theoretical, and discursive tool, see Robert McRuer, *Crip Theory*; Alison Kafer, *Feminist, Queer, Crip*; Tobin Siebers, *Disability Aesthetics*; Julia Miele Rodas, *Autistic Disturbances*.

5 The abandonment of formerly enslaved people to white supremacist violence took barely ten years to develop. As David Blight shows, by 1875, "the will for federal intervention to stop violence and intimidation by 'white liners' against blacks and white Republicans had all but vanished" (135).

6 In *Untimely Democracy: The Politics of Progress after Slavery*, Greg Laski makes a compelling argument for the conceptual traps embedded in the language of democratic progress, especially in terms of antiracist change. While Laski is primarily addressing the phenomenon of Black literary production toward the end of the nineteenth century, his point is well taken vis-à-vis the immediate postwar period as well.

Notes to pages 8–14 203

7 This language was echoed by W. E. B. DuBois in *Black Reconstruction*, speaking in the voice of a self-emancipated slave: "I have been owned like an ox. I stole my own body and now I am hunted by law and lash to be made an ox again" (16).

8 The assertion of God's justice underwriting the work of Reconstruction finds its obverse in Harper's poem in the same volume, "An Appeal to the American People." In this poem, Harper speaks directly to white Americans, reminding them of the loyalty, generosity, courage, and self-sacrifice of African Americans during the war, and pointing out the irony of "the traitor," [s]cowling 'neath his brow of hate . . . / Asking you to weakly yield / All we won upon the field . . . / And to write above our slain / 'They have fought and died in vain.'" Where the elegy to Stevens ends with the triumph of the utopian vision of Reconstruction, "An Appeal to the American People" admonishes its addressees that they should reject this alternate trajectory "[l]est the traitor's iron heel / Grind and trample in the dust / All our new-born hope and trust, / And the name of freedom be / Linked with bitter mockery" (168).

9 By the end of the war, about 180,000, or over one-fifth of Black men under forty-five, served in the Union Army. About 40,000 died, three-quarters of those from disease or infection (Foner 8).

10 Stevens's metaphor of the house was not, one imagines, accidental, but rather invoked Lincoln's house divided.

11 In his Yale commencement speech, Horace Bushnell spelled this out. The Revolutionary War had not generated enough carnage to adequately form an ideal Union since the "sacrifices in the fields of the Revolution united us but imperfectly. We had not bled enough to merge our colonial distinctions, and let out the State-rights doctrine, and make us a proper nation" ("Our Obligations" 326).

12 Needless to say, this binary was less of an issue for Southern Blacks, who demanded justice in the form of land, fair and humane working conditions (including contracted labor), the franchise, and education. It also did not nag at the consciences of many Southern whites, who frequently resorted to one-on-one and/or mob violence against freedpeople, in response to what they saw as insolence and overreach. For a discussion of white anti-Black violence during Reconstruction, see George C. Rable's 1984 history, *But There Was No Peace: The Role of Violence in the Politics of Reconstruction.*

13 Blum overstates here in using the phrase "people of color." White Northerners were motivated to extend the franchise to Black citizens, but, as I show below, most were strongly opposed to expand that right to Chinese Americans or Indigenous people, or to afford Asian immigrants the same rights to naturalization that their European counterparts enjoyed.

14 Even as Reconstruction was dismantled after 1877, radicals still deployed this trope. In 1887, after Grover Cleveland directed the Secretary of War to return all captured Confederate flags to their states of origin, Wisconsin Lucius Fairchild – himself an amputee who lost his left arm at Gettysburg – invoked

the language of disease as a function of reconciliation at the expense of the principles of radical Reconstruction. In a speech to the Grand Army of the Republic, a powerful veterans' organization of which he served as commander-in-chief, Fairchild condemned Cleveland: "May God palsy the hand that wrote the order! May God palsy the brain that conceived it! And may God palsy the tongue that dictated it!" (Ross 207).

15 Laurann Figg and Jane Farrell-Beck provide more granular information about the incidence of different kinds of amputation among Union soldiers: the highest number of amputations were of fingers and/or hands (7,902), which also led to the lowest fatalities. The next most common was amputations of the leg at the thigh (6,369), but the resulting mortality rates were much higher, at over 50 percent (459).

16 See, for example, Frances Clarke, "'Honorable Scars': Northern Amputees and the Meaning of Civil War Injuries," in *Union Soldiers and the Northern Home Front: Wartime Experiences, Postwar Adjustments*, edited by Paul A. Cimbala and Randall M. Miller; David Serlin, *Replaceable You: Engineering the Body in Postwar America*; Colleen Glenney Boggs, "The Civil War's 'Empty Sleeve' and the Cultural Production of Disabled Americans," *J19* 3, no. 1; Allison M. Johnson, *The Scars We Carve: Bodies and Wounds in Civil War Print Culture*.

17 The lyrics of one version were written by Fanny Crosby, the "Blind Poetess," who was a prolific hymnist. Also known as "the Queen of Gospel Song Writers," Crosby wrote over 8,000 hymns, including the perennial favorite "Blessed Assurance." Crosby also published more than a thousand secular poems, earning her the sobriquet "the Blind Poetess." For more information about Crosby, see Edith L. Blumhofer, *Her Heart Can See: The Hymns and Life of Fanny J. Crosby* (Grand Rapids, MI: William Eerdmans, 2005).

18 Both Allison Johnson and Brian Matthew Jordan have written about Bourne and his Left Armed Corps, and Johnson has contributed greatly to the scholarly conversation about this phenomenon with her edited collection of writings from the penmanship competition, *The Left-Armed Corps*.

19 Some writers went even further in their defense of Black Americans. In his competition entry, Iowa Volunteer Infantry first lieutenant William Miller Decamp penned an extended manifesto on Black equality, concluding, "Will any sane man, pretend to say, that [a corrupt and sinful] white man is superior to an honest and well behaved black man? In what respect superior? The idea is absurd! In short, the unkind feeling against the black man is a selfish, ignorant, and vulgar prejudice, the offspring of a narrow, contracted, and ungenerous mind" (qtd. in Johnson, *Left-Armed Corps* 279–80). Decamp goes on to declare that although racially mixed marriages were "not in accordance with my taste," who chooses to marry whom was "simply none of my business; *nor is it any other man's business*" (280). Ultimately, Decamp avers that "it now only remains that the Freedman be endowed with all his Natural rights: Life, Liberty, and the pursuit of Happiness (including the right of Suffrage), as justly set forth in the Declaration of Independence" (281).

Notes to pages 22–25 205

20 The newly emancipated were not the only group whose status as citizens was debated. There was much discussion of the legal status of members of the former Confederacy: Were they still US citizens, albeit former insurrectionists (or, in the radical view, traitors), members of a defeated enemy state, or stateless people who needed to be granted US citizenship?

21 As Leon Litwack chronicles, from the very beginnings of the republic, Black men were excluded by the federal government from serving in militias or carrying the mails, and although they were initially barred from serving in the armed services, the military needs of the War of 1812 countermanded that decree (31–2). Black applicants were generally denied passports, which would acknowledge formal citizenship (54–5). And, of course, Roger Taney's majority decision in *Dred Scott* had the last word on formal citizenship of the United States. In addition to these federal practices, most free Northern Black people were, like their white counterparts, ruled primarily by state and local regulation. Some states and territories prohibited Black immigration, and although the laws were sporadically enforced, they could always be called up to harass Black migrants (Litwack 72). As unpropertied white men gained the franchise throughout the Northeastern and mid-Atlantic states, Black men's ability to vote was increasingly diminished, and even though there was equal right to the franchise in New England, it was honored as much in the breach as in the observance. Only Massachusetts formally allowed Black jurors, but again, that was usually ignored, and Black people were rarely allowed to testify in court as witnesses (Litwack 94).

22 A study by the Pew Research Center surveyed Americans across the racial spectrum about their support for the Black Lives Matter movement first in June 2020, at the height of political protests spurred by the deaths of George Floyd and Breanna Taylor and then again in September 2020. In September, while a majority of American adults still supported the movement (55 percent), that number was a decrease from the June figure of 67 percent. When the PRC divided results by race, the differences were starker. While 60 percent of white Americans expressed at least some support for the movement in June 2020, only 45 percent reported the same level of support in September of the same year (which is to say that a quarter of supporters changed their minds over the course of three months). And reductions were even more marked among white Americans who identified as Republican/leaning Republican: a more than 50 percent decline in support, from 37 to 16 percent. White Democrats' support, by contrast, shrank by only four percentage points, from 92 to 88 percent. Among all Black Americans, regardless of political affiliation, support decreased by a single percentage point from 87 to 86 percent. Most striking is the racial divide among those supporters of Black Lives Matter who said that they *strongly* approved of BLM – while 59 percent of white Americans who identified as Democratic/leaning Democratic and supporting BLM *strongly* supported the movement, over 71 percent of Black Americans across the political spectrum who were supportive expressed strong approval of BLM. Among white people more generally, about 50 percent strongly supported

206 *Notes to pages 25–31*

BLM. www.pewresearch.org/fact-tank/2020/09/16/support-for-black-lives-matter-has-decreased-since-june-but-remains-strong-among-black-americans/ (accessed December 6, 2021).

23 The *New York Times* 1903 review of W. E. B. DuBois's masterwork, *The Souls of Black Folk*, is perhaps a paragon of this attitude. Patronizing throughout, the reviewer defers on the matter of what Black people actually think (especially Southern Black people) to "the Southern-bred white," who "knows by instinct ... fundamental attitudes of race to race" ("The Negro Question" BR7).

24 One of the most insistent Black voices opposed to Chinese exclusion and Indigenous displacement was Frederick Douglass. As Edlie Wong shows, Douglass "embraced difference in formulating an understanding of Americanization as a nonassimilative process that entails a reciprocal diversification and expansion of national life" (104).

25 It should not surprise us that white radicals in the post–Civil War years were not politically consistent in their embrace of other kinds of racist or xenophobic values aside from anti-Black racism. On the one hand, abolitionists had embraced Indigenous rights in the prewar period, linking them in large part to the expansionist ambitions of the Slave Power, and they likened Indian removal to the colonizationist impulse to "repatriate" African Americans to Liberia or Sierra Leone (Joy 218). Both white and Black abolitionists equated African American and Indigenous claims to the United States as a homeland and, in particular, supported the rights of the so-called Five Civilized Tribes (the Cherokee, Creek, Chickasaw, Choctaw, and Seminole), since they had in large part assimilated to Anglo practices (including, ironically, slaveholding). By contrast, their support for Native American self-determination waned considerably during the era of the Indian Wars, which overlapped with and then succeeded the Civil War.

26 Strikingly, a number of African American activists shared the dominant view of Indigenous Americans as savage and/or less evolved than either white or Black people. See, for example, Jessica Wells Cantiello, "Frances E. W. Harper's Educational Reservations: The Indian Question in *Iola Leroy*," *African American Review*, vol. 45, no. 4 (Winter 2012), pp. 575–92.

Chapter 1

1 The carte de visite was an immensely popular format for photography in the American mid-nineteenth century. Originating in France and patented in 1854, the carte was small – usually about 3 × 4 inches – and produced on a specialized camera that generated up to eight images at a time. Cartes de visite initially represented celebrities of one kind or another, but within a few years developed into a popular form of portraiture for ordinary people. Unlike daguerreotypes, which were expensive, cartes took advantage of a new and cheaper technology and cost about a dollar per sheet of eight to twelve. Given

Notes to pages 31–47   207

the accessibility of the cartes, Americans bought millions each year, and since they came in multiples, the images were designed to be shared and circulated. For a detailed discussion of the history and cultural significance of cartes de visite, see Annie Rudd, "Victorians Living in Public: Cartes de Visite as 19th Century Social Media."

2 Early daguerreotypes were formed of a complicated procedure that simplified somewhat over time, but not by much. First, a silver-plated copper plate was polished to a high shine. Then it was sensitized by chemical fumes, at first iodine, but later bromine, chlorine, or a combination of the two. At that point the plate was transferred to the camera and exposed to the light. Finally, the image was developed with a solution of sodium thiosulfate or salt and then toned with gold chloride. Exposure times in the early years of photography were long – anywhere from five to fifteen minutes – but by the mid-1850s, when this picture was taken, had shortened considerably. The silver plate was replaced by a glass one, and the image was printed onto paper with a silver albumen solution, rather than developed directly onto the plate itself, which allowed for multiple prints of a single image.

3 For a nuanced discussion of the ethics of looking in photography, and the ways that looking shades into voyeurism, see *Exposed: Voyeurism, Surveillance, and the Camera since 1870* , edited by Clive Joinson.

4 Not all midcentury US postmortem photography was of white children, but the vast majority was. Although within the budgets of middle-class Americans, even cartes de visite could prove too costly for all but the most affluent Black Americans. Given the racism of the time, the majority of free African Americans outside the South worked in manual or domestic trades, with lower wages than their white counterparts that placed photographs out of their financial reach. Of the hundreds of photographs of dead children that I saw that were taken from about 1850 to 1870 I found not one of a Black child, and only a couple after that period.

5 Gutta-percha is a natural thermoplastic latex, made from the sap of a tree native to Malaysia. While today it is mostly used for filling dental cavities, in the nineteenth century it was an all-purpose material, used for everything from knife handles to insulation for telegraph wires.

6 For a detailed description of antebellum American mourning practices, there is still no better source than Karen Halttunen's now-classic *Confidence Men and Painted Women: A Study of Middle-Class Culture In America 1830–1870* (New Haven, CT: Yale University Press, 1982).

7 For a detailed discussion of mourning fashions and artifacts, see Ann Schofield, "The Fashion of Mourning," in *Representations of Death in Nineteenth-Century US Writing and Culture*, edited by Nancy Frank (London: Taylor and Francis Group, 2007), 157–71.

8 Winifred's rejection of a wholly material heaven is of a piece with her (and Phelps's) gentle repudiation of Swedenborgian thought. Although she finds it "suggestive" and "pretty," she avers that "you can't accept what seem to the uninitiated to be his impossibilities" (171–2).

208   *Notes to pages 47–50*

9   This pleasantness extends in a variety of directions. For example, when she
    and Winifred visit Roy's grave, they find it "looking very pleasant" (84), and
    when they sit at the grave, Winifred mentions that "'It is very pleasant
    here' ... in her pleasant voice" (84). Similarly, Winifred avers that in heaven
    Roy and Mary won't forget the narrative of their mortal lives together, but
    that "Heaven will be not less heaven, but more, for this pleasant
    remembering'" (135).
10 One extension of this belief in the material body in heaven is that our bodies
    shall be their ideal forms. As Aunt Winifred is brushing her long, gray hair she
    sighs, "'Well, when I am in heaven, I shall have my pretty brown hair
    again'" (131).
11 A short but detailed entry in *American Medical Biographies* (ed. Howard
    A. Kelly and Walter L. Burrage [Baltimore: Norman, Remington, 1920],
    123–124), written by his son Reed Brinsmade Bontecou, provides insight into
    Bontecou's life and work. Bontecou describes his father with admiring enthu-
    siasm: "Personally a vigorous and handsome man of genial temperament and
    great originality, he was an indefatigable worker and constant student of his
    profession, keeping himself abreast of its advances, and covering in his sixty
    years of practice an immense field of activity and achievement" (124).
    Bontecou's greatest achievements outside his Civil War service occurred
    earlier in his career: with the help of copious doses of opium he repaired a
    pregnant woman's umbilical hernia, which "spill[ed] almost all her abdominal
    viscera on the ground," and reversed the complete paralysis of a housepainter
    who had broken one of his cervical vertebrae (123). On the Civil War
    battlefield, Bontecou was the first to attempt a shoulder and a knee joint
    resection, and refined amputation practice, decreasing the mortality rate from
    major surgeries (123). Bontecou was widely admired by his colleagues: in
    *Conservative Surgery, with a List of the Medical and Surgical Force of New York
    in the War of Rebellion 1861–2*, Sylvester D. Willard calls him "a graceful and
    accomplished operator, [who] must be ranked among the first American
    surgeons" (36).
12 For a discussion of the complex relationship between discourses of photog-
    raphy and of medicine, see Tanya Sheehan, *Doctored: The Medicine of
    Photography in Nineteenth-Century America* (University Park: Pennsylvania
    State University Press, 2011).
13 Up until midcentury, having one's photograph taken was in and of itself
    uncomfortable, accompanied by forced stillness in a head brace (a practice
    that was continued even as exposure times shrank to a couple of seconds).
14 While Confederate soldiers were often (but not only) motivated by a sense
    that they were fighting to assert their moral superiority, much of the Southern
    discourse around the war was focused on regional integrity and preserving the
    honor of the South. For more details about the discourses around Southern
    involvement in combat, see Gaines M. Foster, *Ghosts of the Confederacy:
    Defeat, the Lost Cause, and the Emergence of the New South* (New York:
    Oxford University Press, 1987).

Notes to pages 52–75 209

15 For a discussion of these conventions, see Alan Trachtenberg, *Reading American Photographs: Images as History, Matthew Brady to Walker Evans* (New York: Hill and Wang, 1989).

16 A large collection of these images are part of the Liljenquist Family Collection of Civil War Photographs at the Library of Congress: www.loc.gov/collec tions/liljenquist-civil-war-photographs/about-this-collection/.

17 The circumstances of his injury are recorded in Charles Walcott's *History of the Twenty-First Regiment Massachusetts Volunteers* (Boston: Houghton, Mifflin, 1882). Walcott had been the commander of the Twenty-First. Drawing on the official report by a Colonel Clark, Walcott reports that at the disastrous battle of Fredericksburg, the Color-Sergeant of the regiment was shot and fell. Plunkett immediately "seized the colors and carried them proudly forward to the farthest point reached by our troops during the battle … [However,] a shell was thrown with fatal accuracy at the colors, which were again brought to the ground wet with the life-blood of the brave Plunkett, both of whose arms were carried away" (150). Plunkett was later awarded the Medal of Honor.

18 For a brief biography of George Rockwood, see http://georgerockwood.com/rockwoodbiography.htm.

19 For a brief biography of J. W. Black and his contributions to photography, see http://historiccamera.com/cgi-bin/librarium2/pm.cgi?action=app_dis play&app=datasheet&app_id=2401.

20 For a detailed discussion of Jeremiah Gurney's life and career, see Christian A. Peterson, *Chaining the Sun: Portraits by Jeremiah Gurney* (Minneapolis: Minnesota Institute of Art, 1999).

21 Wintress's obituary in 1908 called him the "worst wounded man in the army to recover." While he was on picket duty after the second battle of Williamsburg a fellow soldier accidentally discharged his weapon. The bullet "passed upward, forcing fragments of bone through his brain and lobe of his left eye, finally passing through the brain and lobe of the right eye also." While he was unconscious for more than three weeks, doctors removed seventy pieces of bone from his face and head, and at one point he was fed through his eye cavity. His obituary in the July 12 *Washington Post* was entitled "Bullets Couldn't Kill Him."

22 Fredricks and Co. was founded by Charles DeForest Fredricks. A student of Jeremiah Gurney, Fredricks owned studios not only in New York but also in Havana and Paris. His most famous portraits are of John Wilkes Booth.

Chapter 2

1 See www.britannica.com/event/Crimean-War.

2 Thanks to Jeff Allred for pointing me toward Benjamin.

3 Rifled muskets weren't uniformly more effective, though. As Kerr notes, while almost ten inches shorter than their predecessors, they were about 10 percent

210 *Notes to pages 75–78*

heavier (not to mention the weight of the attached bayonet). Plus, under the pressure of fire, soldiers made mistakes in loading and shooting, which rendered their guns about as useful as iron pipes. After Gettysburg, "37,000 muskets were salvaged. Of these, 24,000 were loaded and 18,000 more were loaded more than once. Some had unopened cartridges, others had bullets upside down" (22). In addition, many rifles used black powder, which created dark smoke, making the field almost invisible to combatants. Even after rifles became more commonly muzzle- than barrel-loading, soldiers had a limited amount of ammunition they could use in any given engagement. They carried on average roughly sixty rounds, firing about two rounds per minute. So a soldier would run out of ammunition after about half an hour (although given how cumbersome barrel-loading was, it often took longer). Usually battles would last until soldiers ran out of ammunition and could be relieved by the next line, and they weren't above scavenging cartridges from the dead and wounded (Kerr 24)

4 The *Surgical Memoirs of the War of the Rebellion*, published by the United States Sanitary Commission, put the percentage of lower extremity injuries due to minié balls at about 30 percent. The next most common cause, round, smooth-bore musket balls, was half that. Gunshot to the extremities was by far the greatest cause of injury for soldiers. The Sanitary Commission's statistics put the total number of injuries during that war at 87,822, of which 55,245 (close to two thirds) were located in the extremities.

5 Given the Confederate Army's reduced access to medical supplies, including clean bandages, anesthetics, and, toward the end of the war, adequate food and clean clothing, postsurgical mortality among Confederate troops was always higher, never falling much below 35 percent (although that is a significant reduction from the 50 percent at the beginning of the war). While the South had the advantage in terms of military leadership, the Union could count on more trained surgeons. In either case, as Brian Miller observes, "most surgeons were competent, skilled, and compassionate doctors, operating under sometimes horrifying conditions, and saving thousands of lives and hundreds of limbs" (48).

6 An infection that is now quite rare in the contemporary United States took up several pages of discussion in the Confederate manual: erysipelas. Erysipelas was an acute skin and subcutaneous infection caused by streptococcus bacteria that caused intense pain and often death. Its main symptom was bright red and swollen skin. Just as common was what nineteenth-century doctors called "pyemia" – systemic sepsis caused by strep or staph bacteria finding its way into the blood.

7 Both the Union and Confederate manuals recommend manual exploration of wounds to locate and remove bullets, scraps of clothing blown into the wound, and other debris, ideally with the index finger, but really with any finger that fits into the wound. However, the Confederate manual extends its suggestions for care of injuries, recommending that dressings be changed often to avoid infestations of flies in or near the wound.

Notes to pages 80–95 211

8 This swagger existed on both sides of the Mason-Dixon Line. From the beginning of the war, Confederate surgeons, especially the younger and less experienced, "defined their manhood through an honorable reputation ... Abundant evidence reveals the impatience and bravado of young and eager Confederate doctors early in the war who wanted to cut their teeth in the medical profession and felt they had something to prove" (Miller 38).

9 An excellent example of the Western adventure genre (although not without its own profound ambivalences) is Frances Parkman's *The Oregon Trail: Sketches of Prairie and Rocky-Mountain Life* (1847).

10 As Brian Craig Miller has shown, these narratives are not limited to the Union Army. In his detailed and thorough analysis of Confederate amputees, *Empty Sleeves: Amputation in the Civil War South*, he offers account after account of piles of amputated limbs in Southern field hospitals, which "left a powerful and lasting impression on Confederate soldiers trying to make sense of the unprecedented level of carnage and destruction after a battle" (21).

11 This image of the speaking amputated limb reappears at the end of this chapter in my discussion of "The Case of George Dedlow."

12 For a brief discussion of Morton and polygenism, see my *Technology and the Logic of American Racism* (2000).

13 The *Oxford English Dictionary* finds a usage of the word in this way as late as 1876, in Edward Bulwer-Lytton's *Pausanias, the Spartan*.

14 The *OED* finds this usage as late as 1907.

15 This inseparability between North and South is not only positive. Whitman is clear that the North was equally implicated in the system of slavery as the South due to the inextricability of Southern agribusiness from Northern capitalism. Interestingly, though, he overstates this culpability in a way that seems to exculpate the South: "The North had been just as guilty, if not more guilty; and the East and the West had. The former Presidents and Congresses had been guilty – the Governors and Legislators of every Northern state had been guilty and the Mayors of New York and other northern cities had all been guilty – their hands were all stain'd" (123). While he's not wrong about New York – the city was notoriously anti-abolitionist – or to a certain extent Philadelphia, it's more than a stretch to say that Boston was "just as guilty, if not more guilty" than, say, Richmond or Birmingham. There were riots when the nineteen-year-old fugitive Anthony Burns was arrested in Boston under the 1850 Fugitive Slave Law, and when he was sentenced to be returned to Virginia, the city was placed under virtual martial law.

16 See, for example, David G. Kline, "Silas Weir Mitchell and 'The Strange Case of George Dedlow,'" *Journal of Neurosurgery*, vol. 41, no. 1 (2016), https://doi .org/10.3171/2016.4.FOCUS1573 (accessed January 5, 2021); Joanna Bourke, "Silas Weir Mitchell's 'The Strange Case of George Dedlow,'" *The Lancet*, 373 (2016), pp. 1332–3; Debra Journet, "Phantom Limbs and 'Body-Ego': S. Weir Mitchell's 'George Dedlow,'" *Mosaic*, vol. 23, no. 1 (Winter 1990), pp. 87–99.

212   *Notes to pages 96–103*

17 I was able to find one quadruple amputee, Benjamin Franklin Work. However, he did not lose his limbs in battle. Rather, having survived the battle of Antietam, he was caught in a severe snowstorm in Minnesota two years later. Rescued on Christmas Eve, 1865, Work was brought to Fort Ridgeley. After a couple of weeks, the decomposition of his frozen lower arms and legs was so serious that the fort surgeon had to operate on all four limbs. For a detailed discussion of Work's life, see Marlin Peterson's 2015 self-published book, *Blizzard Ordeal of a Minnesota Cavalryman*.

18 The alcohol used to store specimens was sourced a few different ways. The Provost Marshal – essentially the chief prosecutor of the military – confiscated liquor from troops, usually alcohol that they had taken from the homes of Confederate sympathizers in the course of a campaign. This was turned over to the Army Medical Museum. Brinton also requisitioned alcohol from regiments if necessary. This alcohol was stored in barrels and sent by train and wagon to field hospitals, to be stocked with amputated body parts and sent back up to Washington, DC. Apparently, according to Brinton, railroad workers and military guards soon twigged to this and started tapping the barrels (presumably before they were filled up with bones) to drink and/or smuggle out. Brinton soon put an end to this by adding an emetic to the barrels of spirits (192).

19 While the definition of phantom includes the common meaning of a spirit that haunts the living, it's also defined as a figment of the imagination, and as a hallucination or delusion (*OED.com*).

Chapter 3

1 Briefly: in 1872, the Supreme Court held that the Privileges or Immunities Clause of the Fourteenth Amendment was limited to federal citizenship rather than extending to state citizenship. In other words, the Amendment could be enforced only in federal jurisdictions, such as access to waterways crossing state lines, or the right to run for federal office.

2 Perhaps most notable has been the use of the Fourteenth Amendment to establish rights to privacy, bodily self-determination, and relationship rights. The Fourteenth Amendment was initially used by the Supreme Court in 1965 in *Griswold v. Connecticut*, which established that privacy within marriage was sacrosanct, using the due process clause of the Amendment (rather than the "privileges and immunities" clause, which on its surface makes more sense) to rule that prohibiting married couples from using contraceptives was unconstitutional. A flurry of cases followed *Griswold*: *Loving v. Virginia* in 1967, outlawing miscegenation laws; extending the right to contraception via the equal protection clause in 1972; and, in a case that has faced a series of challenges, *Roe v. Wade*, legalizing abortion. More recently, the Court used the due process and equal protection clauses to legalize same-sex marriage in *Obergefell v. Hodges*. For an overview of uses of the Fourteenth Amendment

Notes to pages 104–107   213

and the history of debates over the various clauses, see https://constitutioncenter.org/interactive-constitution/amendment/amendment-xiv. For an overview of most of these cases, see oyez.com; for a complete listing of all Supreme Court cases, see https://supreme.justia.com/cases/federal/us/.

3 In her entry for Dickinson in *Eminent Women of the Age*, Elizabeth Cady Stanton quotes from a review in the *Fall River Press*: "Her voice is clear and penetrating, without being harsh; her enunciation is very distinct, and at times somewhat rhythmic in its character" (Parton et al. 495). Similarly, Stanton herself expatiates on Dickinson's gifts: "There never was such a furor about an orator in this country. The period of her advent, the excited condition of the people, her youth, beauty, and remarkable voice, all heightened the effect of her genius, and helped to produce this result" (498).

4 A January 29, 1867, letter from her sister Susan, who was also her business manager, reports having booked Dickinson's tour through Ohio, taking her to Cleveland, Akron, Toledo, Oberlin, Delaware, Springfield, and Cincinnati, with possible other dates in Caton and Warren.

5 For a classic, and to my mind unequaled, discussion of white Northern racism, see Leon Litwack's *North of Slavery*. In their narratives, both Frederick Douglass and Harriet Jacobs write at length about the humiliation and even violence they experienced as Black people in Massachusetts and New York, respectively.

6 Elizabeth Cady Stanton's article on Dickinson in *Eminent Women of the Age* traces her power back to her childhood, describing her as "a wayward, willful, intensely earnest, imaginative child, causing herself and her elders much trouble and unhappiness ... With courageous defiance she would submit to punishment rather than rules she thought foolish and unnecessary" (480). This defiance set the stage for Dickinson's fearlessness as a speaker and unwillingness to compromise her principles, which allowed "this noble girl, through all temptations and discouragements, [to] maintain a purity, dignity, and moral probity of character, that reflect honor on herself, and glory on her whole sex" (479). It's striking, too, that the editors of *Eminent Women* decided not to include Dickinson in one of the categories by which the sketches of many of the subjects of the book are classified, such as "Our Pioneer Educators," "Women of the Drama," "The Woman's Rights Movement," "Woman as Physician," and the like. Rather, like Florence Nightingale, Harriet Beecher Stowe, or Julia Ward Howe, she occupies her own category, unclassifiable in relation to other women.

7 Of course, the praise was not universal. Democrats abhorred her and she inspired attacks in the their partisan newspapers, which called her "unwomanly" and "unsexed," and even compared her to Barnum's freaks (Gallman 37).

8 It was also the basis for the Third Enforcement Act of 1871, also known as the Ku Klux Klan Act, which explicitly outlawed violating any person's constitutional rights and interfering with the privileges and immunities of citizenship.

214 *Notes to pages 111–122*

9 As Geoff D. Zylstra has shown, there was a significant struggle over the segregation of Philadelphia streetcars. As white Philadelphians tried to cement white supremacy in the context of the Civil War and then emancipation, "Black residents of Philadelphia protested the discriminatory practices of streetcar companies by riding in the cars, thereby creating a public dialogue about the legitimacy of racial discrimination and using the courts to challenge policies that legalized racial inequality" (681).

10 A useful source of information about African American soldiers is *Freedom's Soldiers: The Black Military Experience in the Civil War*, ed. Ira Berlin, Joseph P. Reidy, and Leslie S. Rowland (1998). In fact, it's very unlikely that black troops would have fought at Newbern, since it took place in March 1862 and Black volunteers were only officially added to combat troops in early 1863.

11 The losses they have already suffered are chronicled in the novel: their mother is injured in a fire set by a racist mob in Philadelphia, and their oldest brother is killed by falling rafters and bricks – "an accident, they said; yet as really murdered as though they had willfully and brutally stricken him down" (175). Francesca's mother dies in grief while giving birth to her and is buried at sea on their trip to England to escape American racism.

12 For a digital facsimile of a lovely printing of Lincoln's Seccond Inaugural Address, go to www.loc.gov/resource/rbpe.15900100/.

13 The novel makes a point of providing examples of Black virtue beyond this scene. For example, in a conversation between Surrey, a Colonel Brooks, and an enlisted man, Whittlesey, about Brooks's conversion to abolitionism, Brooks describes the incident that changed his mind. Looking for the body of a drowned soldier, he and his men find enslaved people who buried the body: one of them "'showed us some traps of the buried officer, among them a pair of spurs, which his brother recognized immediately. When she was quite sure that we were all correct, and that the thing had fallen into the right hands, she fished out of some safe corner his wallet, with fifty-seven dollars in it'" (105). It is this detail that causes Brooks to doubt everything he had believed about Black people: "'I confess I stared, for they were slaves, both of them, and evidently poor as Job's turkey, and it has always been one of my theories that a nigger invariably steals when he gets a chance'" (106). This proof of Black honesty pulls Brooks away from his unexamined racism and toward antislavery.

14 Dickinson is careful to point out that the rioters are "not of native growth, nor American born," blaming the violence on Irish immigrants.

15 This tradition in antislavery activism traces back to the eighteenth century in both Britain and the United States. The Society for the Abolition of Slavery in England adopted the slogan "Am I not a man and a brother?," later accompanied by an image of an enslaved Black man in chains, on one knee, arms extended in an act of pleading, an image designed and popularized by Josiah Wedgwood (Bindman 79). American antislavery activists soon appropriated the slogan and the image for their own abolitionist work – for example, John

Greenleaf Whitter's poem "Our Countrymen in Chains," which first appeared on the front page of *The Liberator* in 1834, was reissued as a broadsheet in 1837 accompanied by the image. In the nineteenth century both sensationalist and sentimental representations of Black pain emerged, with the sentimental winning out by the beginning of the 1840s (for a fascinating discussion of this shift from the sensational to the sentimental, see Carol Lasseer, "Voyeuristic Abolitionism: Sex, Gender, and the Transformation of Antislavery Rhetoric," *Journal of the Early Republic*, 28, no. 1, 2008, pp. 83–114).

16 Sarah Josepha Hale's *Northwood* (1827) was nominally antislavery but is primarily notable for its full-throated advocacy of the mission of the African Colonization Society and its romanticized representation of Thanksgiving (a holiday that Hale was instrumental in establishing). E. D. E. N. Southworth published serialized novels in the antislavery journal *The National Era* (which also serialized *Uncle Tom's Cabin*) in the late 1840s and early 1850s, but, as Paul Christian Jones points out, these texts can "drift into descriptions of the institution that have been read as proslavery apologism even while she attempts to produce antislavery fiction" (56). And Frances Trollope's *Jonathan Jefferson Whitlaw*, while it made a splash among abolition circles, was a success mostly in Trollope's native England.

17 Raymond Williams comments on the difficulty of writing outside generic conventions. In *Resources of Hope* (1989) he discusses the challenges working-class writers historically have had in writing novels at all: "take the case of nineteenth-century working-class writers, who wanted to write about their working lives. The most popular form was the novel, but though they had marvellous material that could go into the novel very few of them wrote good or even any novels." Instead, he observes, these writers crafted autobiographies, since the genres they were most familiar with – "the witness confessing the story of his life or ... the defence speech at the trial ... oral forms" – were "more accessible, forms centred on 'I,' on the single person." By contrast, the novel "with its quite different narrative forms was virtually impenetrable to working-class writers for three or four generations. Indeed, the forms of working-class consciousness are bound to be different from the literary forms of another class" (86).

18 For a detailed discussion of the mechanisms of Johnson's presidential Reconstruction, see Levine.

19 It is not clear whether Dickinson ever gave this speech. It does not appear in the correspondence between Dickinson and her sister Susan that I found, nor does her biographer J. Matthew Gallman mention it. In addition, like the many of the drafts of her speeches, this one begins strongly, but after a few pages is marked by crossings-through, stray sentences, and the like, so the reader can't know, even if she delivered it, how much of the written text found its way into spoken word.

20 Robert S. Levine chronicles the reactions of a number of Reconstruction radicals who reached out to Johnson in an attempt to persuade him to change

216   *Notes to pages 124–139*

course (58–61). Carl Schurz, on the ground in the South, was a witness to the oppression faced by the newly freed, and recommended a significant increase in US troops in the former Confederate States, among other policy changes to empower Black Southerners. Similarly, Charles Sumner, Thaddeus Stevens, and Frederick Douglass initially petitioned Johnson to take up a policy of meaningful Reconstruction until they wholly abandoned hope in the final months of 1865.

21 I am working from Dickinson's handwritten draft, and not all words are clear. I have made my best attempt at transcription.

Chapter 4

1 The size and scale of the work the Bureau took on is astounding. By late 1868, the Bureau had distributed over twenty million rations, moved over 30,000 freedpeople for work or to reunite with family members, opened fifty-six hospitals that treated 500,000 patients annually, and maintained 4,300 schools for a quarter of million students (Harrison 212).

2 The historiography of the Freedmen's Bureau is a story in and of itself. Under the Dunning School, it was regarded as a corrupt and corrupting power that trampled over the rights of white Southerners and invested Black freedpeople with rights and responsibilities they were incapable of handling. In the 1960s and 1970s, when revisionist historians were challenging the reigning interpretations of both the Civil War and Reconstruction, scholars "found what looked like an agency of economic and social control rather than racial uplift. They discovered officers who, far from exhibiting a principled sympathy for the freedpeople, turned out to be disturbingly racist or paternalistic in their approach" (Harrison 206). More recent historians have been more positive about the Bureau and in particular explored its local iterations, in which the work of the Bureau on the ground showed the massive changes it effected. According to these scholars, on the whole agents seem to have been committed and conscientious, if not as antiracist as we might hope. In the majority of cases formerly enslaved people brought to Bureau tribunals, agents found for the freedpeople. For a detailed discussion of the historiography of Reconstruction, see Harrison.

3 This is not to say that Howard's experience is pleasant – the operating room to which he's taken is "a place a little grewsome withal from arms, legs, and hands not yet all carried off" (v. 1, 250).

4 Howard was not contending just with unreconstructed Southerners. This address was given as part of a larger speaking tour he embarked on in early 1866 after a negative evaluation of the Bureau's work that was sponsored and supported by then-president Andrew Johnson. In response, Howard went on the offensive, defending the Bureau in a series of speeches around the Northeast.

5 Howard's observation has been borne out by contemporary historians. Eric Foner points to the (perhaps inevitable) struggle between formerly enslaved

Notes to pages 141–146 217

people and their erstwhile enslavers: "Planters' inability to establish their authority arose from the clash between their determination to preserve the old forms of domination and the freedmen's desire to carve out the greatest possible independence for themselves and their families" (136).

6 This change was not atypical, even for men who were previously agnostic about abolition or even anti-abolitionist. In an 1864 letter to Eliza Scudder, Lydia Maria Child writes about a "Captain ____," who had been a "bitter pro-slavery man violent in his talk against abolitionist and 'niggers.'. . . A few days ago he was going in the cars from Boston to Roxbury, when a colored solder entered the car. Attempting to seat himself he was repulsed by a white man who rudely exclaimed, 'I am not going to ride with niggers.' Captain W. . . . rose up, in all the gilded glory of his naval uniform, and called out, 'Come here, my good fellow! I've been fighting alongside people of your color, and glad enough was I have 'em by my side. Come sit by me'" (180).

7 Tourgée's uncritical estimation of Freedmen's Bureau agents is only partially true, of course. The Bureau was a decidedly mixed bag in which agents "brought to their posts a combination of paternalist assumptions about race and sensitivity to the plight of Blacks, the precise mixture varying with the individual" (Foner 142). In addition, there was quite a bit of turnover both in leadership positions and of agents at the local level: an egalitarian former abolitionist could be replaced by a more conservative and pragmatic agent more inclined to conform to the dictates of white supremacy, and vice versa. Finally, as Eric Foner has shown, Bureau leadership largely subscribed to free labor politics, which did not take into account the exploitive nature of the work contracts freedpeople were pressured to sign, and saw any kind of distribution of aid in the form of food, clothing, and the like as charity that could make them dependent on government aid and contribute to "encouraging idleness" (*North Carolina Assistant Commissioner* n.p.). Many Bureau employees mostly believed in the laissez-faire economic policies dominant at the time, and were convinced that freedpeople would achieve economic mobility through hard work and self-denial.

8 In fact, leaving the employment of a person with whom one had signed a labor contract, or convincing someone else to leave, was a crime under many of the notorious "Black Codes" of the mid-1860s. See Harold Woodman, *New South, New Law: The Legal Foundations of Credit and Labor Relations in the Postbellum Agricultural South* (Baton Rouge: Louisiana State University Press, 1995), for a detailed description of the Black Codes related to employment policy.

9 Tourgée himself was well aware of the violence of the Klan. Two of his associates were murdered by the KKK in 1870 – one of them lynched by hanging and the other shot – and his life was often threatened (Karcher, *Refugee* 5). After 1868, with the rise of the Klan, violence skyrocketed. In nine parishes of Louisiana alone, Howard noted that 227 Black and white supporters of Reconstruction were murdered, 68 beaten and/or wounded by gunshots, and "very many who had disappeared whose fate was not known" (386).

218 *Notes to pages 148–151*

10 An August 27, 1862, letter to the *New York Times* invokes the distinction between "the Union as it was" and "the Union as it ought to be," dismissing the debate between the two as "bosh." According to the writer, "H.R.R.," "Slavery is already dead – beyond the possibility of resurrection." At the end of the letter, the author reiterates the central point: "Slavery is dead – past surgery – and the cry about restoring the Union with Slavery, or without it, amounts to nothing." The Democratic party slogan for the 1864 election was "The Union as it was, and the Constitution as it is." The phrase survived beyond the war into Reconstruction. Thomas Nast's famous engraving, "The Union as It Was/The Lost Cause, Worse than Slavery," explicitly links the nostalgic desire to go back with ongoing efforts by white supremacists to suppress Black votes, control Black labor, and terrorize Black people. It shows a Black couple holding a (possibly dead) baby, flanked by a KKK member and a personification of the White League, a similar vigilante organization. On the ground by the couple's feet are the signs of Reconstruction: a spelling book and a schoolhouse sign, already on fire, and in the background is the image of a Black man hanging from a tree.
11 The pamphlet publication of this letter is in the collection of the Library of Congress. Archivists there have identified "W.W.W." as "possibly Capt. William W. Wise," but there is no indication of the identity of "King," to whom the letter is addressed.
12 W.W.W.'s experience was much like that of Ambrose Bierce, whose "What I Saw of Shiloh" (1892) is a graphic and horrifying narrative of the engagement of his own regiment, the Ninth Indiana, in the battle. Both men were involved in the second day of fighting, having to clamber over the bodies of men killed the previous day.
13 For more information about railway mail delivery during the Civil War, see US Post Office Department, *History of the Railway Mail Service* (Washington, DC: Government Printing Office, 1885).
14 Child was only partially successful in distributing *The Freedmen's Book*. First of all, the market for textbooks for freedpeople's schools was dominated by the American Tract Society and the American Missionary Association, which coordinated the appointment of many teachers in Bureau schools. Second, Child's book was not sufficiently pious and too imbued with antiracist and radical politics to pass muster for the ATS to consider distributing. One difference in particular is telling: while the *Freedmen's Book* is focused on Black achievement and features a number of Black writers, the ATS's *Freedman's Third Reader* has no Black authors, and even its profiles of Black luminaries like Phillis Wheatley and Frederick Douglass are more concerned about the state of their souls than the quality of their politics (Karcher, *First Woman*, 502). In order to try to break the freedpeople's textbook cartel, Child underwrote the cost of publication, covering half of the expenses, and helped significantly with distribution. She also fed whatever profit the books made back into further publication and dissemination. Although freedpeople

Notes to pages 154–157

themselves seemed to prefer her book, it was never taken up by the ATS or the AMA, so sales were disappointing (Karcher, *First Woman* 503).

15 The section that Child excerpts is from a longer work, "Emancipation in the District of Columbia and the British West Indies." Written in the midst of the Civil War, it covers a great deal of ground over the course of several pages: emancipation, John Brown, the war, the Founding Fathers, and more.

16 Child's commitment to Black futurity is echoed in Howard's explanation behind the proliferation of Bureau schools: "The prevailing thought was: The slaves are becoming free; give them knowledge – teach them to read – teach the child!" (vol. 2, 195).

17 As the records of the Freedmen's Bureau show, the schools themselves were a very mixed bag in terms of educational success, the effectiveness of teachers, the availability of students, and the administration of the schools. In one school in Charleston, West Virginia, for example, ideological conflict among the school board led to generalized dysfunction and the disillusionment of the teacher, C. W. Sharpe, who wrote to the Washington, DC, headquarters: "There is a manifest disposition in the trustees – one of whom was a rebel, and, with one exception, all of whom are under the influence of the conserva-tive or anti-negro element, and hostile to the Bureau – to annoy me, to degrade, if possible, and finally to drive me out from here.... It is the manifest intent of the ruling influence here to defeat my object [to educate freedpeople], and, if possible, make the efforts of the Bureau contemptible. Any failure on my part, would be regarded as a disgrace to that branch of government" (*District of Columbia Education* n.p.).

18 Letters to various regional commissions are filled with requests for all kinds of supplies, including woodstoves to heat schoolrooms in winter and even to build or renovate schoolhouses. Schools were bedeviled by shortages of teachers, building supplies, schoolbooks, and furniture, and students them-selves often lacked shoes or warm clothes. A letter from a teacher in Lutherville, Maryland, complained that students, "about fifty children who have no Education whatever, and about one hundred twenty mature Colored People ... will gladly avail themselves of all advantages of school privileges" if the school had basic resources to offer them (*District of Columbia Education* n. p.). Schools did still soldier on, though – one letter from C. W. Sharpe described how "the education of the colored population is *advancing* quite as rapidly as that of the whites. The eagerness of the freedmen to learn atones in great part for the want of the best facilities."

19 The successes of the Bureau schools are stunning. In 1860, over 90 percent of enslaved people were illiterate (Foner 96). Over the course of its involvement in education, it educated roughly 170,000 children and an unknown number of adults (Vaughn 19). The Bureau itself spent about $13 million on educa-tion from 1865 to 1870 (after which public education devolved to the states, counties, and/or municipalities), and voluntary associations such as the AMA spent about the same (Vaughn 12). Over the course of the first five years of

220   *Notes to pages 157–160*

Reconstruction, both emancipated and free Black people and communities invested heavily in education: Eric Foner estimates that by 1870 "Blacks had expended over $1 million on education" (98). At the same time, the Bureau's reach was limited, especially in regard to education. As William Preston Vaughn points out, "what had been accomplished was a mere drop in the bucket when compared to the vast number of Blacks needing instruction" (19). Vaughn estimates that no more than one-tenth of the 1.7 million formerly enslaved children eligible for education actually attended school, and possibly fewer. Other historians argue for higher numbers: John David Smith argues that by 1870 over 250,000 students were attending Bureau schools (39). Of course, it's impossible to know how many of those children and adults then went home to educate family members who weren't able to attend school due to work, which would multiply the indirect effect of Bureau schools.

20 Some Bureau officials remained optimistic despite the resistance and violence. Bureau district officers in North Carolina, for example, held onto the hope that white North Carolinians would adjust to the new order of things. The director of the Western District was cautiously optimistic in February 1866, reporting that "the temper of the whites is settling down into a determination to treat the Blacks with considerable fairness, but not so fairly and justly as we desire. They wish to impress it thoroughly on the blacks that they are inferior and must be kept so by law. Still I hope for gradual improvement" (*North Carolina Assistant Commissioner*, n.p.). In a May 14, 1866, letter from the director of the Central District of the North Carolina Commission, the official holds onto hope that white people can be brought around if they are reassured that the Bureau is not against them: "The whites have been led to believe that the officers of the Bureau were determined to back up the Blacks (Freedmen) right or wrong. Disabuse them of this impression and there will not be any difficulty in carrying out the objects of the Bureau" (n.p.).

21 In his autobiography, Howard makes recourse again and again to the brutal statistics of white violence against freedpeople and Bureau agents. In August of 1866 in North Carolina alone, there were reported to the local office of the Bureau forty-nine cases of "assault whipping, false imprisonment shooting, and other outrages against Blacks" (v. 2, 286). In 1867 Howard notes the "criminal calendar" of Tennessee: "Murders, 20; shootings, 18; rape, 11; other maltreatments, 270. Total outrages of whites perpetrated upon the freedmen, 319 recorded cases" (v. 2, 345).

Chapter 5

1 Philosophers of haptic phenomenology (i.e., the experience of touch) often point to the example of Doubting Thomas, who cannot believe his eyes and has to put his hands on Jesus's wounds in order to believe them to be real.

2 It is an important developmental progression when babies can identify items in a bag by touch only, rather than having to see them. The inability to sense

Notes to pages 162–173 221

objects solely by handling them is a diagnosable neurological disorder called astereognosis (or tactile agnosia if in only one hand), usually caused by a lesion in the parieto-temporo-occipital lobe of the brain. This can cause significant problems in terms of self-care and safety – we handle any number of objects from combs to soap to our own bodies without being able to see them fully (O'Sullivan and Schmitz 988).

3 Only one other cartoon that I can find of Nast's uses the isolated image of a hand – an anti-Tweed drawing in which New York city is crushed by Tweed's enormous thumb. But even there, as I will show below, Nast is borrowing from his own vocabulary of hands as signs of liberation or threat.

4 Several testifiers at the so-called Klan hearings described being whipped or witnessing whippings – this form of violence was not just physically destructive; it also invoked a sort of rhetorical linkage to enslavement through the object of the whip.

5 It's not surprising that this image is of a white veteran. Black soldiers were theoretically legally entitled to the same benefits as their white counterparts. There were, however, many obstacles: Black soldiers were less likely to have been hospitalized than whites, and so lacked official documentation of their injuries. Although the need for wartime medical records was legally obviated in 1890, Black veterans were less likely to apply for pension benefits (probably assuming that they would be denied). Pension applications were lengthy and especially challenging for formerly enslaved people, many of whom were illiterate. Many Black veterans did not have basic information about themselves, such as date of birth, date of marriage or marriage certificate, or enlistment papers. Submitting the application required a fee, another obstacle for people who had not much more than the clothes on their backs. Black pensioners were investigated for fraud at twice the rate of white veterans, and the Grand Army of the Republic was not inclined to advocate for Black veterans, resulting in a huge racial disparity in pensions granted: 29.5 percent of Black applicants versus an average of 70.5 percent for whites. Black women had an even harder time. As Susie King Taylor narrates in *Reminiscence of My Life in Camp*, Black female nurses were classified as "laundresses" and prevented from receiving a pension. For a full discussion of racial disparities for Union veteran pensions, see Sven E. Wilson, "Prejudice and Policy: Racial Discrimination in the Union Army Disability Pension System, 1865–1906," *American Journal of Public Health*, 100, 2010, pp. S56–S65.

6 The best source I could find describing the Gettysburg reunion of 1888 is part of the larger website of the Gettysburg National Military Park: https://npsgnmp.wordpress.com/2015/10/16/the-grand-reunion-of-1888/.

7 While the twenty-fifth anniversary was well attended, the fiftieth reunion in 1913 received much more attention. Almost 60,000 veterans and their families attended, again primarily from the Union side. Newspapers from around the country reported on the activities, and the governor of

222 *Notes to pages 175–183*

Pennsylvania and President Woodrow Wilson gave the culminating addresses on July 4.

8 This is not to say that all newspaper accounts were this breathlessly positive. The Republican-affiliated *Harrisburg* (Pennsylvania) *Telegraph* cast a more jaundiced eye on the proceedings. In an article entitled "Desecrating the Gettysburg Reunion," the newspaper reprinted a story from the *Reading Times* and quoted a James McKinney "returned from the Gettysburg reunion." McKinney reported that "there will never be a reunion of the blue and the gray. Everything is solid South. He says that on Wednesday evening a Union flag was floating across Baltimore pike ... and yesterday morning it was drooping from the rope in a thousand shreds."

9 The "Gratz Brown" whose name is inscribed on the small step on which Greeley rests his left foot is Benjamin Gratz Brown, who was Greeley's Liberal Republican running mate.

10 The classic history of Andersonville, Ovid Futch's *History of Andersonville Prison*, is a detailed archival study of the prison.

11 The US Colored Troops were mobilized only a couple of months before Gettysburg but did not fight there. Given that the bulk of Black troops were formerly enslaved Southerners, the USCT were deployed to battles farther south, in Missouri, South Carolina, and Virginia.

12 This brings to mind Walt Whitman's poem "Over the Carnage Rose Prophetic a Voice," in which the poet celebrates the reunion of North and South, and the coming together of East and West. Whitman's rhetoric is much like Gordon's: "Be not dishearten'd, affection shall solve the problems of freedom yet, / Those who love each other shall become invincible, / They shall yet make Columbia victorious."

13 German immigrants participated significantly in abolitionist movements before and emancipationist projects after the Civil War. As Eric Foner remarks, Germans, "many of them exiles from the failed revolution of 1848, who identified the Slave Power with the landed aristocracy of Europe, gave the democratic revolution a significant base of white support" (41) (Carl Schurz, who came to the United States in 1852 and subsequently served as a general in the Union Army, a US senator from Missouri, and secretary of the interior under Rutherford Hayes, is an excellent example of this).

14 This conflation of Lindau with the past is present when he is first introduced: "His long soft beard and moustache had once been fair, and they kept their tone of yellow in the gray to which they had turned. His eyes were full, and his lips and chin shaped the beard to the noble outline which shows in the beards the Italian masters liked to paint for the Last Supper. His carriage was erect and soldierly, and March presently saw that he had lost his left hand" (74). The novel aligns Lindau with the past in several ways: first, as his previously blond hair shows in the present gray; second, in his resemblance to a painting by Italian Renaissance artists; and third all the way back to the Last Supper. His "soldierly" carriage is pushed into the past with March's "present" recognition that Lindau's hand has been amputated, a callback to the Civil War.

Notes to pages 183–195   223

15 Not all the characters in the novel fall so easily into this revisionist version of enslavement. Alma Leighton, an artist and daughter of Col. Woodburn's landlady, argues against the justification of slavery: "'Still, I can't believe it was right to hold people in slavery, to whip them and sell them. It never did seem right to me'" (152).

16 Indeed, the (re)establishment of white supremacy after Reconstruction was, as Desmond S. King and Stephen G. N. Truck show, as much a Northern phenomenon as a Southern one: "Southern white supremacy was constructed *in conjunction with*, rather that *in opposition to*, developments in the rest of the country after Reconstruction. In the national government, federal officials did not just acquiesce in the Southern counter-revolution, but promoted a nationwide order of white supremacy" (214).

17 Thank you to Sophie Bell for the germ of this idea.

18 For a detailed discussion of tract visitors, see Cynthia S Hamilton, "Spreading the Word: The American Tract Society, *The Dairyman's Daughter*, and Mass Publishing," *Book History*, 14, 2011, pp. 25–57.

19 King and Truck detail the incidence of murder of Black people by lynching in the North and South, and come to the conclusion that adjusting for Black population, lynchings were as common in the North as they were in the South. That is, the percentage of the Black population lynched in each region was the same; it was just the number of people lynched up North was smaller, given the smaller density of population.

Conclusion

1 This assertion answers Heather O'Connell's question in "More than Rocks and Stone: Confederate Monuments, Memory, Movements, and Race": "Are Confederate monuments a response to (Black) mobilization for equality and/ or are they a reflection of the privileged position of Whites to assert their perspective on the public landscape?" (1480). The answer, I would argue, is both, since the two are inextricable.

2 Veneration of Lee was a constant even before his death in 1870, but it intensified afterward, and grew to epic proportions after the end of Reconstruction.

3 Kirk Savage points to the centrality of Lee to the pantheon of Confederate statuary: "the equestrian image of Lee stood for nothing less than the moral authority of the Confederacy and of white power in general" (135), which goes part of the way in explaining why the threatened removal of a statue of Lee was the occasion for the white nationalist "Unite the Right" march in Charlottesville in 2017.

4 As Karen L. Cox shows, these monuments were expensive. Even local statues of generic Confederate soldiers ran up to $4,000, and more elaborate statuary like the Jefferson Davis monument in Richmond cost $70,000. Other large monuments could cost between $50,000 and $65,000 (56).

224 *Notes to pages 195–199*

5 O'Connell traces the building of Confederate monuments decade by decade. Before 1900, the new monuments installed represented only about 6 percent of the total, as contrasted with 1900–20, which saw about half of all Confederate memorials erected throughout the South. After 1920, monument construction dropped significantly: only 9 percent of statuary was installed between 1920 and 1930, and even less between 1930 and 1960. There is a brief blip in the decade 1960–70, but still only 6 percent of all monuments. Oddly, there is also a brief rise in the number of memorials constructed in 2000–10, although less than in 1960–70, perhaps in reaction to 9/11 and the concomitant rise in right-wing radicalism.

6 The Liberty Place monument, a white obelisk, was installed in 1891, seventeen years after the actual battle. Its role in enforcing and maintaining white supremacy was made clear by an inscription on the obelisk's pedestal that was added in 1932: "UNITED STATES TROOPS TOOK OVER THE STATE // GOVERNMENT AND REINSTATED THE USURPERS // BUT THE NATIONAL ELECTION NOVEMBER 1876 // RECOGNIZED WHITE SUPREMACY IN THE SOUTH // AND GAVE US OUR STATE" (Maxson 57).

7 In fact, in late 2021, Ralph Northam, outgoing governor of Virginia, had the pedestal disassembled and removed (see "Protesters transformed Richmond's Robert E. Lee memorial. Now they mourn the loss of their most powerful icon of resistance," *Washington Post*, December 11, 2021).

Bibliography

Abbott, S. G. "Memorial Day Address." *New Hampshire Sentinel*, June 4, 1890, p. 1.

Adams, Nehemiah. *Agnes and the Key to Her Little Coffin, by Her Father.* Boston: S. K. Whipple, 1857.

Alcott, Louisa May. *Hospital Sketches.* Boston: James Redpath, 1863.

Alexander, Harriet. "'Our Great Country Being Ripped Apart': Donald Trump Criticises 'Foolish' Removal of Confederate Monuments in New Tweets." *Daily Telegraph*, August 17, 2017. www.telegraph.co.uk/news/2017/08/17/donald-trump-says-removal-confederate-monuments-great-country/. Accessed July 8, 2022.

Altschuler, Sari. *The Medical Imagination: Literature and Health in the Early United States.* Philadelphia: University of Pennsylvania Press, 2018.

Anthony, Susan B. Letter, August 6, 1866. Anna E. Dickinson Papers, New-York Historical Society.

Armstrong, Tim. *The Logic of Slavery: Debt, Technology, and Pain in American Literature.* New York: Cambridge University Press, 2012.

Asen, Robert. "A Discourse Theory of Citizenship." *Quarterly Journal of Speech*, vol. 90, no. 2, 2004, pp. 189–211.

Avins, Alfred, editor. *The Reconstruction Amendments Debates: The Legislative History and Contemporary Debates in Congress on the 13th, 14th, and 15th Amendments.* Richmond: Virginia Commission on Constitutional History, 1967.

Aynes, Richard L. "The 39th Congress (1865–1867) and the 14th Amendment." In *Infinite Hope, Finite Disappointment: The Story of the First Interpreters of the Fourteenth Amendment,* edited by Elizabeth Reilly. Akron, OH: University of Akron Press, 2011, pp. 56–73.

Badger, Henry. *The Empty Sleeve.* Toledo: W. W. Whitney, 1864.

Barnes, Albert Rev. "Peace and Honor: A Thanksgiving Sermon." *The National Preacher*, vol. 15, no. 1, 1866, pp. 1–12.

Bell, Charles. *The Hand: Its Mechanisms and Vital Endowments as Evincing Design.* London: William Pickering, 1834.

Benjamin, Walter. *Illuminations.* Edited by Hannah Arendt. New York: Schocken Books, 1968.

Bibliography

Bentley, Nancy. "Reconstruction and the Cruel Optimism of Citizenship." *American Literary History*, vol. 30, no. 3, 2018, pp. 608–15.

Berlant, Lauren. *The Queen of America Goes to Washington City: Essays of Sex and Citizenship*. Durham, NC: Duke University Press, 1997.

Bindman, David. "Am I Not a Man and a Brother? British Art and Slavery in the Eighteenth Century." *Res*, vol. 26, 1994, pp. 68–82.

Blight, David W. *Race and Reunion: The Civil War in American Memory*. Cambridge, MA: Harvard University Press, 2001.

Blum, Edward J. *Reforging the White Republic: Race, Religion, and American Nationalism, 1865–1898*. Baton Rouge: Louisiana State University Press, 2005.

Boggs, Colleen Glenney. "The Civil War's 'Empty Sleeve' and the Cultural Production of Disabled Americans." *J19*, vol. 3, no. 1, 2015, pp. 41–65.

Bond, James E. *No Easy Walk to Freedom: Reconstruction and the Ratification of the Fourteenth Amendment*. London: Praeger, 1997.

Bourdieu, Pierre. *In Other Words: Toward a Reflexive Sociology*. Translated by Matthew Adamson. Stanford, CA: Stanford University Press, 1990.

"Breakers Ahead: Lecture by Miss Anna E. Dickinson at the Cooper Institute." *New York Times*, December 11, 1867, p. 5.

Brinton, John H. *Personal Memoirs of John H. Brinton, Major and Surgeon U.S.V., 1861–1865*. New York: Neale Publishing, 1914.

Bromwich, Jonah Engel. "What Does It Mean to Tear down a Statue?" *New York Times*, June 11, 2020, updated June 24, 2020. nytimes.com/2020/6/11/style/confederate-statue-columbus-analysis.html. Accessed July 7, 2020.

Bucklin, Sophronia E. *In Hospital and Camp: A Woman's Record of Thrilling Incidents among the Wounded in the Late War*. Philadelphia: John E. Potter and Company, 1869.

Burbick, Joan. *Healing the Republic: The Language of Health and the Culture of Nationalism in Nineteenth-Century America*. New York: Cambridge University Press, 1994.

Burgess, N. G. "Taking Portraits after Death." *The Photographic Fine Art Journal*, vol. 80, 1855, p. 80.

Burke, Devin. "'Good Bye, Old Arm': The Domestication of Veterans' Disabilities in Civil War Era Popular Songs." In *The Oxford Handbook of Music and Disability Studies*, edited by Blake Howe, Stephanie Jensen-Moulton, Neil Lerner, and Joseph Straus. New York: Oxford University Press, 2015, pp. 423–44.

Bushnell, Horace. "Our Obligations to the Dead." 1865. In *Building Eras in Religion*. New York: Charles Scribner's Sons, 1881, pp. 319–35.

The Vicarious Sacrifice: Grounded in Principles of Universal Obligation. New York: Charles Scribner, 1866.

Castronovo, Russ. "Deconstructing Reconstruction." *American Literary History*, vol. 30, no. 3, 2018, pp. 616–26.

Necro Citizenship: Death, Eroticism, and the Public Sphere in the Nineteenth-Century United States. Durham, NC: Duke University Press, 2001.

Bibliography

Cervetti, Nancy. *S. Weir Mitchell, 1829–1914: Philadelphia Literary Physician.* State College: Pennsylvania State University Press, 2012.

Child, Lydia Maria. *The Freedmen's Book.* Boston: Ticknor & Fields, 1865.

Letters of Lydia Maria Child. Boston: Houghton Mifflin, 1883.

Christmas, Danielle. "Weaponizing Silent Sam: Heritage Politics and the Third Revolution." In *Reading Confederate Monuments*, edited by Maria Seger. Jackson: University Press of Mississippi, 2022, pp. 99–117.

Cimbala, Paul A. "The Freedmen's Bureau, the Freedmen, and Sherman's Grant in Reconstruction Georgia, 1865–1867." *The Journal of Southern History*, vol. 55, no. 4, 1989, pp. 597–632.

Under the Guardianship of the Nation: The Freedmen's Bureau and the Reconstruction of Georgia, 1865–1870. Athens: University of Georgia Press, 1997.

Clarke, Frances. "'Honorable Scars': Northern Amputees and the Meaning of Civil War Injuries." In *Union Soldiers and the Northern Home Front: Wartime Experiences, Postwar Adjustments*, edited by Paul A. Cimbala and Randall Miller. New York: Fordham University Press, 2002.

Coe, S. L., and George Cooper. *Old Arm Good Bye.* Chicago: H. M. Higgins, 1866.

Congressional Globe. Senate, 39th Congress, May 24, 1866.

Cox, Karen L. *Dixie's Daughters: The United Daughters of the Confederacy and the Preservation of Confederate Culture.* Gainesville: University Press of Florida, 2003.

The Cripple, vol. 1, no. 1, October 8, 1864.

The Cripple, vol. 1, no. 4, October 29, 1864.

Crouch, Barry A. "Black Education in Civil War and Reconstruction Louisiana: George T. Ruby, the Army, and the Freedmen's Bureau." *Louisiana History: The Journal of the Louisiana Historical Society*, vol. 38, no. 3, 1997, pp. 287–308.

Curtis, Michael Kent. "Albion Tourgée: Remembering Plessy's Lawyer on the 100th Anniversary of *Plessy v. Ferguson.*" *Constitutional Commentary*, vol. 13, no. 2, 1996, pp. 187–99.

Cuyler, Theodore. *The Empty Crib: The Memorial of Little Georgie, with Words of Consolation for Bereaved Parents.* New York: Baker and Taylor, 1868.

Darda, Joseph. "'The Sacrificial Enterprise': Negotiating Mutilation in W. D. Howells' *A Hazard of New Fortunes.*" *American Literary Realism*, vol. 46, no. 3, 2014, pp. 210–29.

Davis, Cynthia J. *Bodily and Narrative Forms: The Influence of Medicine on American Literature 1845–1915.* Stanford, CA: Stanford University Press, 2000.

Davis, Robert Leigh. *Whitman and the Romance of Medicine.* Berkeley: University of California Press, 1997.

Dedmun, J. W., and P. A. Hanaford. *The Empty Sleeve.* Boston: Oliver Ditson, 1866.

"Desecrating the Gettysburg Reunion." *Harrisburg Telegraph*, July 7, 1888, p. 1.

Bibliography

Devine, Shauna. *Learning from the Wounded: The Civil War and the Rise of American Medical Science*. Chapel Hill: University of North Carolina Press, 2017.

Dickinson, Anna E. "Draft of Speech on Andrew Johnson." Anna E. Dickinson Papers, New-York Historical Society. Undated.

Speeches and Writings File 1868–1907. Anna E. Dickinson Papers, New-York Historical Society. Undated.

A Tour of Reconstruction: Travel Letters of 1874. Edited by J. Matthew Gillman. Lexington: University Press of Kentucky, 2011.

What Answer? Boston: Ticknor & Fields, 1869.

Dickinson, Emily. *The Letters of Emiliy Dickinson*. Edited by Thomas H. Johnson. Cambridge, MA: Belknap Press of Harvard University Press, 1958.

Dickinson, Susan. Letter, January 29, 1867, Scrapbook, Anne E. Dickinson Papers, New-York Historical Society.

District of Columbia Education, Registered Letters Received, Entered in Register 1, P-Y, Jan. 1868–Dec. 1869, Part 1. https://transcription.si.edu/project/14871. Accessed March 2019.

Donald, Bernice Bouie. "When the Rule of Law Breaks Down: Implications of the 1866 Memphis Massacre for the Passage of the Fourteenth Amendment." *Boston University Law Review*, vol. 99, no. 6, 2018, pp. 1607–76.

Douglass, Frederick. "Govern with Magnanimity and Courage: An Address Delivered in Philadelphia, Pennsylvania on 6 September1866." In *The Frederick Douglass Papers*, series 1, vol. 4, edited by John W. Blassingame and John R. McKivigan. New Haven, CT: Yale University Press, 1991, pp. 139–46.

Edelstein, Sari. *Adulthood and Other Fictions: American Literature and the Unmaking of Age*. New York: Oxford University Press, 2018.

Edwards, Laura F. "The Civil War and Reconstruction." In *The Cambridge History of Law in America, vol. 2: The Long Nineteenth Century (1789–1920)*, edited by Michael Grossberg and Christopher Tomlins. Cambridge: Cambridge University Press, 2008, pp. 313–44.

"The Eloquence of Anna Dickinson." *Western Musical Review*, December 1, 1869. Scrapbook, Anna E. Dickinson Papers, New-York Historical Society.

Eng, David L., and David Kazanjian. "Introduction." In *Loss: The Politics of Mourning*, edited by David L. Eng and David Kazanjian. Berkeley: University of California Press, 2003, pp. 1–28.

Epps, Garrett. "The Antebellum Political Background of the 14th Amendment." In *Infinite Hope, Finite Disappointment: The Story of the First Interpreters of the Fourteenth Amendment*, edited by Elizabeth Reilly. Akron, OH: University of Akron Press, 2011, pp. 11–34.

Faulkner, Carol. *Women's Radical Reconstruction: The Freedmen's Aid Movement*. Philadelphia: University of Pennsylvania Press, 2004.

Faust, Drew Gilpin. *This Republic of Suffering: Death and the American Civil War*. New York: Alfred A. Knopf, 2008.

Bibliography

Figg, Laurann, and Jane Farrell-Beck. "Amputation in the Civil War: Physical and Social Dimensions." *Journal of the History of Medicine and Allied Sciences,* vol. 48, no. 4, pp. 454–75.

Folsom, Ed. "'A yet more terrible and more deeply complicated problem': Walt Whitman, Race, Reconstruction, and American Democracy." *American Literary History*, vol. 30, no. 3, 2018, pp. 531–57.

Foner, Eric. *Reconstruction: America's Unfinished Revolution, 1863–1877.* 1988. New York: Harper Perennial Classics, 2014.

Foster, Gaines M. *Ghosts of the Confederacy: Defeat, the Lost Cause, and the Emergence of the New South.* New York: Oxford University Press, 1987.

Foster, Travis M. *Genre and White Supremacy in the Postemancipation United States.* New York: Oxford University Press, 2019.

Foulke, William Dudley. *Life of Oliver P. Morton, Including His Important Speeches*, vol. 2. Indianapolis: Bowen-Merrill, 1899.

Francis, Jacqueline. "Bearden's Hands." In *Studies in the History of Art*, vol. 71, Symposium Papers XLVIII: "Romare Bearden, American Artist." Washington, DC: Center for Advanced Study in the Visual Arts, 2011, pp. 119–42.

Frank, Lucy. "'Bought with a Price': Elizabeth Stuart Phelps and the Commodification of Heaven in Postbellum America." *ESQ: A Journal of the American Renaissance*, vol. 55, no. 2, 2009, pp. 165–83.

Franke, Katherine M. "Becoming a Citizen: Reconstruction Era Regulation of African American Marriages." *Yale Journal of Law and Humanities*, vol. 11, no. 2, 1999, pp. 251–309.

Freemon, Frank R. *Gangrene and Glory: Medical Care during the American Civil War.* Madison, NJ: Fairleigh Dickinson University Press, 1998.

Gallagher, Shaun. "The Enactive Hand." In *The Hand: An Organ of the Mind*, edited by Zdrarko Radman et al. Cambridge, MA: Harvard University Press, pp. 209–25.

Gallman, J. Matthew. *America's Joan of Arc: The Life of Anna Elizabeth Dickinson.* New York: Oxford University Press, 2006.

Garnet, Henry Highland. *A Memorial Discourse by Rev. Henry Highland Garnet,, Delivered in the Hall of the House of Representatives, Washington City, D.C., on Sabbath, February 12th, 1865.* Philadelphia: Joseph M. Wilson, 1865.

Garrison, William Lloyd. *No Compromise with Slavery: An Address Delivered at the Broadway Tabernacle, New York, February 14, 1854.* New York: American Anti-Slavery Society, 1854.

"Gettysburg: A Continuation of the Celebration Yesterday." *Macon* (GA) *Telegraph*, July 3, 1888, p. 1.

"Gettysburg Field: The Turning Point of the War of Rebellion." *Wilkes-Barre News*, July 4, 1888, p. 1.

Goldstein, Alyosha. "Possessive Investment: Indian Removals and the Affective Entitlements of Whiteness." *American Quarterly*, vol. 66, no. 4, 2104, pp. 1077–84.

Bibliography

"Green Clad Gettysburg. Twenty-Fifth Anniversary of the Decisive Contest." *Philadelphia Inquirer*, July 2, 1888, p. 1.

Gross, S. D. *A Manual of Military Surgery; or, Hints on the Emergencies of Field, Camp, and Hospital Practice*. Philadelphia: J. B. Lippincott, 1861.

Gustafson, Melanie Susan. *Women and the Republican Party 1854–1924*. Champaign-Urbana: University of Illinois Press, 2001.

Halloran, Fiona Deane. *Thomas Nast: The Father of Modern Political Cartoons*. Chapel Hill: University of North Carolina Press, 2013.

Harper, Frances Ellen Watkins. *A Brighter Coming Day: A Frances Ellen Watkins Harper Reader*. Edited by Frances Smith Foster. New York: Feminist Press of CUNY, 1990.

Harris, Cheryl. "Whiteness as Property." *Harvard Law Review*, vol. 106, 1993, pp. 1707–71.

Harris, M. Keith. *Across the Bloody Chasm: The Culture of Commemoration among Civil War Veterans*. Baton Rouge: Louisiana State University Press, 2014.

Harrison, Robert. "New Representations of a 'Misrepresented Bureau': Reflections on Recent Scholarship on the Freedmen's Bureau." *American Nineteenth Century History*, vol. 8, no. 2, 2007, pp. 205–29.

Hartman, Saidiya. *Scenes of Subjection: Terror, Slavery, and Self-Making in Nineteenth-Century America*. New York: Oxford University Press, 1997.

Hasegawa, Gary R. *Mending Broken Soldiers: The Union and Confederate Programs to Supply Artificial Limbs*. Carbondale: Southern Illinois University Press, 2012.

Hayward, G. M. *Good-Bye Old Arm!* Baltimore: George Willig, 1865.

Holmes, Oliver Wendell. "The Human Wheel, Its Spokes and Felloes." *Atlantic Monthly*, vol. 12, no. 67, 1863, pp. 567–80.

Howard, Oliver Otis. *Autobiography of Oliver Otis Howard*, 2 vols. New York: Baker & Taylor, 1907.

Howells, William Dean. *A Hazard of New Fortunes*. 1890. New York: Penguin Books, 1994.

Hyde, Carrie. *Civic Longing: The Speculative Origins of U.S. Citizenship*. Cambridge, MA: Harvard University Press, 2018.

"It's Again a Tented Field: Sickles and Longstreet at Gettysburg." *New York Times*, July 1, 1888, p. 1.

Jackson, Cassandra. "Rewriting the Landscape: Black Communities and the Confederate Monuments They Inherited." In *Reading Confederate Monuments*, edited by Maria Seger. Jackson: University Press of Mississippi, 2022, pp. 191–212.

Jackson, Holly. *American Blood: The Ends of the Family in American Literature, 1850–1900*. New York: Oxford University Press, 2014.

American Radicals: How Nineteenth-Century Protest Shaped the Nation. New York: Crown, 2019.

Jarman, Baird. "The Graphic Art of Thomas Nast: Politics and Propriety in Postbellum Publishing." *American Periodicals*, vol. 20, no. 2, 2010, pp. 156–89.

Bibliography

"Jeanne D'Arc: Lecture by Miss Anna Dickinson." *The New Brunswick Daily Times.* Undated (1870?). Scrapbook, Anna E. Dickinson Papers, New-York Historical Society.

Johnson, Allison M. *The Left-Armed Corps: Writings by Amputee Civil War Veterans.* Baton Rouge: Louisiana State University Press, 2022.

    The Scars We Carve: Bodies and Wounds in Civil War Print Culture. Baton Rouge: Louisiana State University Press, 2019.

Johnson, Charles F. *The Civil War Letters of Charles F. Johnson, Invalid Corps.* Edited by Fred Pelka. Amherst: University of Massachusetts Press, 2004.

Jones, Paul Christian. *Unwelcome Voices: Subversive Fiction in the Antebellum South.* Knoxville: University of Tennessee Press, 2005.

Jordan, Brian Matthew. "'Living Monuments': Union Veteran Amputees and the Embodied Memory of the Civil War." *Civil War History,* vol. 57, no. 2, 2011, pp. 121–52.

    Marching Home: Union Veterans and Their Unending Civil War. New York: Liveright, 2014.

Joy, Natalie. "Cherokee Slaveholders and Radical Abolitionists: An Unlikely Alliance in Antebellum America." *Common-place: The Interactive Journal of Early American Life,* vol. 10, no. 4 (July 2010). https://commonplace.online/article/cherokee-slaveholders-radical-abolitionists/. Accessed July 23, 2021.

Karcher, Carolyn L. *First Woman In the Republic: A Cultural Biography of Lydia Maria Child.* Durham, NC: Duke University Press, 1994.

    A Refugee from His Race: Albion W. Tourgée and His Fight against White Supremacy. Chapel Hill: University of North Carolina Press, 2016.

Kennedy-Nolle, Sharon D. *Writing Reconstruction: Race, Gender, and Citizenship in the Postwar South.* Chapel Hill: University of North Carolina Press, 2015.

Kerr, Richard E., Jr. "Wall of Fire: The Rifle and Civil War Infantry Tactics." Unpublished MA thesis, US Army Command and General Staff College, Fort Leavenworth, 1990.

Kete, Mary Louise. *Sentimental Collaborations: Mourning and Middle-Class Identity in Nineteenth-Century America.* Durham, NC: Duke University Press, 2000.

King, Desmond S., and Stephen G. N. Tuck. "De-Centering the South: America's Nationwide White Supremacist Order after Reconstruction." *Past and Present,* no. 194, 2007, pp. 213–54.

Laski, Gregory. *Untimely Democracy: The Politics of Progress after Slavery.* New York: Oxford University Press, 2018.

Lasser, Carol. "Voyeuristic Abolitionism: Sex, Gender, and the Transformation of Antislavery Rhetoric." *Journal of the Early Republic,* vol. 28, no. 1, 2008, pp. 83–114.

Lawson, Melinda. *Patriot Fires: Forging a New American Nationalism in the Civil War North.* Lawrence: University Press of Kansas, 2002.

Levine, Robert S. *The Failed Promise: Reconstruction, Frederick Douglass, and the Impeachment of Andrew Johnson.* New York: W. W. Norton & Company, 2021.

Litwack, Leon F. *North of Slavery: The Negro in the Free States.* Chicago: University of Chicago Press, 1965.

Livermore, Mary A. *My Story of the War: A Woman's Narrative of Four Years' Personal Experience.* Hartford, CT: J. D. Worthington, 1889.

Long, Lisa A. "'The Corporeity of Heaven': Rehabilitating the Civil War in *The Gates Ajar.*" *American Literature*, vol. 64, no. 4, 1997, pp. 781–811.

Luciano, Dana. *Arranging Grief: Sacred Time and the Body in Nineteenth-Century America.* New York: New York University Press, 2007.

Magliocca, Gerard N. *American Founding Son: John Bingham and the Invention of the Fourteenth Amendment.* New York: New York University Press, 2013.

Manual of Military Surgery: Prepared for the Use of the Confederate States Army. By Order of the Surgeon General. Richmond, VA: Ayres and Wade, 1863.

Marrs, Cody. "Three Theses on Reconstruction." *ALH*, vol. 30 no. 3, 2018, pp. 407–20.

Marten, James. *Sing Not War: The Lives of Union and Confederate Veterans in Gilded Age America.* Chapel Hill: University of North Carolina Press, 2011.

Mathiesen, Erik. *The Loyal Republic: Traitors, Slaves, and the Rendering of Citizenship in Civil War America.* Chapel Hill: University of North Carolina Press, 2018.

Maxson, J. David. "'Second Line to Bury White Supremacy': Take 'Em Down Nola Monument Removal, and Residual Memory." *Quarterly Journal of Speech*, vol. 106, no. 1, 2020, pp. 48–71.

McClay, Wilfred M. "Of Statues and Symbolic Murder." *First Things*, July 26, 2020. firstthings.com/web-exclusives/2020/06/of-statues-and-symbolic-murder. Accessed June 8, 2022.

McGarry, Molly. *Ghosts of Futures Past: Spiritualism and the Cultural Politics of Nineteenth-Century America.* Berkeley: University of California Press, 2008.

Miller, Brian Craig. *Empty Sleeves: Amputation in the Civil War South.* Athens: University of Georgia Press, 2015.

"Miss Dickinson at the Cooper Institute." *The National Antislavery Standard*, vol. 24, no. 39, February 6, 1864, p. 3.

"Miss Dickinson's Address." *The Liberator*, vol. 33, no. 2, 1863, p. 15.

"Miss Dickinson's Lecture Last Evening." Unidentified source. 1864? Anna E. Dickinson Papers, New-York Historical Society.

"Miss Dickinson Speaks." *The Liberator*, vol. 34, no. 7, 1864, p. 28.

Mitchell, David T., and Sharon L. Snyder. *Narrative Prostheses: Disability and the Dependencies of Discourse.* Ann Arbor: University of Michigan Press, 2000.

Mitchell, Koritha. *From Slave Cabins to the United House: Homemade Citizenship in African American Culture.* Urbana: University of Illinois Press, 2020.

Mitchell, S. Weir. "The Case of George Dedlow." In *The Autobiography of a Quack and Other Stories.* New York: Century Company, 1900.

Injuries of the Nerves and Their Consequences. Philadelphia: J. B. Lippincott, 1872.

Moore, Frank, editor. *The Civil War in Song and Story, 1860–1865.* New York: P. F. Collier, 1889.

Bibliography

Morris, Angela L. "Take 'Em Down 901: The Kairos of Progressive Activism during a National Rise in Racist Rhetoric." *Spark: A 4C4 Journal*, vol. 1, no. 1, March 2019. Sparkactivism.com/volume-1-intro. Accessed July 7, 2022.

Morton, Oliver P. *Oration of Hon. O. P. Morton, Address of Major General George G. Meade, and Dedication Ode for the National Cemetery at Gettysburg, July 1, 1869, by Bayard Taylor.* Washington, DC: Gettysburg National Monument Association, 1870.

Mzezwa, Tariro. "The Woman Who Took Down a Confederate Flag on What Comes Next." *New York Times*, June 15, 2020, p. A12.

Nabers, Deak. *Victory of Law: The Fourteenth Amendment, the Civil War, and American Literature, 1852–1867.* Baltimore: Johns Hopkins University Press, 2006.

"The Negro Question: Essays and Sketches Touching upon It by a Colored Writer." *New York Times*, April 25, 1903, BR7.

"Negro Suffrage: The New Agitations of the Anti-Slavery Society." *New York Times*, May 13, 1865, p. 8.

Nelson, Megan Kate. *Ruin Nation: Destruction and the American Civil War.* Athens: University of Georgia Press, 2012.

Nelson, William E. *The Fourteenth Amendment: From Political Principle to Judicial Doctrine.* Cambridge, MA: Harvard University Press, 1988.

Newman, Kathy. "Wounds and Wounding in the American Civil War." *Yale Journal of Criticism*, vol. 6, no. 2, 1993, pp. 63–86.

North Carolina Assistant Commissioner, Reports of Operations, Statistical Reports, Oct. 1865–Oct. 1866. https://transcription.si.edu/project/13751. Accessed March 2019.

Novak, William J. "The Legal Transformation of Citizenship in Nineteenth-Century America." In *The Democratic Experiment: New Directions in American Political History*, edited by Meg Jacobs, William J. Novak, and Julian E. Zelizer. Princeton, NJ: Princeton University Press, 2003, pp. 85–119.

Nudelman, Franny. *John Brown's Body: Slavery, Violence, and the Civil War.* Chapel Hill: University of North Carolina Press, 2004.

O'Connell, Heather. "More than Rocks and Stone: Confederate Monuments, Memory Movements, and Race." *Social Forces*, vol. 100, no. 4, 2022, pp. 1479–502.

Olmstead, Frederick Law. *Hospital Transports: A Memoir of the Sick and Wounded from the Peninsula of Virginia in the Summer of 1862.* Boston: Ticknor and Fields, 1863.

"On Gettysburg's Field: Auspicious Opening of the Great Reunion." *New York Times*, July 2, 1888, p. 1.

O'Sullivan, Susan B., and Thomas J. Schmitz. *Physical Rehabilitation: Assessment and Treatment.* Philadelphia: F. A. Davis, 2000.

Parton, Jane, et al., editors. *Eminent Women of the Age: Being Narratives of the Lives and Deeds of the Most Prominent Women of the Present Generation.* Hartford, CT: S. M. Betts, 1868.

Bibliography

Paterson, Mark. *The Sense of Touch: Haptics, Affects, and Technologies.* New York: Taylor and Francis Group, 2007.

Perhamus, Lisa M., and Clarence M. Joldersma. "What Might Sustain the Activism of This Moment? Dismantling White Supremacy, One Monument at a Time." *Journal of Philosophy of Education*, vol. 54, no. 5, 2020, pp. 1314–32.

Phelps, Elizabeth Stuart. *The Gates Ajar.* Boston: Fields, Osgood, 1869.

Phillips, Phillip, and Fanny Crosby ("The Blind Poetess"). *Good-By, Old Arm! A Pathetic Song and Chorus.* Cincinnati: John Church, Jr., 1865.

Preston, R. A. "A Letter from a British Military Observer of the American Civil War." *Military Affairs*, vol. 16, no. 2, 1952, pp. 49–60.

Proceedings of the National Convention of Colored Men; held in the City of Syracuse, N.Y.; October 4, 5, 6, and 7, 1864; with the Bill of Wrongs and Rights; and the Address to the American People. Boston: J. S. Rock and Geo. L. Ruffin, 1864.

Putzi, Jennifer. *Identifying Marks: Race, Gender, and the Marked Body in Nineteenth-Century America.* Athens: University of Georgia Press, 2006.

Quarles, Benjamin. *Black Abolitionists.* New York: Oxford University Press, 1969.

Quigley, Paul. "Introduction." In *The Civil War and the Transformation of Citizenship*, edited by Paul Quigley. Baton Rouge: Louisiana State University Press, 2018, pp. 1–17.

Radman, Zdravko, et al. *The Hand: An Organ of the Mind.* Cambridge, MA: Harvard University Press.

Ray, Angela G. *The Lyceum and Public Culture in the Nineteenth-Century United States.* East Lansing: Michigan State University Press, 2005.

Redpath, James. *The Public Life of John Brown, with an Autobiography of His Youth.* Boston: Thayer and Eldridge, 1860.

Reidy, Joseph P. "The African American Struggle for Citizenship Rights in the Northern United States during the Civil War." In *Civil War Citizens: Race, Ethnicity, and Identity in America's Bloodiest Conflict*, edited by Susannah J. Ural. New York: New York University Press, 2010, pp. 213–36.

Reilly, Elizabeth, editor. *Infinite Hope, Finite Disappointment: The Story of the First Interpreters of the Fourteenth Amendment.* Akron, OH: University of Akron Press, 2011,

Reynolds, Larry J. *Righteous Violence: Revolution, Slavery, and the American Renaissance.* Athens: University of Georgia Press, 2011.

Rhode, Michael G. "The Rise and Fall of the Army Medical Museum and Library." *Washington History*, vol. 18, no. 1, 2006, pp. 78–97.

"R.H.X." "Formation of Colored Regiments." *The Weekly Anglo-African*, vol. 1, no. 9, 1861, p. 1.

Richards, David A. J. *Conscience and the Constitution: History, Theory, and Law of the Reconstruction Amendments.* Princeton, NJ: Princeton University Press, 1993.

Richardson, Heather Cox. *The Death of Reconstruction: Race, Labor, and Politics in the Post–Civil War North, 1865–1901.* Cambridge, MA: Harvard University Press, 2001.

Bibliography

Richmond City Council Chief of Staff. "Richmond City Council Requests Research Review Matrix." September 9, 2021. www.rva.gov/richmond-city-council/confederate-monuments-disposition. Accessed July 12, 2022.

Ritchie, Daniel. "War, Religion, and Anti-Slavery Ideology: Isaac Nelson's Radical Abolitionist Examination of the American Civil War." *Historical Research*, vol. 89, no. 246, 2016, pp. 799–823.

Rogers, Blair O. "Reed B. Bontecou, M.D.: His Role in Civil War Surgery and Medical Photography." *Aesthetic Plastic Surgery*, vol. 24, 2000, pp. 114–29.

Rogosin, Elizabeth. "Huldah Gordon and the Question of Former Slaves' Citizenship." In *The Civil War and the Transformation of American Citizenship*, edited by Paul Quigley. Baton Rouge: Louisiana State University Press, 2018, pp. 21–43.

Ross, Sam. *The Empty Sleeve: A Biography of Lucius Fairchild*. Madison: State Historical Society of Wisconsin, 1964.

Roth, Wolff-Michael. *First-Person Methods: Toward an Empirical Phenomenology of Experience*. Rotterdam: Sense Publishers, 2012.

Ruby, Jay. *Secure the Shadow: Death and Photography in America*. Cambridge, MA: MIT Press, 1995.

Samuels, Shirley. *Facing America: Iconography and the Civil War*. New York: Oxford University Press, 2004.

Sánchez-Eppler, Karen. *Dependent States: The Child's Part in Nineteenth-Century America*. Chicago: University of Chicago Press, 2005.

Savage, Kirk. *Standing Soldiers, Kneeling Slaves: Race, War, and Monument in Nineteenth-Century America*. Princeton, NJ: Princeton University Press, 1997.

Schantz, Mark S. *Awaiting the Heavenly Country: The Civil War and America's Culture of Death*. Ithaca, NY: Cornell University Press, 2008.

Schmidt, James M., and Guy R. Hasegawa, editors. *Years of Change and Suffering: Modern Perspectives of Civil War Medicine*. Roseville, MN: Edinborough Press, 2009.

Schneider, Gregory S. "Protesters Transformed Richmond's Robert E. Lee Memorial. Now They Mourn the Loss of Their Most Powerful Icon of Resistance." *Washington Post*, December 11, 2021. www.washingtonpost.com/dc-md-va/2021/12/11/richmond-lee-statue-pedestal-dismantled/. Accessed July 14, 2022.

Schnog, Nancy. "'The comfort of my fancying': Loss and Recuperation in The Gates Ajar." *Arizona Quarterly*, vol. 49, no. 1, Spring 1993, pp. 21–47.

Schuller, Kyla. *The Biopolitics of Feeling: Race, Sex, and Science in the Nineteenth Century*. Durham, NC: Duke University Press, 2018.

Schultz, Jane E. *Women at the Front: Hospital Workers in Civil War America*. Chapel Hill: University of North Carolina Press, 2004.

Schurz, Carl. *The Reminiscences of Carl Schurz*, 3 vols. New York: McClure Company, 1907.

Report on the Condition of the South. 1865. New York: Arno Press, 1969.

236 Bibliography

Secor, Anna. "'There Is an Istanbul That Belongs to Me': Citizenship, Space, and Identity in the City." *Annals of the Association of American Geographers*, vol. 94, no. 2, 2004, pp. 352–68.

Serlin, David. "Cripping Masculinity: Queerness and Disability in US Military Culture, 1800–1945." *GLQ*, vol. 9, no. 2, 2003, pp. 149–79.

Replaceable You: Engineering the Body in Postwar America. Chicago: University of Chicago Press, 2004.

Shaffer, Donald R. *After the Glory: The Struggles of Black Civil War Veterans*. Lawrence: University Press of Kansas, 2004.

Sigourney, Lydia Maria. *Poems*. Philadelphia: Key and Biddle, 1834.

Sizer, Lyde Cullen. *The Political Work of Northern Women Writers and the Civil War, 1850–1872*. Chapel Hill: University of North Carolina Press, 2000.

Smith, Adelaide W. *Reminiscences of an Army Nurse during the Civil War*. New York: Greaves Publishing, 1911.

Smith, James McCune. "Citizenship." *The Anglo-American Magazine*, vol. 1, no. 5, 1859, pp. 144–50.

Smith, John David. *We Ask Only for Even-Handed Justice: Black Voices from Reconstruction, 1865–1877*. Amherst: University of Massachusetts Press, 2014.

Snoby, Paulette. *April's Revolution: A Modern Perspective of American Medical Care of Civil War Soldiers and African Slaves*. Bloomington: Indiana University Press, 2014.

"Sometimes." "Anna E. Dickinson's Book." *The Christian Recorder*, vol. 8, no. 35, 1868, p. 1.

Spires, Derrick. *The Practice of Citizenship: Black Politics and Print Culture in the Early United States*. Philadelphia: University of Pennsylvania Press, 2019.

Stanton, Elizabeth Cady, Susan B. Anthony, and Matilda Joslyn Gage, editors. *History of Woman Suffrage*, vol 2. Rochester, NY: Charles Mann, 1881.

Stearns, Amanda Akins. *The Lady Nurse of Ward E*. New York: Baker and Taylor, 1909.

Stevens, Thaddeus. *Reconstruction: Speech of the Hon. Thaddeus Stevens, Delivered in the City of Lancaster, September 7th 1865*. Lancaster, PA: Examiner and Herald Print, 1865.

Stokes, Claudia. *The Altar at Home: Sentimental Literature and Nineteenth-Century American Religion*. Philadelphia: University of Pennsylvania Press, 2014.

Sumner, Charles. "Creation of the Freedmen's Bureau: A Bridge from Slavery to Freedom." 1865. In *Complete Works*, vol. 11. Boston: Shepard and Lee, 1900, pp. 301–50.

"Rejoicing in the Decline of the Rebellion." 1864. In *Complete Works*, vol. 11. Boston: Shepard and Lee, 1900, pp. 414–17.

"Slavery and the Rebellion: One and Inseparable." 1864. In *Complete Works*, vol. 11. Boston: Shepard and Lee, 1900, pp. 434–81.

"Sunday at Gettysburg." *The Times* (Philadelphia), July 2, 1888, p. 1.

Bibliography

Tallis, Raymond. *The Hand: A Philosophical Inquiry into Human Being.* Edinburgh: Edinburgh University Press, 2003.

Taylor, Susie King. *Reminiscences of My Life in Camp.* 1902. Athens: University of Georgia Press, 2006.

Thomas, Brook. "Complicating Today's Myth of the Myths of the Lost Cause: The Calhoun Monument, Reconstruction, and Reconciliation." In *Reading Confederate Monuments*, edited by Maria Seger. Jackson: University Press of Mississippi, 2022, pp. 21–42.

Tourgée, Albion W. *Bricks without Straw.* 1880. Edited by Carolyn Karcher. Durham, NC: Duke University Press, 2009.

A Veteran and His Pipe. Chicago: Belford, Clark, 1886.

Trachtenberg, Alan. *Reading American Photographs: Images as History, Matthew Brady to Walker Evans.* New York: Hill and Wang, 1989.

Tuggle, Lindsay. *The Afterlives of Specimens: Science, Mourning, and Whitman's Civil War.* Iowa City: University of Iowa Press, 2017.

Uliano, Dick. "Richmond City Council Votes on Confederate Statue Measure." *WTOP News*, October 8, 2018. wtop.com/virginia/2018/ how-richmond-city-council-voted-in-measure-on-confederate-statues. Accessed July 8, 2022.

"United at Gettysburg: A Grand Reunion of the Blue and the Gray." *New York Times*, July 3, 1888, p. 1.

US Sanitary Commission. *A Record of the Metropolitan Fair in Aid of the United States Sanitary Commission Held at New York in April 1864.* New York: Hurd and Houghton, 1867.

US Sanitary Commission. *Surgical Memoirs of the War of the Rebellion.* Edited by Frank Hastings Hamilton. New York: Hurd and Houghton, 1871.

US Surgeon General's Office. *The Medical and Surgical History of the War of Rebellion, 1861–1865,* 6 vols. Washington, DC: Government Printing Office, 1870.

VanderHaagen, Sara C., and Angela G. Ray. "A Pilgrim-Critic at Places of Public Memory: Anna Dickinson's Southern Tour of 1875." *Quarterly Journal of Speech,* vol. 100, no. 3, 2014, pp. 348–75.

Vaughn, William Preston. *Schools for All: The Blacks and Public Education in the South, 1865–1877.* Lexington: University Press of Kentucky, 2014.

Verboon, Caitlin. "'The Fire Fiend,' Black Firemen, and Citizenship in the Urban South." In *The Civil War and the Transformation of American Citizenship*, edited by Paul Quigley. Baton Rouge: Louisiana State Press, 2018, pp. 159–77.

"Victories of Peace: The Reunion of Friends and Whilom Foes." *Philadelphia Inquirer,* July 3, 1888, p. 1.

Walcott, Charles F. *History of the Twenty-First Regiment Massachusetts Volunteers in the War for the Preservation of the Union, 1861–1865.* Boston: Houghton, Mifflin, 1883.

Walker, Brandon. "Dissenting Opinion: Stop Tearing down the Statues." *Brigham Young University Scroll.* advance-lexis-com.proxy.wexler.hunter

.cuny.edu/api/document?collection=news&id=urn:contentItem:6073-NFF1-JBSN-31HB-00000-00&context=1516831. Accessed July 7, 2022.

Weinstein, Cindy. "Heaven's Tense: Narration in *The Gates Ajar.*" *Novel*, vol. 45, no. 1, 2012, pp. 56–70.

"Wendell Phillips: What He Asks of Congress." *New York Times*, December 3, 1869, p. 2.

Whiles, Lee Ann. *The Civil War as a Crisis in Gender: Augusta, Georgia 1860–1890*. Athens: University of Georgia Press, 1995.

"Whited Sepulchres." 1870? Scrapbook, Anna E. Dickinson Papers, New-York Historical Society.

Whitman, Walt. *Memoranda during the War*. 1876. Edited by Peter Coviello. New York: Oxford University Press, 2004.

Willard, Sylvester D. *Conservative Surgery, with a List of the Medical and Surgical Force of New York in the War of Rebellion, 1861–2*. Albany, NY: Charles van Benthuysen, 1862.

Williams, Caroline Randall. "You Want a Confederate Monument? My Body Is a Confederate Monument." *New York Times*, June 28, 2020, p. SR4.

Williams, Raymond. *Marxism and Literature*. London: Oxford University Press, 1977. *Resources of Hope: Culture, Democracy, Socialism*, edited by Robin Gable. London: Verso Books, 1989.

Wilson, Susan. "Prejudice and Policy: Racial Discrimination in the Union Army Disability Pension System, 1865–1906." *American Journal of Public Health*, vol. 100, 2010, pp. 556–65.

Wong, Edlie. *Racial Reconstruction: Black Inclusion, Chinese Exclusion, and the Fictions of Citizenship*. New York: New York University Press, 2015.

Wood, Barry D. "Opinion: Pulling Down Confederate Statues Is a Disgrace." *Atlanta Journal-Constitution*. June 9, 2017. www.ajc.com/news/opinion/pulling-down-confederate-statues-disgrace/odcE5dSwEl4f8AcnlwOW5L/. Accessed July 17, 2022.

Yellott, Jock. "The Battle over History Never Ceases." *Bacon's Rebellion*, March 14, 2020. baconsrebellion.com/wp/the-battle-over-history-never-ceases;#more-86743. Accessed July 7, 2022.

Young, Elizabeth. "Footnotes: Amputation and Reconstruction in Reed Bontecou's Civil War Photography." *Mississippi Quarterly*, vols. 70–71, no. 4, Fall 2017/2018, pp. 487–504.

Zandy, Janet. *Hands: Physical Labor, Class, and Cultural Work*. New Brunswick, NJ: Rutgers University Press, 2004.

Zittlau, Andrea. "Pathologizing Bodies: Medical Portrait Photography in Nineteenth-Century America." *Iconographies of the Calamitous in American Visual Culture*. Special issue of *Amerikastudien*, vol. 58, no. 4, 2013, edited by Ingrid Gessner and Susanne Leikam, pp. 543–58.

Zylstra, Geoff D. "Whiteness, Freedom, and Technology: The Racial Struggle over Philadelphia's Streetcars, 1859–1867." *Technology and Culture*, vol. 52, no. 4, 2011, pp. 678–702.

Index

54th Massachusetts Infantry Regiment (Massachusetts 54th), 83, 119

abolitionism, 3, 112, 122
abolitionists, 2–3, 6–9, 111, 118, 202, 206
Adams, Nehemiah, 35–6
  Agnes and the Key to Her Little Coffin, 35–6
Agassiz, Louis, 83
Agnes and the Key to Her Little Coffin (Adams), 35–6
Alcott
  Louisa May, 87
Alcott, Bronson, 88
Alcott, Louisa May, 27, 72, 88–90
  Hospital Sketches, 27, 88–90
American Missionary Association (AMA), 151, 218
American Tract Society (ATS), 151–2, 218
amputation
  of Black soldiers, 111–12
  of Confederate monuments, 191, 196–8
  discourses of, 2, 15, 50, 58, 162
  as guarantee of Black citizenship, 19–20, 25, 67, 103
  and irrecoverable past, 25, 33, 67, 147
  as irreparable, 26, 84, 172
  and masculinity, 16
  meaning of for Southern soldiers, 143, 147
  meaning of for Southerners, 145–6
  medical descriptions of, 77–9
  mortality rates for, 76
  nation, 15, 201
  in payment for slavery, 9, 20, 25, 110, 113, 115–16, 136, 139, 147
  permanence of, 20, 27
  as permanent, 56, 60
  rates of, 1, 15, 72, 75, 83, 89
  as sign of newly non-racist nation, 135
  as sign of permanent change, 14, 51, 54, 72, 83–4, 101, 146
  as sign of the present, 28, 55

stump of, 50
  as symbol of the promise of Black emancipation, 2, 115, 142, 177
  as trope for antiracism, 198
amputee
  as agent of racial justice, 144–5
  in *Bricks without Straw*, 144
  as emblem of the hopes of Reconstruction, 144
  omnipresence of, 15
  staffing the Freedmen's Bureau, 142–3
  as symbol of racial justice, 144
amputees
  Black, 67–9
  in *Bricks without Straw*, 137, 142–3
  as emblem of the hopes of Reconstruction, 5
  in photographs, *See* photography of amputees
  as reminder of the costs of the Civil War, 1
  as sign of Union victory, 5
  staffing the Freedmen's bureau, 142
  as symbol of the excision of slavery, 2, 14
antebellum past
  nostalgia for, 49, 129, 137, 139–40, 147, 156, 183, 194
antebellum period
  nostalgia for, 49, 139, 183, 195
Anthony, Susan B., 107
Army Medical Museum, 27, 72, 80–1, 92–3, 99, 101
Army Military Museum, 91
Asen, Robert, 23
Atlanta Journal-Constitution, 192

Bacon's Rebellion (blog), 192
Badger, Henry, 17
Ball, Thomas, 164
Banneker, Benjamin, 153
Barthes, Roland, 51
Bass, Bree Newsome, 191, 196
Beecher, Henry Ward, 6
Bell, James Madison, 154

240   *Index*

Benjamin, Walter, 73
Berdan, Hiram, 175
Berlant, Lauren, 20
Bingham, John, 107
Black, J. W., 60
Black Codes, 124
Black legislators, 128, 180, 194
Black Lives Matter, 199–200
Blaine, James, 25
Blight, David W., 3, 6, 11, 132, 178, 183
Blum, Edward, 6
Boggs, Colleen Glenney, 16
Bond, James E., 109
Bontecou, Reed Brockway, xi, 31, 50–7
    Gunshot Wounds Illustrated, 54
    photograph of Charles H. Wood,
      51–5
    photograph of John Parmenter, 32–4, 55–8
    as pioneer of medical photography, 49
Bourdieu, Pierre, 123, 158
Bourne, William Oland, 17, 19, 159
Brady, Matthew, 49, 149
Bricks without Straw (Tourgée), 28, 105, 136–7,
    141–3, 156
    amputation in, 142–3, 146, 158
    representation of Black self-determination,
      141, 144
Brinton, John, 72, 80–2, 90–2, 94
    Personal Memoirs, 27, 80–1, 91–4
Brown, John, 2, 9, 60, 111, 153
Brown, William Wells, 25
Bucklin, Sophronia, 81, 83
Burbick, Joan, 14
Burgess, N. G., 41
Burke, Devin, 17
Bushnell, Horace, 4, 7, 9, 11

Calhoun, John, 86
carte de visite, 31, 34, 54, 58–9, 62
"Case of George Dedlow, The," 27, 95
"Case of George Dedlow, The" (Mitchell), 73,
    100–1, 173
Castronovo, Russ, 21, 23
Chauvin, Derek, 191
Chicago Tribune, 170
Child, Lydia Maria, 136, 151, 158, 217
children
    dead, 26, 31, 35, 90
    consolation literature for, 36–7
    discourses of, 35–6
    ethics of representing, 34
    photography of, *See* photography,
      postmortem
Christian Recorder, The, 117
Christmas, Danielle, 193

citizenship
    Black, 2–3, 12, 14, 19–20, 23, 25, 49, 67, 69,
      103–4, 107, 120, 122–3, 125, 132–3,
      151, 158, 162, 164
    "critical," 24
    barriers to, 69
    Black claims to, 5, 20, 155
    and education, 153
    as guaranteed by the Fourteenth
      Amendment, 20, 104, 126
    history of claims to, 21
    homemade, 21
    nation's brief commitment to, 5
    necessity to destroy Slave Power,
      108–9
    as opposed to necro-citizenship, 21
    regional specificity of, 22
    as result of white loss, 115, 123, 125, 129
    second class, 112, 114
    and self-sacrifice, 116, 121
    as public engagement, 24
    and relationship to the state, 23
    US, 21, 23–5, 30, 67, 113
    defined by Fourteenth Amendment, 22,
      103, 109, 126
    opacity of, 22
citizenship, US
    racially equal, 6
Civil Rights Act of 1875, 128
Cleveland
    Grover, 170
Columbia (allegorical figure), 67, 69, 132,
    154–5, 157, 162, 165, 181, 222
Committee of Fifteen, 108
Compromise of 1877, 169
Confederacy, 2, 108, 116, 128–9, 142, 148, 175,
    180, 195, 199
    commitment to extend slavery, 149
    creation of Southern identity, 22
    defeat of, 22, 130, 140, 147
    nostalgia for, 128, 130
    ongoing belief in, 147–8
    pardon for former members, 124
    political power of, 169
    refusal to accept defeat of, 196
    right to the franchise, 103
    secession by, 86
    White House of, 129
Confederate army, 76, 79, 147, 149–50
    amputation in, 96
    Army of Northern Virginia, 161, 174
    in *Bricks without Straw*, 142
    murder of Black soldiers, 114
    in Nast's "Compromise with the South,"
      181

Index

soldiers
  experiences of, 1
  surrender of, 1, 6
  in *What Answer?*, 117–18, 122
Confederate monuments, 194–5
  as ahistorical, 193
  ahistoricism of, 195
  of Jefferson Davis, 198
  location of, 195
  of Nathan Bedford Forrest, 198
  pedestal of Lee monument, 199
  of Robert E. Lee, 195, 199
  removal of, 191–2
  support for, 191–3
  as symbols of white supremacy,
    193–4
Confederate veterans, 182
  at Gettysburg reunion, 161, 173–4
Coviello, Peter, 84–5
Crimean war, 71, 74, 78, 88
Cripple, The, 16
Crutch, The, 16

Dadmun, J. W., 17
Daniel, Larry, 149
Darda, Joseph, 184
Davis, Jefferson, 129–30, 194
Davis, Robert Leigh, 85
death, 87, 90
  child, 35–41
    in the poetry of Lydia Sigourney, 38–41
  of children, 45
  in the Civil War, 33, 96
  denial of, 35, 42, 45, 47
  in *The Empty Crib*, 36–7
  in *The Gates Ajar*, 46–8
  impermanence of, 37
  as impermanent, 42, 44, 96
  meaning of, 35
  meanings of, 34
  as omnipresent, 35
  in photographs, *See* photography, postmortem
  poetry about, 37
  and promise of heaven, 37
  reunion after, 34, 36, 47
  as a way to preserve status quo, 41
Democrats, 11, 166–8, 170, 180, 190, 205, 213
  Congressional, 168
  and Congressional control, 127
  Copperheads, 12, 162
  opposition to extending pensions, 170
  opposition to Reconstruction, 12, 167
  Southern, 169
Dickinson, Anna, 3, 20, 27, 67, 87, 104–6, 109, 118, 122, 194, 201

commitment to Black male franchise, 107
commitment to racial equality, 126
and commitment to Reconstruction, 123
as orator, 105
sentimentalism in, 116–18
takedown of Andrew Johnson, 110–24
tour of the South, 127–32
What Answer?, 104
Dickinson, Emily, 73–4
disability, xii, 4–5, 14, 16, 28, 62, 65, 67, 69,
  110, 120, 137, 143, 145–6, 170, 172,
  184
Disability Studies, 4
disabled, 16, 19
Donald, Bernice Bouie, 108
Douglass, Frederick, 1, 3, 8, 20, 104, 106, 112,
  155–6, 202, 206, 213, 216, 218
Drum Taps (Whitman), 85

Edelstein, Sari, 4
education
  in "Knowledge is Power," 130
  for all Americans, 5, 30, 137, 141
  Black delight in, 157
  as creating informed Black citizenry, 130, 135
  free and public, 140–1, 170
  as hallmark goal of Freedmen's Bureau, 14,
    135
  Lydia Maria Child's views on, 152–3, 156
  progressive plan for Reconstruction, 5
  reinforcing racist tropes, 151
  as reparation, 157
  as reparative project, 152
  as target of white supremacists, 158
Education
  as abstract possession, 135
  as hallmark goal of Freedmen's Bureau, 152
educational
  as hallmark goal of Freedmen's Bureau, 136
Edwards, Laura, 22
Emancipation Memorial, 164
Emerson, Ralph Waldo, 106
Empty Crib, The (Cuyler), 35–7
empty sleeve, 17, 28, 60, 62, 64, 115, 144, 188
  and Alfred Stratton, 65
  and Thomas Plunkett, 60, 62
"Empty Sleeve" (song)
  J. W. Dadmun and P. A. Hanaford version, 17
  Henry Badger version, 17
Epps, Garrett, 108
erysipelas, 78, 210
eschatology, 87, 90–1, 94

Faust, Drew Gilpin, 33, 88
field artillery, 15, 77, 91

242 *Index*

Fifteenth Amendment, 7, 22–3, 127
First Things, 192
Floyd, George, 191, 199, 205
Folsom, Ed, 87
Foner, Eric, 8, 11, 127, 170, 202–3, 216–17,
    219, 222
Fool's Errand, A (Tourgée), 141
Forrest, Nathan Bedford, 198
Fort Wagner, 83, 119
Foster, Travis M., 14
Fourteenth Amendment, 7, 21, 23–4, 103–4,
    108–10, 123, 126–7, 132, 212
  debates over, 24, 107–8, 125
  defining citizenship, 22
  as guarantee of Black citizenship, 104
  as instrument of Black citizenship, 103, 105,
    107, 126
  ratification of, 127
  text of, 103, 118
Francis, Jacqueline, 160
Frank, Lucy, 44
Franke, Katherine, 23
Freedman's Book, The (Child), 136–7, 151–2,
    154–6
  celebrating Black achievement, 153, 155
  to foster Black pride, 156
  narrating usable Black history, 154, 156
  on the wickedness of slavery, 154
Freedmen's Bureau, 4, 26, 28, 134–7, 146
  benefits for poor white people, 140
  in *Bricks without Straw*, 144–5
  creation of, 11, 135
  and education, 14, 135, 151–2, 156
  as instrument for change, 134–5, 140
  services provided by, 134–5
  staffed by amputees, 132, 134, 136–7, 142–4,
    147, 151, 156
  struggles over, 137, 142, 145, 157
  vision for, 135–6
  vision of, 135
freedpeople, 14, 23, 124, 129, 134–6, 143–4,
    151–3, 216–17, 219–20
  debt owed to, 10
  Freedmen's Bureau services for, 135
  Freedmen's Bureau support of, 136, 216
  as model Americans, 11
  needs of, 134
  precarity of, 169, 182
  rights of, 103, 108
  schools for, 130, 151–2, 156–7
  and self-determination, 144
  self-determination of, 132, 156, 178
  violence against, 14, 169, 203
Freemon, Frank R., 75
Fuller, Charles E., 177

Gallman, J. Matthew, 128
Gardner, Alexander, 49
Garnet, Henry Highland, 8
Garrison, William Lloyd, 8–9, 104
The Gates Ajar (Phelps), 45–9, 67, 96
  as consolation literature, 48
Gettysburg, 82
  address, 180
  battle of, 79, 82, 138, 177–8
    25th anniversary reunion, 29, 161, 173–8,
      180–1
  as "American" experience, 178
  depoliticized, 178
  rewriting reality of, 181
  National Cemetery, 7
Gilman, Charlotte Perkins, 73
  The Yellow Wall-paper, 73
Goldstein, Alyosha, 8
Goldstein, Clarence, 196
Goler, Robert I., 95
Gordon, John P., 179–80
Graetz, Friedrich, 171–2, 178
Grand Army of the Republic (GAR),
    170, 173–4, 177
Grant, Ulysses S., 197
Greeley, Horace, 36, 175–7

Halloran, Fiona Deans, 161
Hamilton, Robert, 21
Hamilton, Thomas, 21
Hanaford, P. A., 17
hands, 159–61
  in "The Insatiable Glutton,"
    172–3, 178, 186
  amputated, 1, 17, 81
  human uniqueness in, 159
  multiple functions of, 160
  and proprioception, 159
  shaking, *See* handshakes
  in Thomas Nast's work, 29
handshakes, 161, 174, 178, 180, 182
  "over the bloody chasm," 178
  over the "bloody chasm," 175, 178–80
  between Confederate and Union veterans,
    173–5, 177, 180–1
  meanings of, 174
  rewriting meaning of Civil War,
    174, 177
  rewriting reality of the Civil War, 178
Harper, Frances E. W., 8, 153
  "An Appeal to the American People," 203
  "Words for the Hour," 7
  eulogy for Thaddeus Stevens, 10
Harper's Weekly, 12–13, 16, 29, 69, 161, 180
Harris, Cheryl, 8

Index

Harris, M. Keith, 177
Hartman, Saidiya, 12, 151–2
Hawes, Josiah Johnson, 31–2, 42
Hayes, Rutherford B., 166, 169, 222
Hazard of New Fortunes, A (Howells), 29, 161, 182, 184, 186
heaven, 27, 49, 65
  as "pleasant," 47
  as better for children, 40
  and the body, 42
  as domestic, 96
  earth visible from, 46
  joys of, 40
  and Little Agnes, 36
  materiality of, 46–8, 101
  promise in, 39
  promise of, 37–8, 97
  reunion in, 36, 38–40, 42, 45, 48
  and temporality, 46
Heaven, 49
  reunion in, 40
Helber, Steve, 199
Hewitt, Abram, 166
Hewitt, Edward O., 71–2
History of Woman Suffrage, 106
Holmes, Oliver Wendell, Sr., 15–16
Homer, Winslow, 16
Hospital Sketches (Alcott), 27, 88–90
hospitals, 49, 60
  field, 54, 71–2, 79–81, 86, 89, 149, 172
  Harewood, 49, 51, 55
  makeshift, 80–1
  military, 82, 84–5, 88, 91
  pre-Civil War function of, 88
  Turner's Lane, 73
  Union Hotel, 88
  United States Army Hospital for Injuries and Diseases of the Nervous System ("Stump Hospital"), 95, 100
Howard, Oliver Otis, xii, 4, 28, 87, 136–41, 144, 148, 151–3, 158, 208, 217, 219
  In the, 26
  amputation experience of, 137–40, 149
  analysis of ideological shift in Civil War, 149–50
  commitment to Black equality, 137, 139
  commitment to the Union, 138
  and Freedmen's Bureau, 135
  and the Freedmen's Bureau, 136, 140
  military experience of, 138
  reports of anti-Black violence, 157
  view of Reconstruction, 140
  visit to Port Royal, 152
Howe, Abigail Gould, 37
Howells, William Dean, 29

A Hazard of New Fortunes, 29, 161, 182–90
Hyde, Carrie, 22

Indian Wars, the, 26
Injuries of the Nerves and Their Consequences (Mitchell), 100
"The Insatiable Glutton" (cartoon), 171

J. Gurney & Son, 62
Jackson, Andrew, 197
Jackson, Cassandra, 193
Jackson, Holly, 109
Jim Crow, 29, 180, 194
Johnson, Allison M., 50, 204
Johnson, Andrew, 26, 135
  Anna Dickinson's takedown of, 123–5
  as depicted by Thomas Nast, 162
  impeachment of, 107
  pardons of former Confederates, 124
  radicals' hopes for, 123–4
  and Reconstruction, 123
Johnston, Albert Sidney, 149
Jordan, Brian Matthew, 14, 16

Karcher, Carolyn L., 136
Kellogg, William Pitt, 197
Kennedy-Nolle, Sharon D., 22
Kete, Mary Louise, 37, 42
Kimball, James, 157
Ku Klux Klan, 6, 13–14, 146–7, 158, 169, 198, 213

Landrieu, Mitch, 192–3
Lee, Robert E.
  heroizing of, 128–9, 131, 196
  nostalgia for, 128, 194
  statues of, 130, 192, 194–5, 198–9
Left Armed Corps, 14, 19, 159
left-handed penmanship competitions, 17–19
Lewis, John Randolph, 143–4
limb
  phantom, 73, 95, 100–1
limbs, 82
  as "rejected members," 86
  afterlives of, 72–3, 90, 93–5
  amputated, 9, 26–7, 60, 71–2, 75, 79–82, 88, 90–2, 95
  amputation of, 15
  anthropomorphized, 90, 99
  in the Army Medical Museum, 72
  assigned numbers, 92, 99
  claimed by previous owners, 92
  as claimed by soldiers, 94
  as detritus, 80
  discarded, 91, 97

Index

limbs (cont.)
  effect of new technology on, 75
  exhuming, 93
  as government property, 93–4
  as inanimate objects, 89, 100–1
  as interchangeable, 80
  as medical specimens, 91–2
  mixed promiscuously, 82, 84, 88, 91
  as payment for slavery, 3
  piles of, 3, 27–8, 56, 72, 80–4, 86–7, 90–1,
    93, 102, 147, 149, 172, 211
  preservation process, 91
  reanimated, 99, 101
  resurrection of, 100
  searching for their bodies, 90–1
  signs of irreversible change, 72
  strewn, 82–5
  surgery on, 86, 89
Lincoln, Abraham, 108, 114–15, 124, 148, 164,
  178, 180, 203
  second inaugural address, 114
Livermore, Mary, 81
Long, Lisa A., 48
Longstreet, James, 174–5
Lost Cause, 175, 193–5, 198, 201, 218
Luciano, Dana, 45
lyceum, 3, 104, 106, 127

"A MAN KNOWS A MAN" (cartoon), 69
Manual of Military Surgery (Confederate), 76–9
Manual of Military Surgery (Union), 76–9
Marrs, Cody, 6
Marten, James, 170
Massachusetts Anti-Slavery Society, 8
Mathisen, Erik, 21
Maxson, J. David, 194, 197–8
McClay, Wilfred M., 192
McGarry, Molly, 96
McNulty, William, 64
Memoranda during the War (Whitman), 27, 81,
  84–7
Memphis, TN, 108, 162, 197–9
Memphis massacre, 108
Meyers, Leonard, 109
Miller, Brian Craig, 76, 202, 211
minié ball, 72–5, 77, 79, 91, 139
  difference from older musket ball, 74
  greater accuracy of, 75
  increased damage by, 74
  increased damage from, 74–5, 77
Minié, Claude-Étienne, 74
Mitchell, David T., 4–5
Mitchell, Koritha, 21, 195
Mitchell, S. Weir, 27, 72–3, 95, 211
  "The Case of George Dedlow," 27, 73, 95–101

Injuries of the Nerves and Their
  Consequences, 100
  as neurologist, 100
  and phantom limb, 100
Morton, Oliver P., 7
Morton, Samuel, 83

Nabers, Deak, 109
narrative prosthesis, 4
Nast, Thomas, 4, 12–13, 29, 68–9, 160–1, 163,
  165, 167–70, 172, 175–7, 180–1, 190,
  218, 221
  "Andrew Jackson's Reconstruction and How
    It Works," 162
  "Compromise – Indeed!," 166–8
  "Compromise with the South – Dedicated to
    the Chicago Convention," 180–1
  "Franchise and Not This Man?," 67–70
  "Let Us Clasp Hands Across the Bloody
    Chasm," 175–6
  "To Thine Own Self Be True," 162–4
  "A Truce – Not a Compromise," 162–4, 169
  style of, 162
Nelson, Megan Kate, 15
New Orleans, 162, 192, 194, 197
New York Draft Riots, 105, 120, 126, 161
New York Sanitary Commission Metropolitan
  Fair, 62
New York Times, 124, 174, 191, 206, 218
Nightingale, Florence, 88
Nott, Josiah, 83
nurses, 27, 72, 80–2, 84, 88–9, 221

O'Connell, Heather, 195
"Old Arm Good Bye," 17

Panic of 1873, 127
Parmenter, John, 32–4, 55–8
Paying Investment , A (Dickinson), 133
pension agents, 172
Perhamus, Lisa M., 196
Phelps, Elizabeth Stuart, 45
  The Gates Ajar, 46–9
  and Spiritualism, 96
Philadelphia Inquirer, 175
Phillips, Wendell, 2, 25, 111, 124, 202
photography
  of amputees, 3, 26, 32–5, 49–67
  commercial, 49–50
  ethics of, 34–5
  group portrait of Thomas Plunkett, Charles
    McNulty, and David Wintress, 62–4
  as medical instrument, 34, 50
  as sign of irreversible loss, 49
  medical, 34

Index 245

of Alfred Stratton, 64–7
sign of irreversible loss, 51, 62
of Thomas Plunkett, 59–64
postmortem
of children, 26–7
denial of finality of death, 41–2
Plunkett, Thomas, 58, 60–4
polygenism, 83
Port Royal Experiment, 152
Posey, Alexander, 157
prisons
Andersonville, 176
libby, 129, 131
Salisbury, 131–2
Puck magazine, 170–1

Quigley, Paul, 22

radicals
in the 39th Congress, 133
Black, 6–8, *See also* Frederick Douglass, Henry
Highland Garnett, Frances E.W. Harper,
James McCune Smith
collaboration with white radicals, 2
solidarity with Chinese immigrants, 26
Black and white collaboration, 5
Republican, 11, 14
shared commitment to justice, 23
shared goal of Black citizenship, 20
white, 3–4, 7–8, 10, 20, *See also* Horace
Bushnell, Lydia Maria Child, Anna
Dickinson, Wendell Phillips, Thaddeus
Stevens, Charles Sumner, Albion
Tourgée
in *Bricks without Straw*, 28
collaboration with Black radicals, 2
commitment to Black citizenship, 103
commitment to racial equality, 10
condemnation of Presidential
Reconstruction, 124
disillusionment with Andrew Johnson, 124
failings of, 201
former abolitionists, 2
and Freedmen's Bureau, 134, 151
hopes for Reconstruction, 19, 24
inability to understand Black experience, 5
insistence on remaking the nation, 11
insistence on total break with the past, 29
kinda, 190
learning from Black counterparts, 6
and Port Royal Experiment, 152
refusal of "The Union as It Was," 14
resistance to reconciliation, 2, 12, 196
resistance to white supremacy, 5
seeing the US as rotted by slavery, 9

support for Chinese exclusion, 25
support for Indigenous genocide, 26
use of amputation as a metaphor, 3, 26,
112, 135
vision of Reconstruction Amendments, 23
Radicals
refusal of "The Union as It Was," 12
Republican, 12
Ray, Angela G., 106
reconciliation
Confederate rejection of, 148
discourse of, 179
at the expense of Black liberation, 34
as focus of Gettysburg reunion, 177
Henry Ward Beecher's support for, 6
Northern white complicity in, 14
post-Civil War desire for, 2, 194
post-war resistance to, 176
and rolling back of Reconstruction, 133
as supposed theme of Robert E. Lee statue, 192
Union rejection of after 1863, 149
Union veterans' resistance to, 177
Whitman's embrace of, 87
Reconstruction
in *Bricks without Straw*, 147
aiding poor whites, 140–1
Albion Tourgée and, 136–7, 148
amputee as signifier for, 2–4, 112, 151, 178
Andrew Jackson's betrayal of, 162
Andrew Johnson's betrayal of, 124
in *Bricks without Straw*, 28, 136, 146
and citizenship, 24
Committee on, 108
Congressional, 8, 12, 26, 107
Democratic opposition to, 166–7, 169
dismantling of, 5, 29, 132, 159, 161, 178, 201
goal of Black citizenship, 20, 103
obscuring results of, 179–80, 182
as ongoing battle, 7
in opposition to reconciliation, 2, 12, 123
post, 3, 182, 193, 195, 199, 201
Presidential, 123–4, 126
as product of the past, 186
radical hopes for, 3
radical vision, 140
radical vision of, 2–5, 7, 10, 23, 25–6, 28–9,
123, 134, 136, 140, 143, 162, 164, 188,
196, 199
reparative role of, 6
reparative work of, 153
resistance to, 6, 34, 127, 132, 139
reversal of, 14, 127, 133, 158, 168–9, 177
shifting balance of power, 6
Southern resistance to, 147
Southern view of, 145

246 *Index*

Reconstruction (cont.)
  stakes of, 20, 169, 185
  struggle over, 11, 29, 190
  successes, 141
  successes of, 131–2, 158, 167, 170
  support by Freedmen's Bureau agents, 143
  Thomas Nast and, 160–1
  waning support for, 6, 25
  white people's role in, 151
  white radical role in, 2–3, 5
  Whitman's views on, 87
Reconstruction Amendments, 23, 25
Remond, Charles Lenox, 5
Republican
  and *Harper's Weekly*, 161
  radical, 129
  Southern hatred for, 129
Republicans, 7, 11, 104, 166, 169
  on Committee on Reconstruction, 108
  in Congress, 127
  Greeley as candidate for, 175
  moderate, 11–12
  opposition to, 161
  radical, 11–12, 14, 24–5, 105, 108–9, 120,
    124, 135
  support of Union pensions, 170
reunion
  of battle of Gettysburg, *See* Gettysburg, battle of
  after death, 36, 39–42, 45, 47, 49, 67, 101
  between North and South, 87
  of North and South, 6, 178
Rhode, Michael G., 83
Richards, David A. J., 126
Richmond, VA, 127–31, 192, 194, 197,
  199–200, 211, 223
rifles, *See* field artillery
Robinson, Rufus L., 19
Rockwood Photographic Studio, 59–60
Rockwood, Elihu P., 59
Rockwood, George Gardner, 59
Rogosin, Elizabeth, 23
Roof, Dylann, 191
Roth, Wolff-Michael, 159
Ruby, Jay, 41

Sanborn, Thomas, 19
Sánchez-Eppler, Karen, 35
Sancho, Ignatius, 153
Savage, Kirk, 164, 194, 196
Schafhert, Frederick, 91
Schantz, Mark S., 35, 46
Schnog, Nancy, 48
Schuller, Kyla, 121
Schurz, Carl, 12, 82, 216, 222
Second Line to Bury White Supremacy, 197

sentimental
  in *What Answer?*, 67
sentimentalism
  amputee photographs' resistance to, 64
  Conrad Dryfoos's, 187
  denial of finality of death, 42
  denying finality of death, 37
  in Hazard of New Fortunes, 190
  Howells's distaste for, 189
  of neo-Confederates, 193
  Sigourney and, 37, 46
  of slavery, 104
  tropes of, 20, 33, 37–8
  in *What Answer?*, 114, 116–18, 120–1, 123
Sharp, C. W., 157
Shaw, Robert Gould, 83, 120
Sheehan, Tanya, 50
Sheridan, Philip, 26
Sherman, William T., 138
Sickles, Daniel E., 175, 178–80
Sigourney, Lydia Howard Huntley, 35, 37–41,
  46–7
skull and crossbones, 13, 176
skulls, 77, 83, 169
Slaughterhouse cases, 103
slavery, 120
  abolition of, 5, 8–9, 20, 28, 50, 107, 109
  anti-, 2, 6, 8–9, 20, 25, 34, 87, 104, 123, 126,
    151, 185, 214
  as challege to God's plan, 10
  as crime of theft against enslaved person, 8
  as disease or infection, 2, 14, 25
  extension of, 9
  Garnet's discussion of, 8
  history of, 2, 8, 29
  institution of, 6
  losses of, 2, 6
  marriage under, 23
  as national sin, 8, 10
  as opposed to American liberty, 112
  post-, 24
  pro-, 86, 105
  reach of, 109
  realities of, 5
  as rot, 9, 11
  sin of, 114
  in *Uncle Tom's Cabin*, 117
  white atonement for, 1, 3, 9, 12, 14, 17, 116
  "Slave Power," the, 3, 9, 108–9, 112, 118, 206,
    222
slavery, losses of, 110, 153
Smith, Gerrit, 104, 123
Smith, James McCune, 20
Snyder, Sharon L., 4–5
Society of the Army of the Potomac, 173

Index 247

song sheets, 17
Sons of Confederate Veterans, the, 194
South
  change in, 139
  debate over Confederate monuments, 192
  identity of, 139
  post-war, 137
South Carolina, 127, 132, 152, 191, 222
South, the
  African Americans in, 7, 110, 116, 126, 141, 196
  belief in its superiority, 132
  belief in their superiority, 145, 147
  change in, 130
  and Confederate monuments, 197
  Confederate monuments in, 194
  Dickinson's tour of, *See* Dickinson, Anna:tour of the South
  and enslavement, 28, 122, 147
  enslaving, 8
  guilt of, 9, 114
  Hesden LeMoyne's antipathy for, 142, 146
  historical revisionism by, 201
  historical revisionism of, 194
  identity of, 22
  investment in white supremacy, 156, 158
  legislative refusal to ratify Reconstruction Amendments, 12
  migration of Black and white teachers to, 156
  and national belonging, 22
  need for change, 8
  political power of, 118, 125
  post-war, 12
  Reconstruction and, 140
  Reconstruction of, 11
  resistance to Black self-determination, 12
  resistance to reconstruction, 12, 14, 129, 145, 147, 158
  revanchism of, 132, 180, 186, 190
  secession by, 86
  society of, 8
  in Thomas Nast cartoon, 181
  withdrawal of Union troops from, 166, 170
Southworth, Albert Sands, 31–2, 42, 215
Spires, Derrick, 21, 24
spiritualism, 27, 96, 98, 101
spiritualism's, 27
Stanton, Elizabeth Cady, 105, 213
Stearns, Frazar, 73–4
Stevens, Thaddeus, 4, 8–12, 19, 108, 201, 216
  Frances Harper's eulogy for, 10
Stowe, Harriet Beecher, 20, 35, 118, 122
Stratton, Alfred A., 65–6
Sumner, Charles, 9, 11, 19, 25, 216

surgeons, 27, 50, 71–2, 75–9, 82, 88, 91, 95, 150, 208, 210–11
surgical manual
  military, 75–6

Take 'Em Down 901, 198, 200
Take 'Em Down Nola (TEDN), 197
Tallis, Raymond, 160, 174
Tammany Hall, 161
Taylor, Susie King, 27, 83, 89
Taylor, Susie Taylor, 84
the Tennessee Heritage Protection Act, 198
Tennessee State Bill 263, 200
Thirteenth Amendment, 7, 107
Thomas, Brook, 194
Thompson, Erin L., 191
Tilden, Samuel J., 166, 168–9
Tour of Reconstruction, A (Dickinson), 104, 128, 133
Tourgée, Albion W., xi, 3–4, 12, 19, 28, 87, 103, 136–7, 141–5, 148, 151–4, 156, 201
  Bricks without Straw, 28, 136–43
  career of, 141
  experience in Civil War, 141
  radicalization of, 137
  A Veteran and His Pipe, 19
Tuggle, Lindsay, 94
Tuttle, John, 81
Twain, Mark (Samuel L. Clemens), 106
Tweed, William M. "Boss," 161

U.S. Civil War
  and the "good death," 33
  to abolish slavery, 112, 119, 179
  amputees, *See* amputees
  battles
    Antietam, 71, 79, 138, 149, 212
    Bull Run, 141, 149
    Chancellorsville, 85, 115, 138
    Fair Oaks, 137–40, 149
    Fredericksburg, 58, 60, 62, 64, 81, 84–5, 90, 138
    Gettysburg, *See* Gettysburg:battle of
    Newbern, 73
    Shiloh, 79, 81, 149–50
    Vicksburg, 79
  as break from the past, 11
  chaos of, 82
  destructive power of, 1, 9, 15, 45, 51, 62, 67, 72–3, 76, 79, 83–4, 108, 172
  and disability, 14, 16
  disavowal of in *A Hazard of New Fortunes*, 182
  discourses of, 159
  as dividing line between past and future, 14
  to end slavery, 17, 19
  God as combatant in, 10

Index

U.S. Civil War (cont.)
  as harbinger of permanent change, 72
  hospitals, *See* hospitals
  meanings of, 2, 4, 26
  mortality rates, 71, 75, 83
  need for medical personnel, 88
  new technology in, 15, 72, 74, 77, 91
  in payment for slavery, 9–10, 104, 113, 115,
    125, 142
  political potential of, 29
  post-, 3, 5–6, 8, 11, 15, 20, 29, 132, 169, 172
  pre-, 2–3, 6, 21, 28–9, 46, 67, 172
  as preparation for Black equality, 7, 125
  radicalizing experience of, 4
  Southern narratives of, 140, 145
  trauma of, 11
  Whitman's ambivalence about, 87
U.S. Constitution, 3, 12, 21, 24, 28, 107–9, 118,
    127
U.S. National Library of Medicine, 51
Uncle Tom's Cabin, 20, 35, 117, 121, 123
Union
  death for, 94
  loyalty oath to, 124
Union army
  and amputation, 76, 85
  Army of the Potomac, 161, 177
  Black troops in, 69, 84, 112–13
    unequal pay for, 114
  defeats in, 149
  defeats of, 60, 73
  occupation of the South, 140, 152
  prisoners of war, 176
  at Shiloh, 150
  soldiers in, 9, 110
  Tourgée's service in, 137
  victories by, 119, 179
  in *What Answer?*, 105, 110, 115, 119–20
  withdrawal from the South, 166, 170
  amputation in, 96
  Black troops in, 115
  medical personnel in, 95
  officers in, 81
Union sveteran
  amputees, 25
Union veterans, 190
  amputee, 3–4
  amputees, 14, 16
    Black, 19
    masculinity of, 16
  demonization of, 3
  demonized, 5
  amputees, 2–3, 20, 28, 131, 134, 142–3, 174
    Black, 20, 67
    committed to racial equality, 17

left handed penmanship competitons, 17
  masculinity of, 16
  in popular culture, 17, 20
  Black, 67, 162
  demonized, 170–1
  at Gettysburg reunion, 161, 173–5
  pensions
    racial inequality in distribution, 84
  pensions for, 49, 170
  photographs of, 58
  radicalized, 144
  returning home, 16
  shaking hands with Confederate veterans, 29
  supporting reconciliation, 192
Union, the, 139
  "the Union as It Was," 12, 14, 28, 103, 137,
    148, 151, 158
  and abolition of slavery, 138
  battle lines, 69, 71
  Confederate secession from, 86
  equal rights within, 69, 84, 126
  maintained by slavery, 6
  post-war, 3
  preservation of, 12, 22, 50, 127, 149, 161, 177
  radical vision for, 14
  reconstruction of, 143, 145
  rotted by slavery, 9, 11, 108
  sacredness of, 17
  sacrifice on behalf of, 173
  Southern antipathy towards, 132
  support for, 147–8, 161
  supporters of, 145
"Unite the Right" rally, 197
United Daughters of the Confederacy (UDC),
    194–5
US Civil War
  as vehicle for racial equality, 113

Valentine, Edward Virginius, 129–30
VanderHaagen, Sara C., 128
Verboon, Caitlin, 23
Veteran and His Pipe, A (Tourgée), 19
Veteran's Reserve Corps, 143
veterans
  Confederate, 29, 143, 181
violence
  anti-black, 6, 12–14, 108, 116, 146, 157, 170,
    191
  vigilante, 146–7
  domestic, 154
  freedom from, 154
  as a legacy of slavery, 154
  of the New York Draft Riots, 105
  police, 188
  political, 112, 127, 190

Index

racist, 25, 29
of slavery, 10, 120–2, 136, 147, 152, 154, 168
threats of, 169
of U.S. history, 200
of war, 56, 108, 149

Walker, Brandon, 191
Warner, Susan, 35
Washburne, Elihu, 125
Weekly Anglo-African, 21
Wells, Ida B., 198
What Answer? (Dickinson), 27, 67, 104–5, 107,
  109–18, 120–3, 125–7, 132–3, 190
White League, the, 13, 197
white supremacy, 5–6, 11, 13–14, 26, 29, 34,
  49, 84, 108, 110, 112–13, 116, 118,
  126, 130, 132, 135–6, 144–5, 147,
  158, 169, 183, 186, 191, 195–201,
  214, 217, 223
  as embodied in Confederate monuments, 193, 195

Whitman, Walt, 27, 60, 72, 81, 84–5, 172
  Calamus, 87
  faith in democracy, 85
  Memoranda During the War, 81, 84–7
The Wide Wide World (Warner), 35
Wild, Edward, 143
Williams, Raymond
  structures of feeling, 24
  theory of formations, 4
Wintress, David, 50, 62–4
Wong, Edlie, 25
Wood, Barry D., 192
Wood, Charles H., 54

Yates, Richard, 109
The Yellow Wall-paper (Gilman), 73
Young, Elizabeth, 55

Zandy, Janet, 159
Zittlau, Andrea, 50

Recent books in this series *(continued from page ii)*

185. ALEXANDER MENRISKY
 Wild Abandon: American Literature and the Identity Politics of Ecology
184. HEIKE SCHAEFER
 American Literature and Immediacy: Literary Innovation and the Emergence of Photography, Film, and Television
183. DALE M. BAUER
 Nineteenth-Century American Women's Serial Novels
182. MARIANNE NOBLE
 Rethinking Sympathy and Human Contact in Nineteenth-Century American Literature
181. ROB TURNER
 Counterfeit Culture
180. KATE STANLEY
 Practices of Surprise in American Literature after Emerson
179. JOHANNES VOELZ
 The Poetics of Insecurity
178. JOHN HAY
 Postapocalyptic Fantasies in Antebellum American Literature
177. PAUL JAUSSEN
 Writing in Real Time
176. CINDY WEINSTEIN
 Time, Tense, and American Literature
175. CODY MARS
 Nineteenth-Century American Literature and the Long Civil War
174. STACEY MARGOLIS
 Fictions of Mass Democracy in Nineteenth-Century America
173. PAUL DOWNES
 Hobbes, Sovereignty, and Early American Literature
172. DAVID BERGMAN
 Poetry of Disturbance
171. MARK NOBLE
 American Poetic Materialism from Whitman to Stevens
170. JOANNA FREER
 Thomas Pynchon and American Counterculture
169. DOMINIC MASTROIANNI
 Politics and Skepticism in Antebellum American Literature
168. GAVIN JONES
 Failure and the American Writer
167. LENA HILL
 Visualizing Blackness and the Creation of the African American Literary Tradition
166. MICHAEL ZISER
 Environmental Practice and Early American Literature

165. ANDREW HEBARD
The Poetics of Sovereignty in American Literature, 1885–1910
164. CHRISTOPHER FREEBURG
Melville and the Idea of Blackness
163. TIM ARMSTRONG
The Logic of Slavery
162. JUSTINE MURISON
The Politics of Anxiety in Nineteenth-Century American Literature
161. HSUAN L. HSU
Geography and the Production of Space in Nineteenth-Century American Literature
160. DORRI BEAM
Style, Gender, and Fantasy in Nineteenth Century American Women's Writing
159. YOGITA GOYAL
Romance, Diaspora, and Black Atlantic Literature
158. MICHAEL CLUNE
American Literature and the Free Market, 1945–2000
157. KERRY LARSON
Imagining Equality in Nineteenth-Century American Literature
156. LAWRENCE ROSENWALD
Multilingual America: Language and the Making of American Literature
155. ANITA PATTERSON
Race, American Literature, and Transnational Modernism
154. ELIZABETH RENKER
The Origins of American Literature Studies: An Institutional History
153. THEO DAVIS
Formalism, Experience, and the Making of American Literature in the Nineteenth Century
152. JOAN RICHARDSON
A Natural History of Pragmatism: The Fact of Feeling from Jonathan Edwards to Gertrude Stein
151. EZRA TAWIL
The Making of Racial Sentiment: Slavery and the Birth of the Frontier Romance
150. ARTHUR RISS
Race, Slavery, and Liberalism in Nineteenth-Century American Literature
149. JENNIFER ASHTON
From Modernism to Postmodernism: American Poetry and Theory in the Twentieth Century
148. MAURICE S. LEE
Slavery, Philosophy, and American Literature, 1830–1860
147. CINDY WEINSTEIN
Family, Kinship and Sympathy in Nineteenth-Century American Literature